DRACULA
SON OF THE
DRAGON
BY
Sable & Salgood

Dramatis Personae

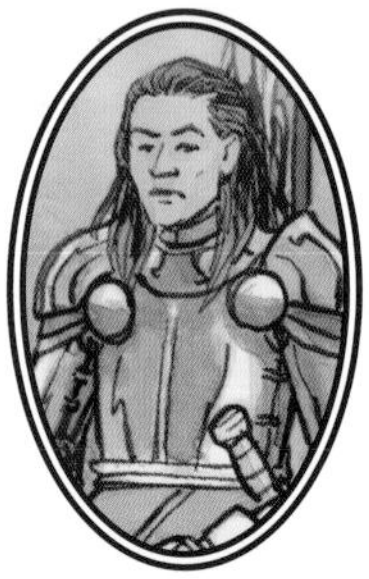

VLAD DRACULA, a.k.a. **VLAD THE IMPALER**, a.k.a. **VLAD ȚEPEȘ**, a.k.a. **SON OF THE DRAGON** (c. 1431–1477): Voivode (ruler) of Wallachia, 1448, 1456–1462, and 1476. Inspiration for Bram Stoker's Count Dracula. Was he a vampire himself? Protagonist of our story.

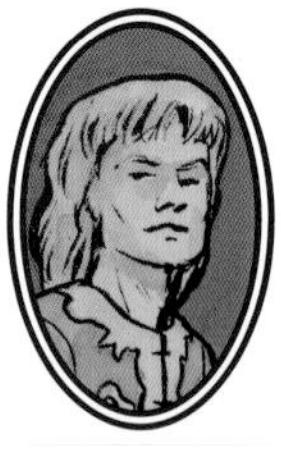

RADU, a.k.a. **RADU BEY**, a.k.a. **RADU THE HANDSOME/THE BEAUTIFUL/THE FAIR** (c. 1437/39–1475): Younger, legitimate brother of Vlad Dracula. Ruler of Wallachia, 1473–1474. Imprisoned with Dracula by the Ottomans during his youth, he eventually defected to their side.

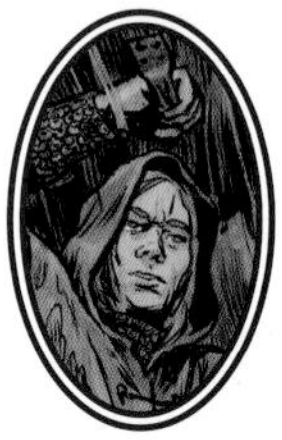

MIRCEA II (c. 1428–1447): Older, legitimate brother of Vlad Dracula. Temporary ruler of Wallachia in 1442.

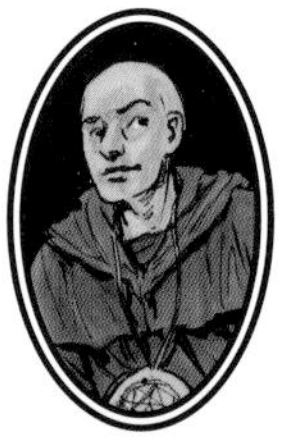

VLAD IV CĂLUGĂRUL, a.k.a. **VLAD THE MONK** (c. 1425–1495): Son of Vlad Dracul and an abbess, illegitimate brother to Vlad Dracula, Mircea, and Radu. Ruler of Wallachia, 1481 and 1482–1495.

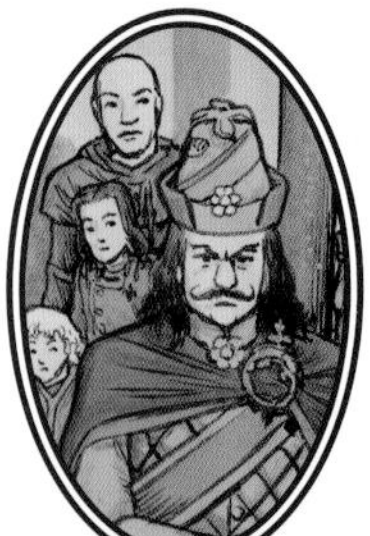

VLAD II DRACUL (c. 1395–1447): Father of Radu, Vlad Dracula, Mircea, and Vlad the Monk. Ruler of Wallachia, 1443–1447. Founding member of the Order of the Dragon.

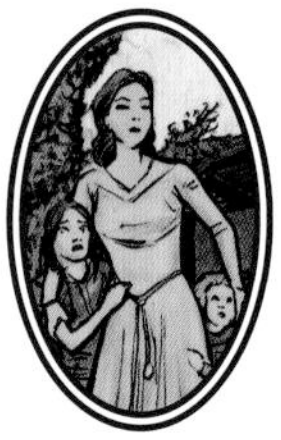

VASILISA MARIA MUSAT, a.k.a. **CNEAJNA** (c. 1394–1462/64/72): Princess of Moldavia, of the Musatin dynasty of neighboring Moldovia. Vlad Dracula and Radu's mother.

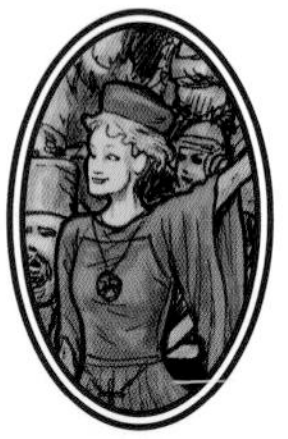

DOAMNA CĂLȚUNA (dates unknown): Mistress of Vlad Dracul, later Mother Eupraxia (abbess) and mother of Vlad the Monk.

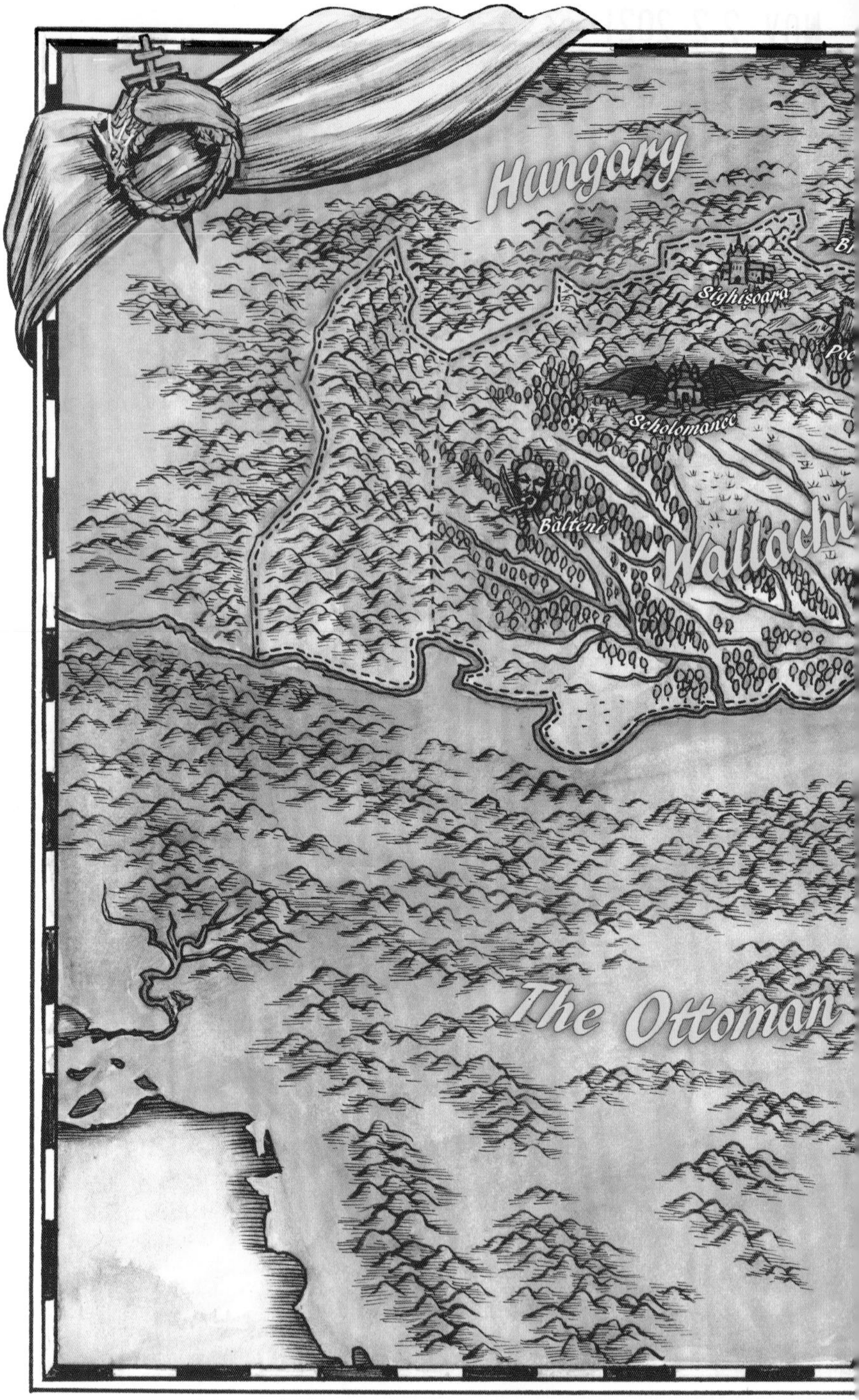

Hungary
Sighisoara
Scholomance
Bălteni
Wallachi
The Ottoman

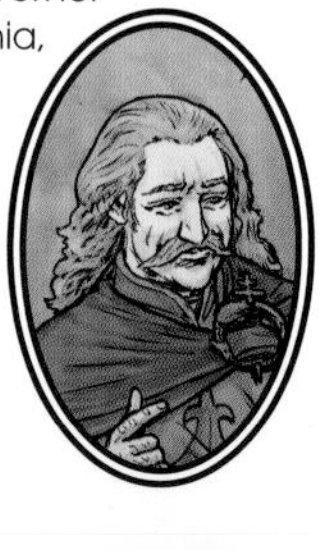

JOHN HUNYADI (c. 1406–1456): Hungarian statesman, crusader against the Ottoman Turks, member of the Order of the Dragon. Governor of Transylvania, regent of Hungary. Friend and later rival to the Draculas.

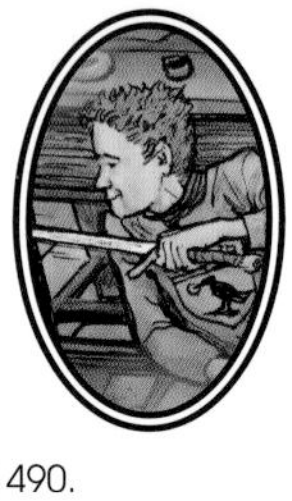

MATTHIAS CORVINUS (c. 1443–1490): Son of John Hunyadi, classmate of Vlad Dracula, and king of Croatia and Hungary, 1458–1490. Also disputed duke of Bohemia and contested duke of Austria.

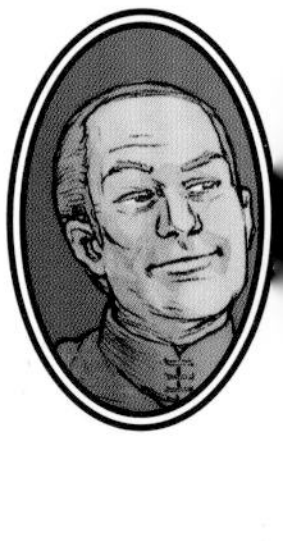

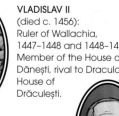

VLADISLAV II (died c. 1456): Ruler of Wallachia, 1447–1448 and 1448–1456. Member of the House of Dănești, rival to Dracula's House of Drăculești.

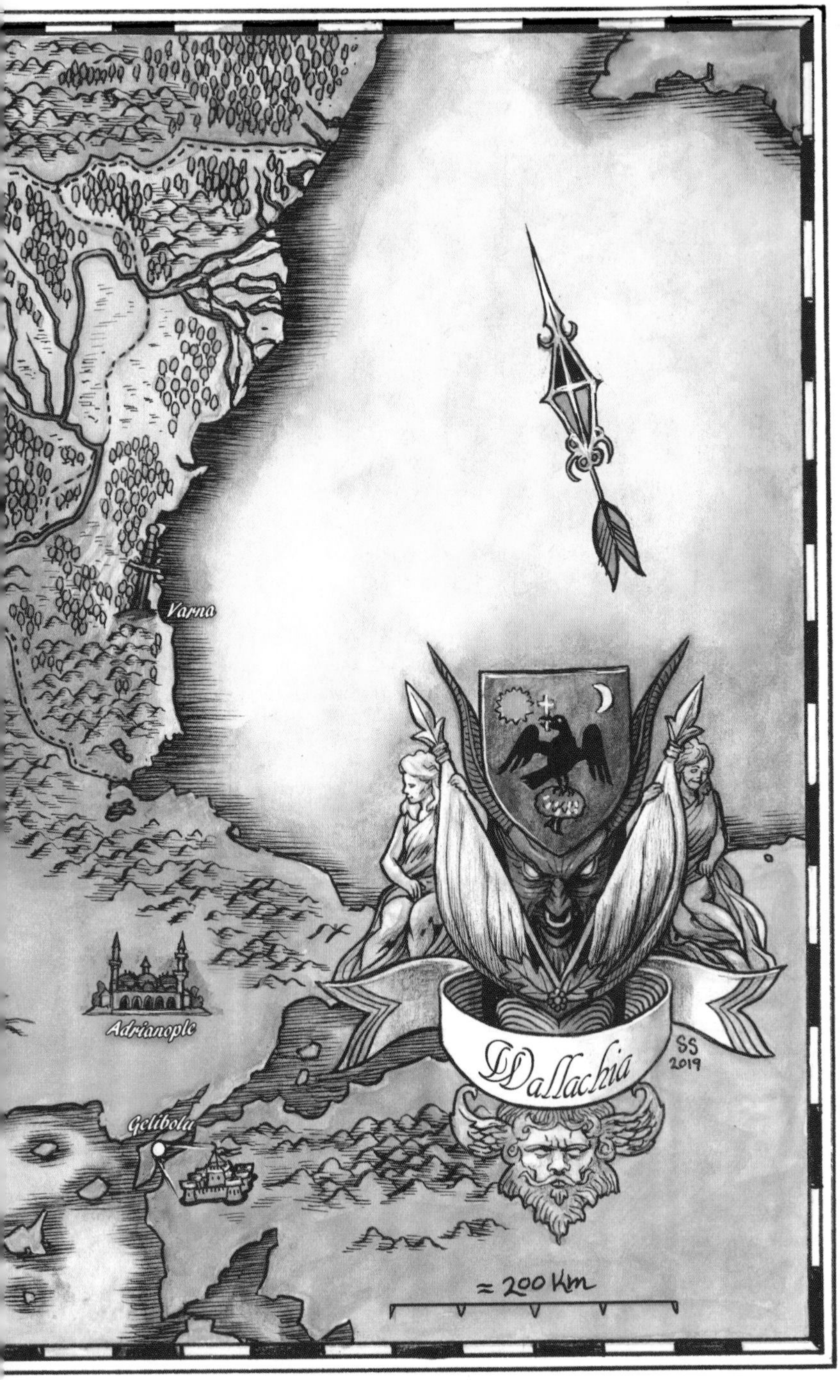
Varna
Adrianople
Gelibola
Wallachia
SS
2019
≈ 200 Km

EMPEROR SIGISMUND
(c. 1368–1437):
Holy Roman Emperor, 1433–1437, founder of the Order of the Dragon.

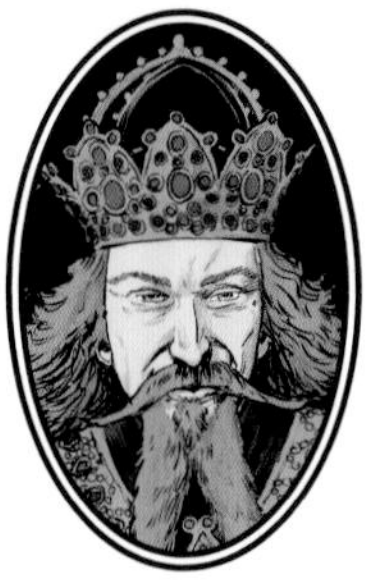

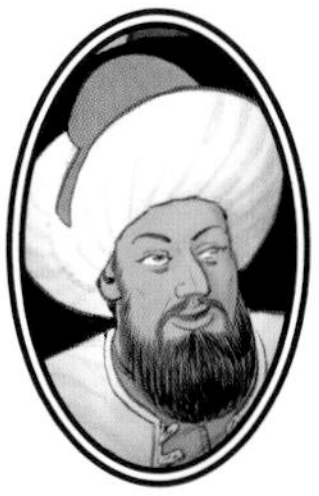

SULTAN MURAD II
(c. 1404–1451):
Sultan of the Ottoman Empire, 1446–1451, during both Vlad Dracul and Dracula's reigns. Held Vlad Dracula and Radu hostage to ensure Vlad Dracul's loyalty.

SULTAN MEHMED II,
a.k.a. **MEHMED THE CONQUEROR**
(c. 1432–1481):
Son and successor of Sultan Murad II, he ruled the Turks from 1451 to 1481. As a young man, he was educated alongside Dracula and Radu during their imprisonment. As sultan, he would conquer Constantinople and much of southeastern Europe, becoming Dracula's greatest enemy.

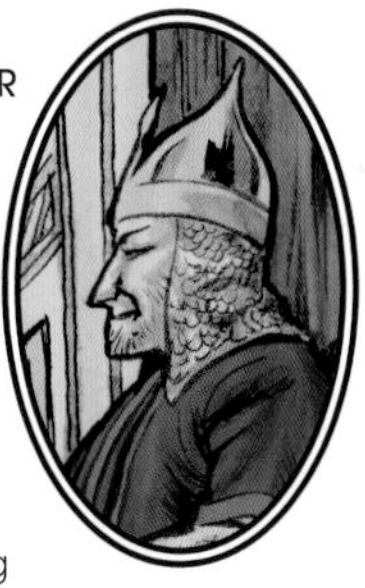

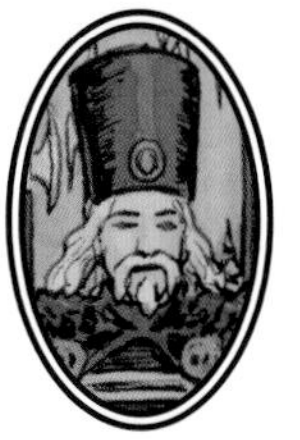

CHANCELLOR CAZAN
(dates unknown):
One of the boyars that remained loyal to Vlad II Dracul, he went on to present Vlad Dracul's sword to Vlad Dracula at the Ottoman court.

STEFAN BRANKOVIĆ,
a.k.a. **STEFAN THE BLIND**
(c. 1417–9 Oct. 1476):
Despot of Serbia, 1458–1459. He and his brother . . .

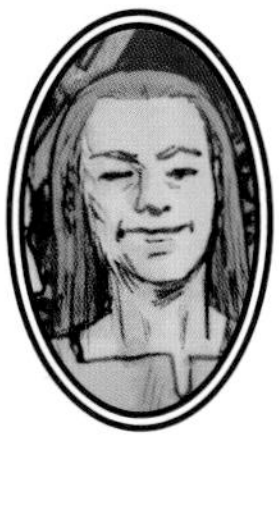

GRGUR BRANKOVIĆ
(c. 1415–16 Oct. 1459):
. . . were fellow hostages, along with Radu and Dracula, of Sultan Murad II. Unlike Dracula and Radu, they were not treated well by the sultan, both blinded with hot pokers.

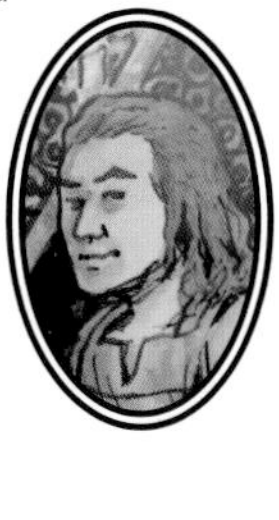

ALEXANDRA
(c. 1429–1444):
A student at the Scholomance, classmate of young Dracula and chosen by the devil as his prize pupil. Then deployed by Vlad Dracul as a secret weapon.

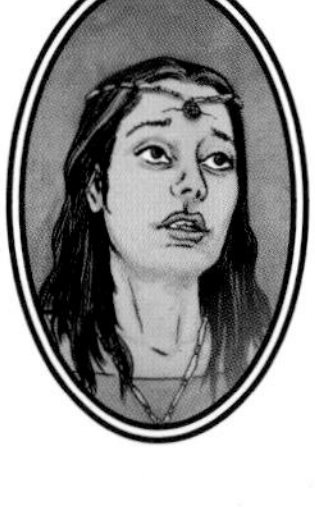

President and Publisher Mike Richardson
Editor Daniel Chabon
Assistant Editors Chuck Howitt and Konner Knudsen
Designer Kathleen Barnett
Digital Art Technician Jason Rickerd

Published by Dark Horse Books | A division of Dark Horse Comics LLC | 10956 SE Main Street, Milwaukie, OR 97222

Comic Shop Locator Service: comicshoplocator.com

Dracula: Son of the Dragon

Art used with permission: page 90 © Robbi Rodriguez; page 91 © Kevin Mellon; page 92 © Leandro Fernández; page 95 © James Romberger; page 97 © Paul Azaceta; page 99 © Richard Pace; page 100 © Jeremy Haun; page 106 © Nathan Fox.

This volume collects Dracula: Son of the Dragon.

Library of Congress Cataloging-in-Publication Data

Names: Sable, Mark, writer. | Sam, Salgood, artist.
Title: Dracula, son of the dragon / Mark Sable, Salgood Sam.
Description: First edition. | Milwaukie, OR : Dark Horse Books, 2021. |
    Summary: "A blood-soaked epic of the real-life Vlad the Impaler's
    transformation into the vampire . Part historical fiction, part
    horror fantasy, this graphic novel is brought to you by writer Mark
    Sable (The Dark, Graveyard of Empires, Unthinkable) and artist Salgood
    Sam (Dream Life, Therefore Repent, Sea of Red)"-- Provided by publisher.

Identifiers: LCCN 2021009696 | ISBN 9781506724423 (trade paperback)
Subjects: LCSH: Graphic novels.
Classification: LCC PN6727.S136 D73 2021 | DDC 741.5/973--dc23
LC record available at https://lccn.loc.gov/2021009696

First edition: September 2021
Trade paperback ISBN: 978-1-50672-442-3

1 3 5 7 9 10 8 6 4 2
Printed in China

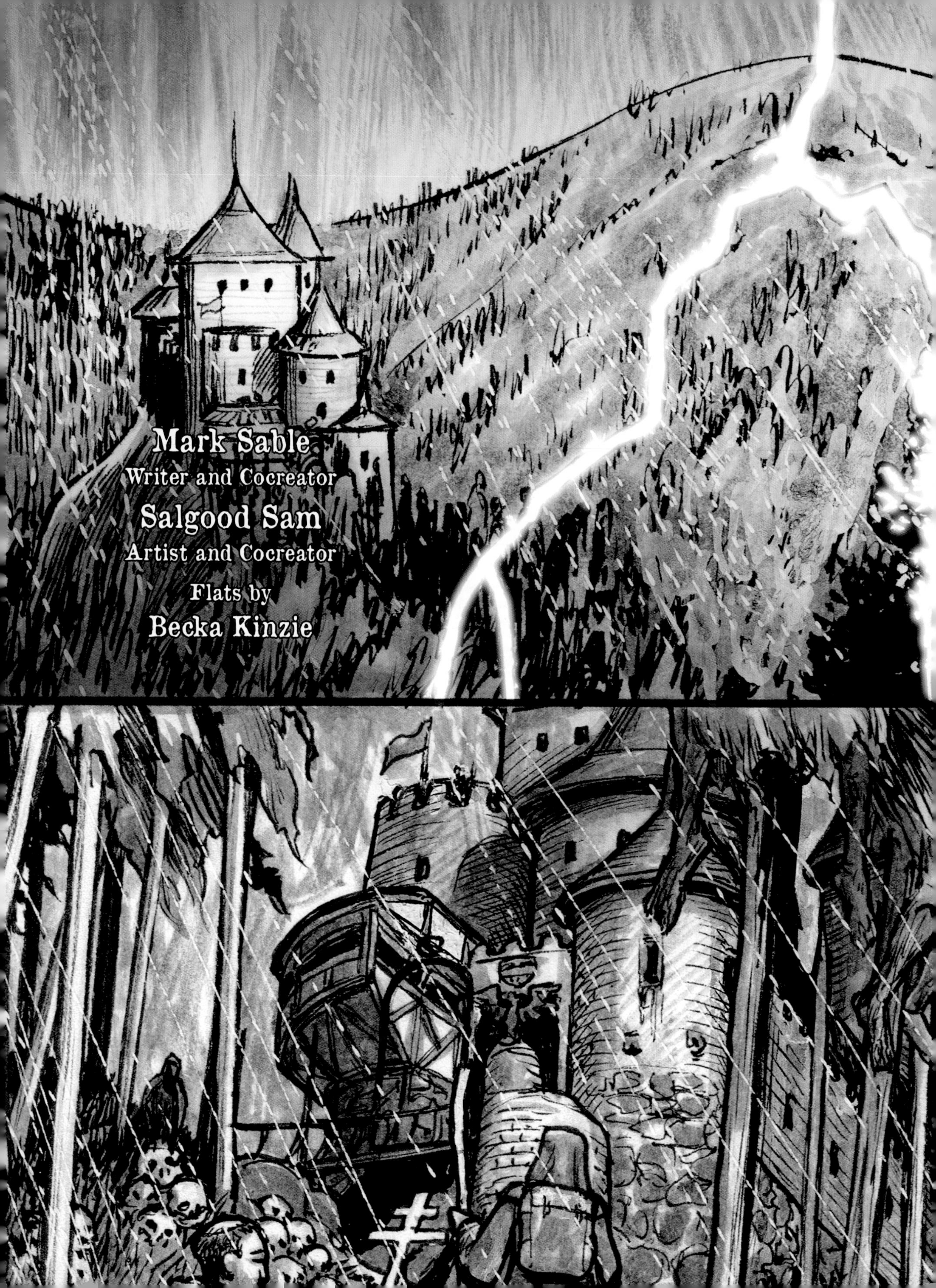
Mark Sable
Writer and Cocreator
Salgood Sam
Artist and Cocreator
Flats by
Becka Kinzie

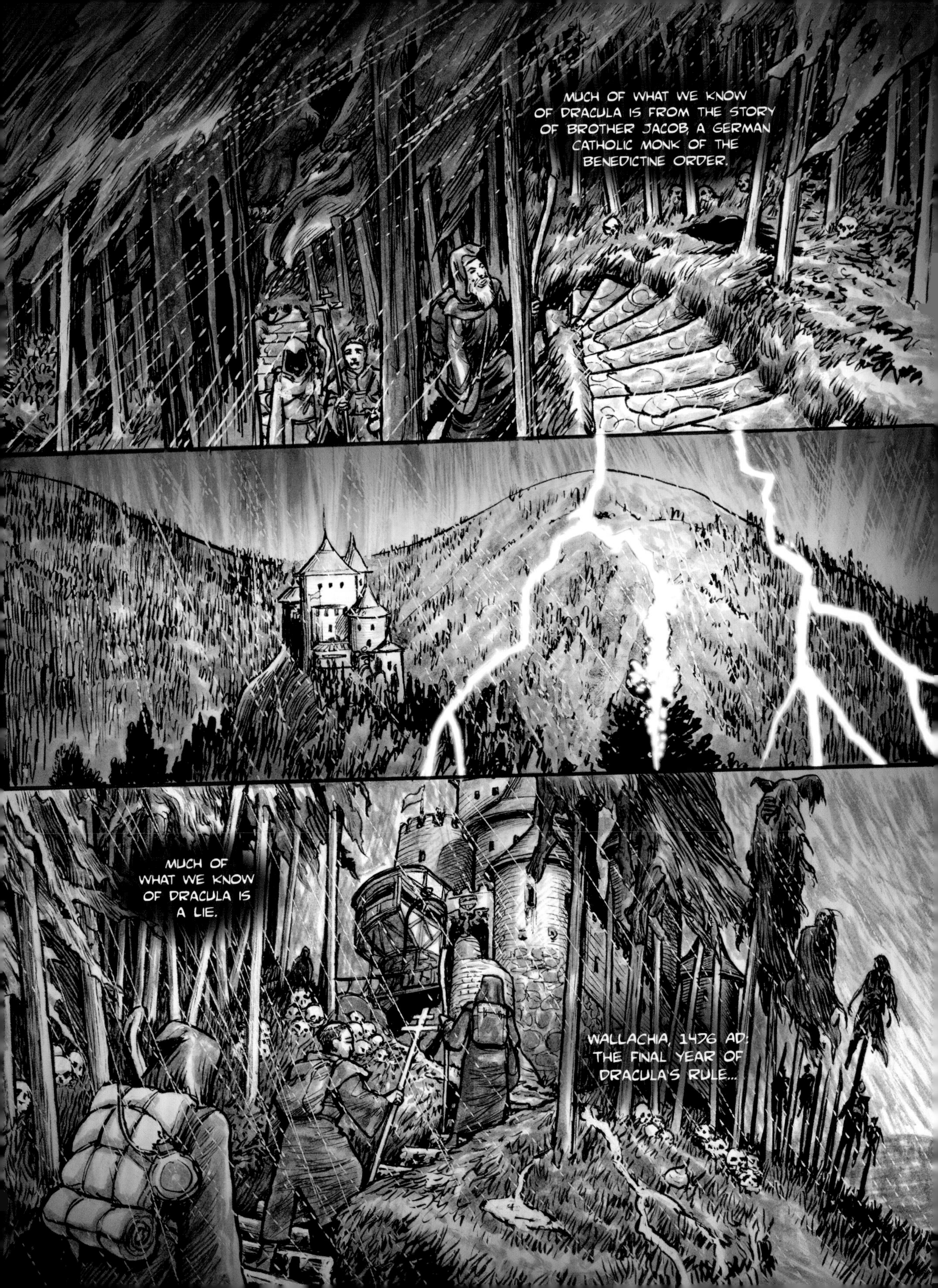
MUCH OF WHAT WE KNOW OF DRACULA IS FROM THE STORY OF BROTHER JACOB, A GERMAN CATHOLIC MONK OF THE BENEDICTINE ORDER.
MUCH OF WHAT WE KNOW OF DRACULA IS A LIE.
WALLACHIA, 1476 AD: THE FINAL YEAR OF DRACULA'S RULE...

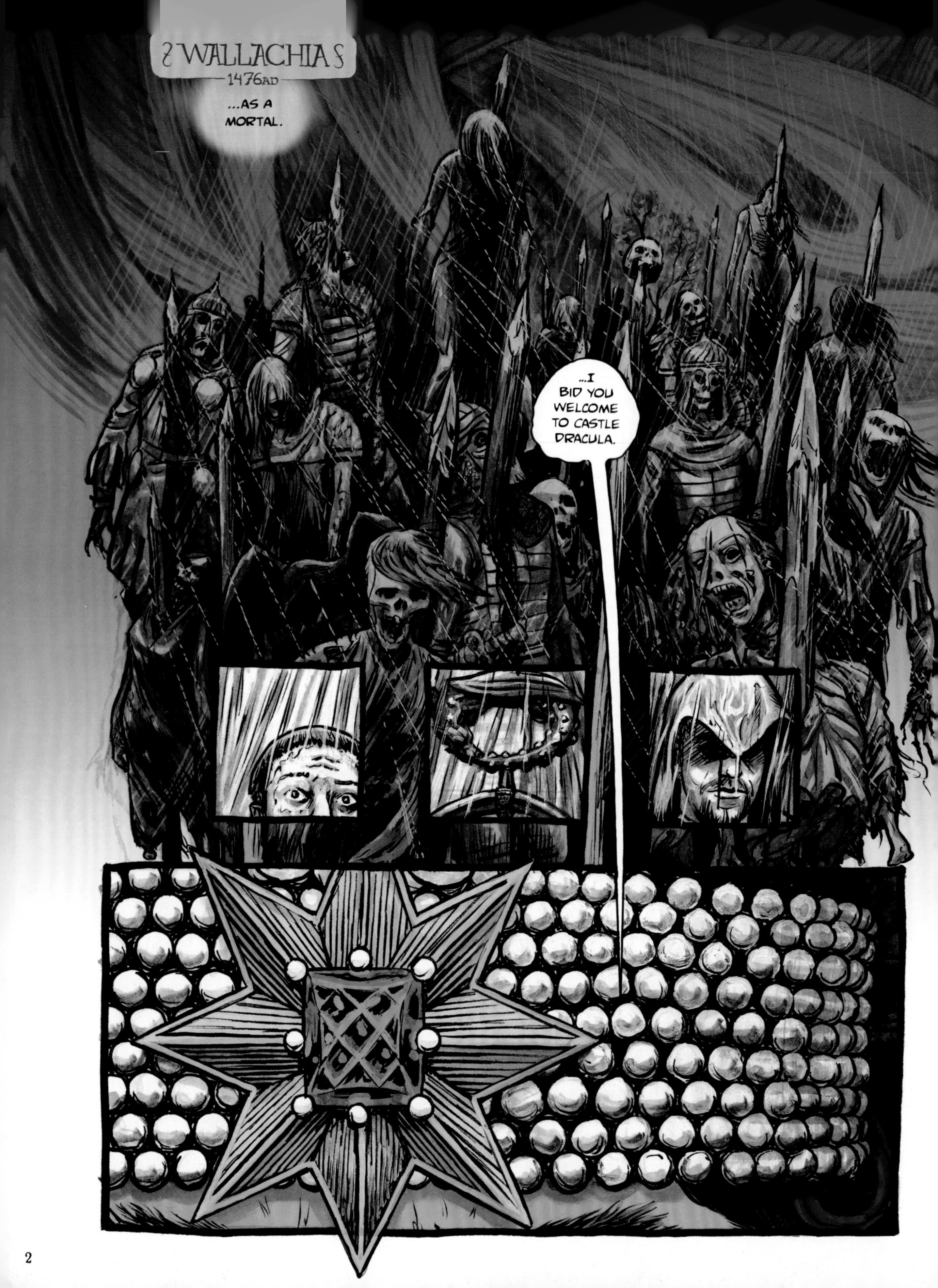
WALLACHIA
1476AD
...AS A MORTAL.
...I BID YOU WELCOME TO CASTLE DRACULA.

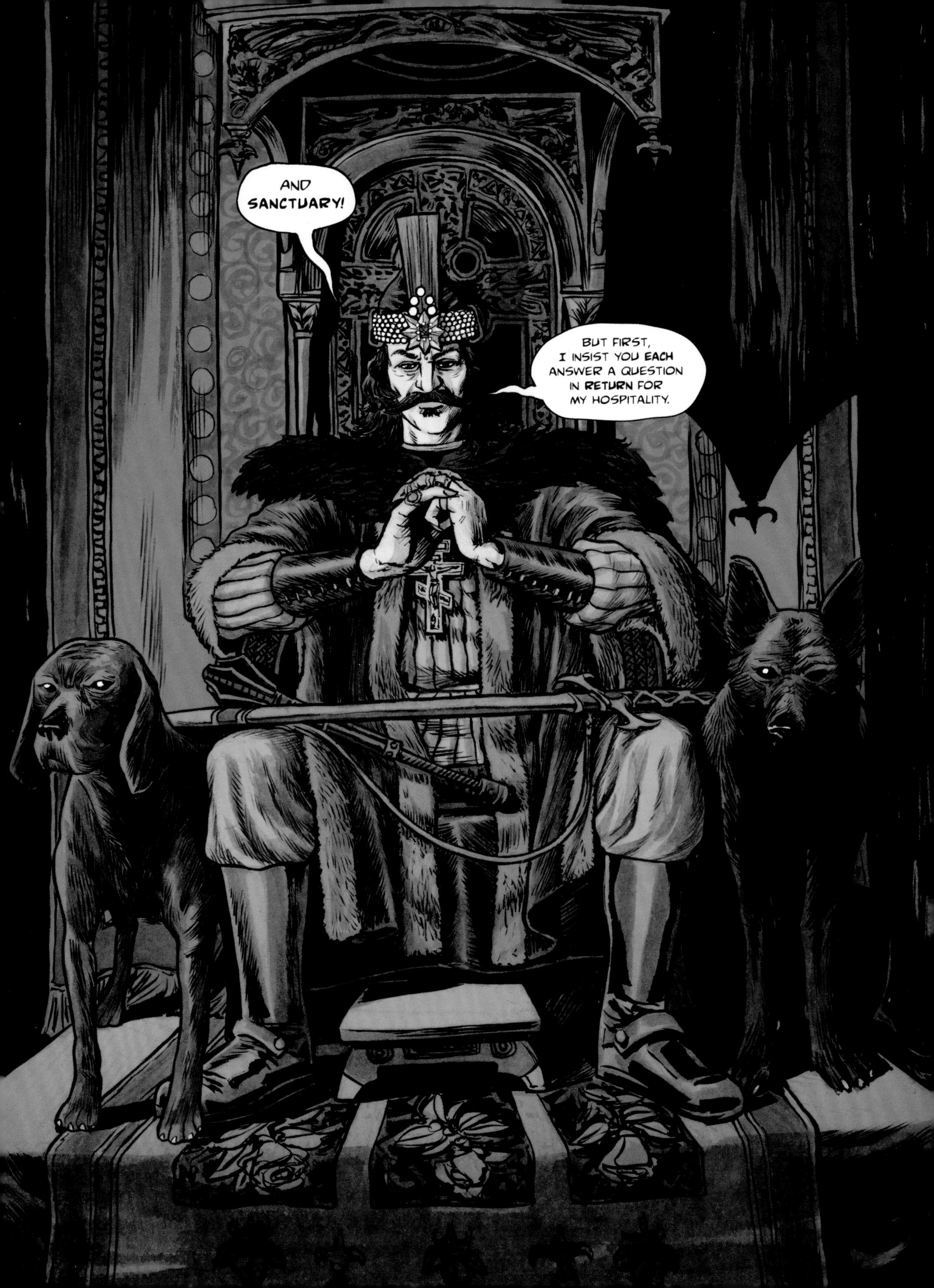
AND SANCTUARY!
BUT FIRST, I INSIST YOU EACH ANSWER A QUESTION IN RETURN FOR MY HOSPITALITY.

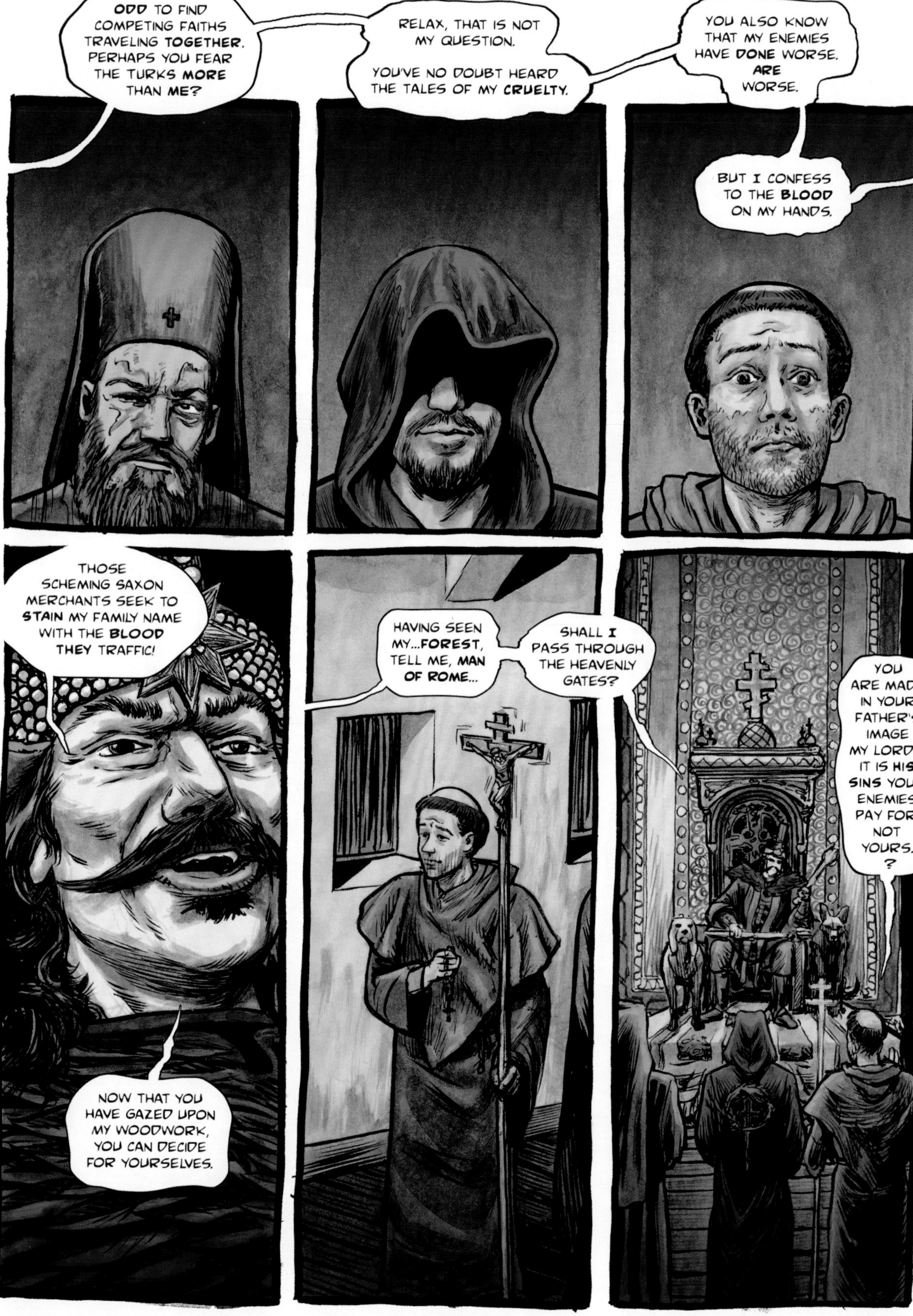
ODD TO FIND COMPETING FAITHS TRAVELING TOGETHER. PERHAPS YOU FEAR THE TURKS MORE THAN ME?
RELAX, THAT IS NOT MY QUESTION.
YOU'VE NO DOUBT HEARD THE TALES OF MY CRUELTY.
YOU ALSO KNOW THAT MY ENEMIES HAVE DONE WORSE. ARE WORSE.
BUT I CONFESS TO THE BLOOD ON MY HANDS.
THOSE SCHEMING SAXON MERCHANTS SEEK TO STAIN MY FAMILY NAME WITH THE BLOOD THEY TRAFFIC!
NOW THAT YOU HAVE GAZED UPON MY WOODWORK, YOU CAN DECIDE FOR YOURSELVES.
HAVING SEEN MY...FOREST, TELL ME, MAN OF ROME...
SHALL I PASS THROUGH THE HEAVENLY GATES?
YOU ARE MADE IN YOUR FATHER'S IMAGE MY LORD! IT IS HIS SINS YOUR ENEMIES PAY FOR, NOT YOURS... ?

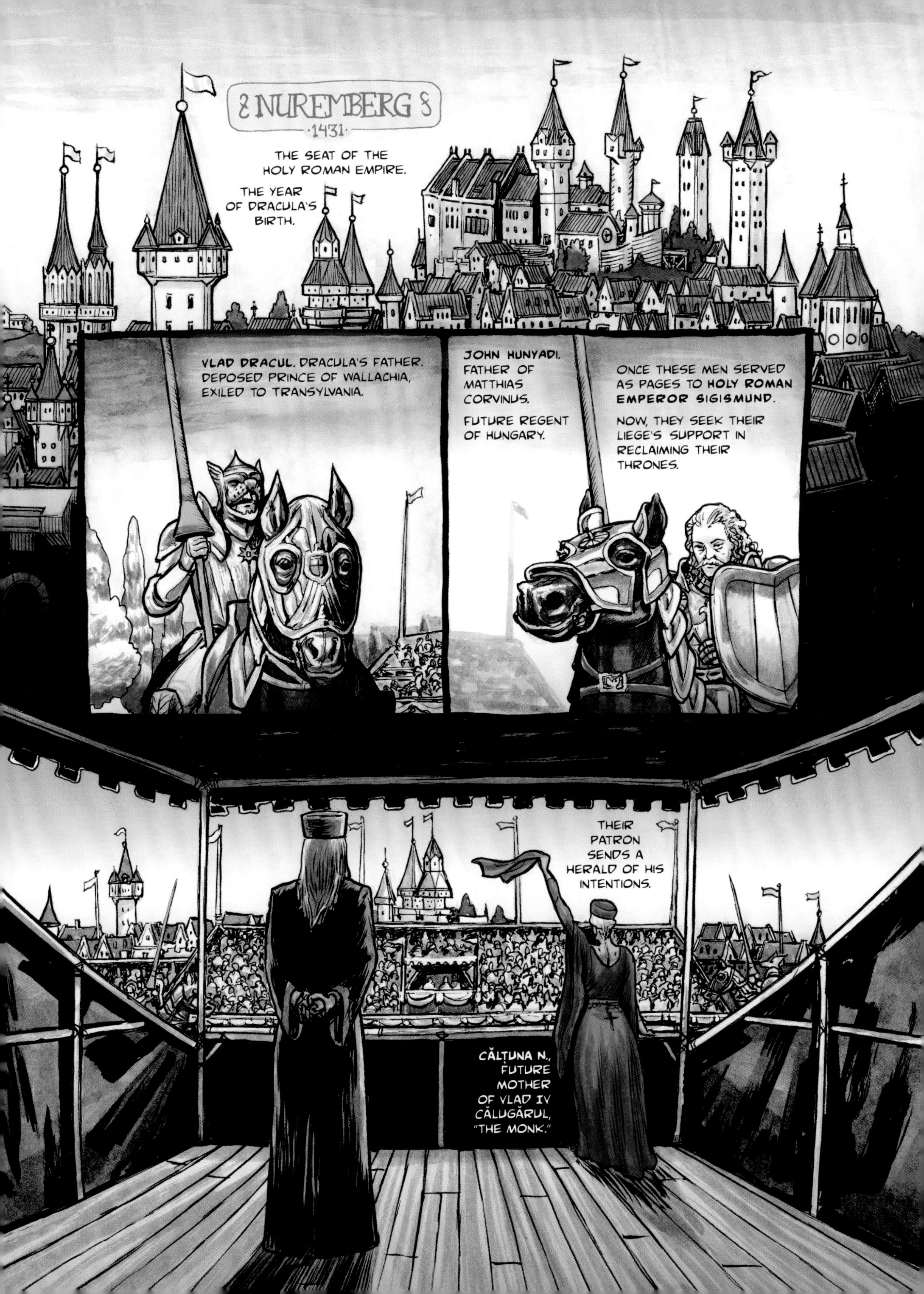
NUREMBERG
1431
THE SEAT OF THE HOLY ROMAN EMPIRE.
THE YEAR OF DRACULA'S BIRTH.
VLAD DRACUL, DRACULA'S FATHER. DEPOSED PRINCE OF WALLACHIA, EXILED TO TRANSYLVANIA.
JOHN HUNYADI, FATHER OF MATTHIAS CORVINUS.
FUTURE REGENT OF HUNGARY.
ONCE THESE MEN SERVED AS PAGES TO **HOLY ROMAN EMPEROR SIGISMUND**.
NOW, THEY SEEK THEIR LIEGE'S SUPPORT IN RECLAIMING THEIR THRONES.
THEIR PATRON SENDS A HERALD OF HIS INTENTIONS.
CĂLȚUNA N., FUTURE MOTHER OF VLAD IV CĂLUGĂRUL, "THE MONK."

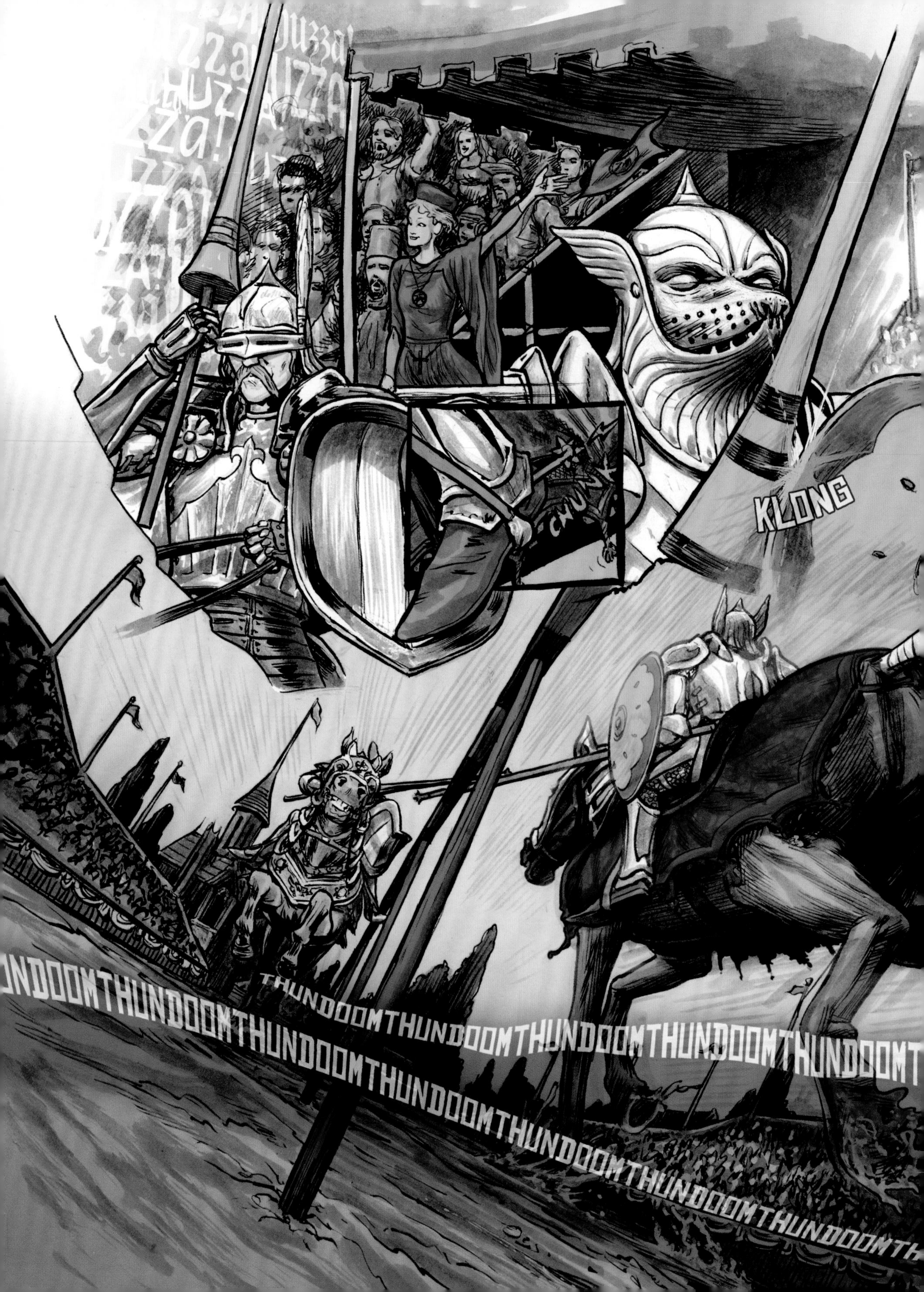

KLONG
THUNDOOMTHUNDOOMTHUNDOOMTHUNDOOMTHUNDOOMT

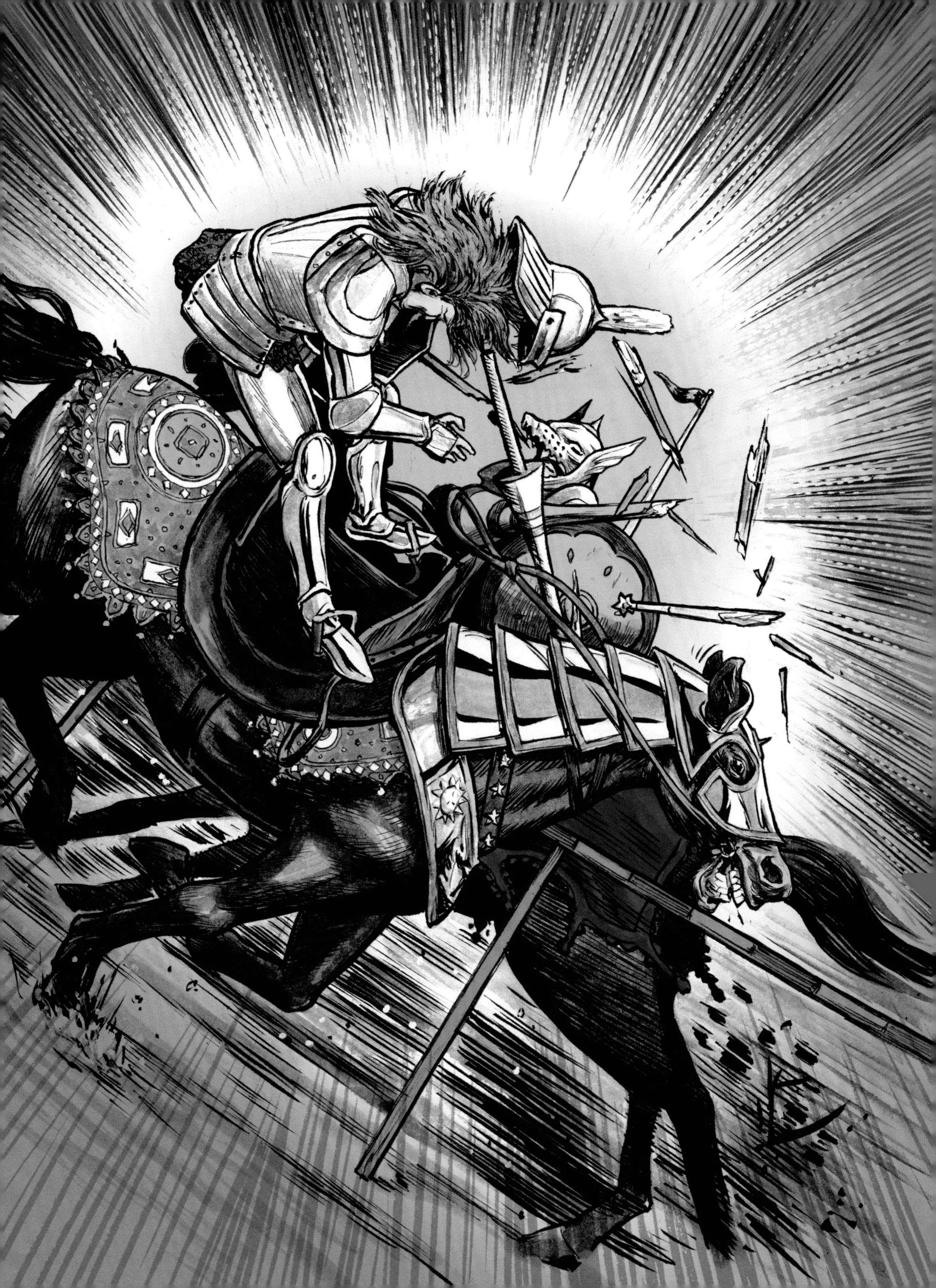

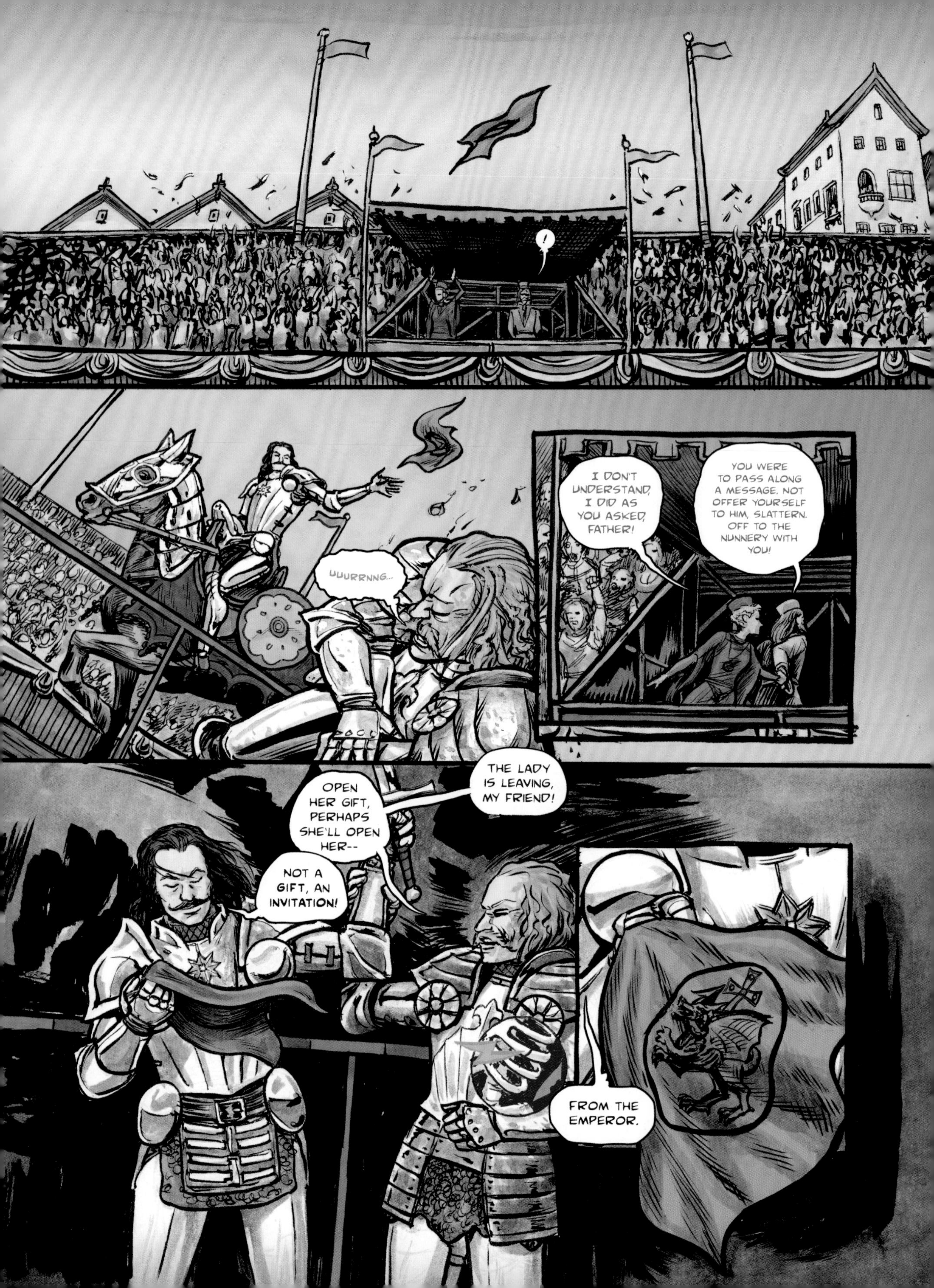
!
UUURRNNG...
I DON'T UNDERSTAND, I DID AS YOU ASKED, FATHER!
YOU WERE TO PASS ALONG A MESSAGE. NOT OFFER YOURSELF TO HIM, SLATTERN. OFF TO THE NUNNERY WITH YOU!
THE LADY IS LEAVING, MY FRIEND!
OPEN HER GIFT, PERHAPS SHE'LL OPEN HER--
NOT A GIFT, AN INVITATION!
FROM THE EMPEROR.

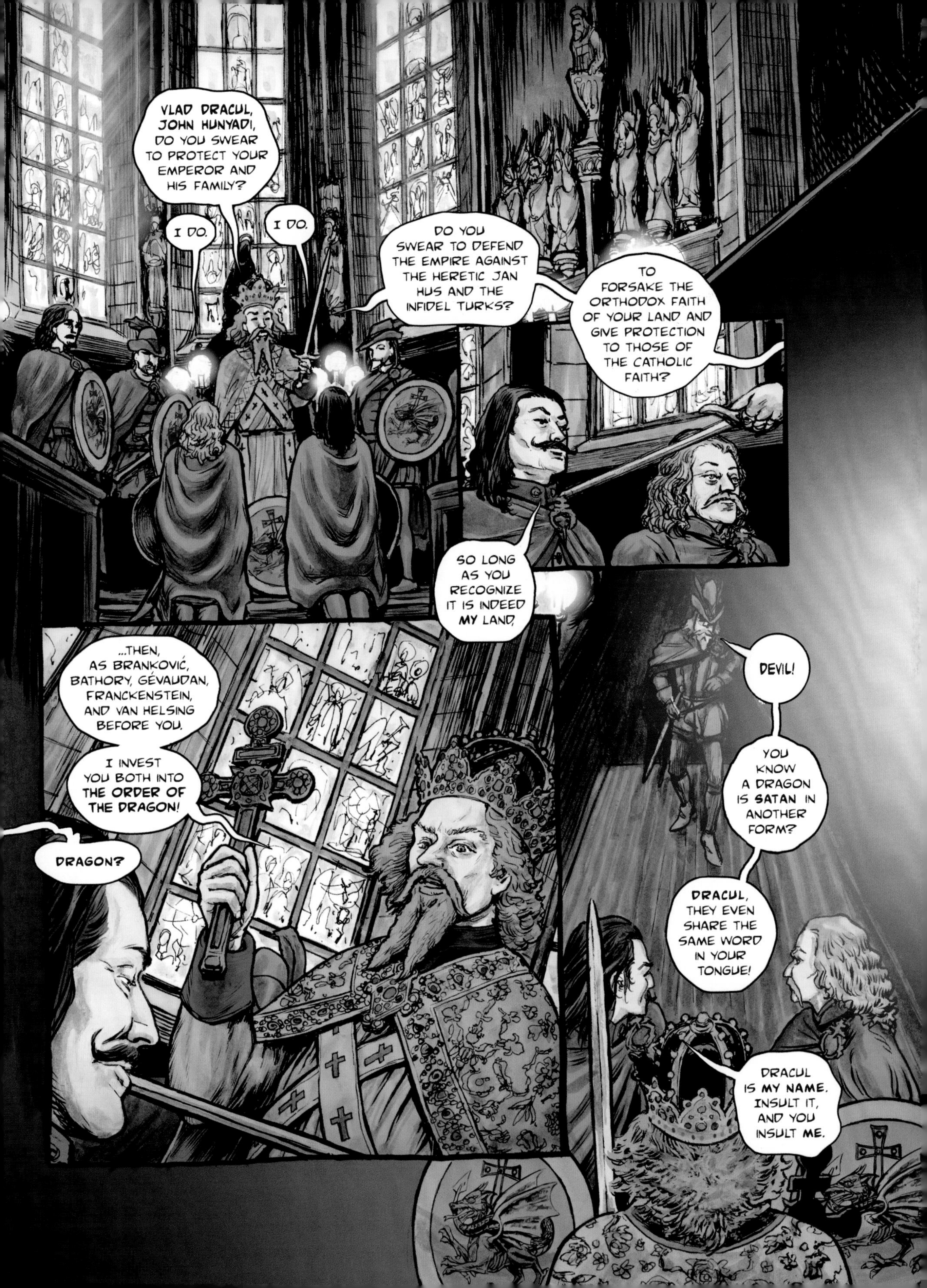
VLAD DRACUL, JOHN HUNYADI, DO YOU SWEAR TO PROTECT YOUR EMPEROR AND HIS FAMILY?
I DO.
I DO.
DO YOU SWEAR TO DEFEND THE EMPIRE AGAINST THE HERETIC JAN HUS AND THE INFIDEL TURKS?
TO FORSAKE THE ORTHODOX FAITH OF YOUR LAND AND GIVE PROTECTION TO THOSE OF THE CATHOLIC FAITH?
SO LONG AS YOU RECOGNIZE IT IS INDEED MY LAND.
...THEN, AS BRANKOVIĆ, BATHORY, GÉVAUDAN, FRANCKENSTEIN, AND VAN HELSING BEFORE YOU.
I INVEST YOU BOTH INTO THE ORDER OF THE DRAGON!
DRAGON?
DEVIL!
YOU KNOW A DRAGON IS SATAN IN ANOTHER FORM?
DRACUL, THEY EVEN SHARE THE SAME WORD IN YOUR TONGUE!
DRACUL IS MY NAME. INSULT IT, AND YOU INSULT ME.

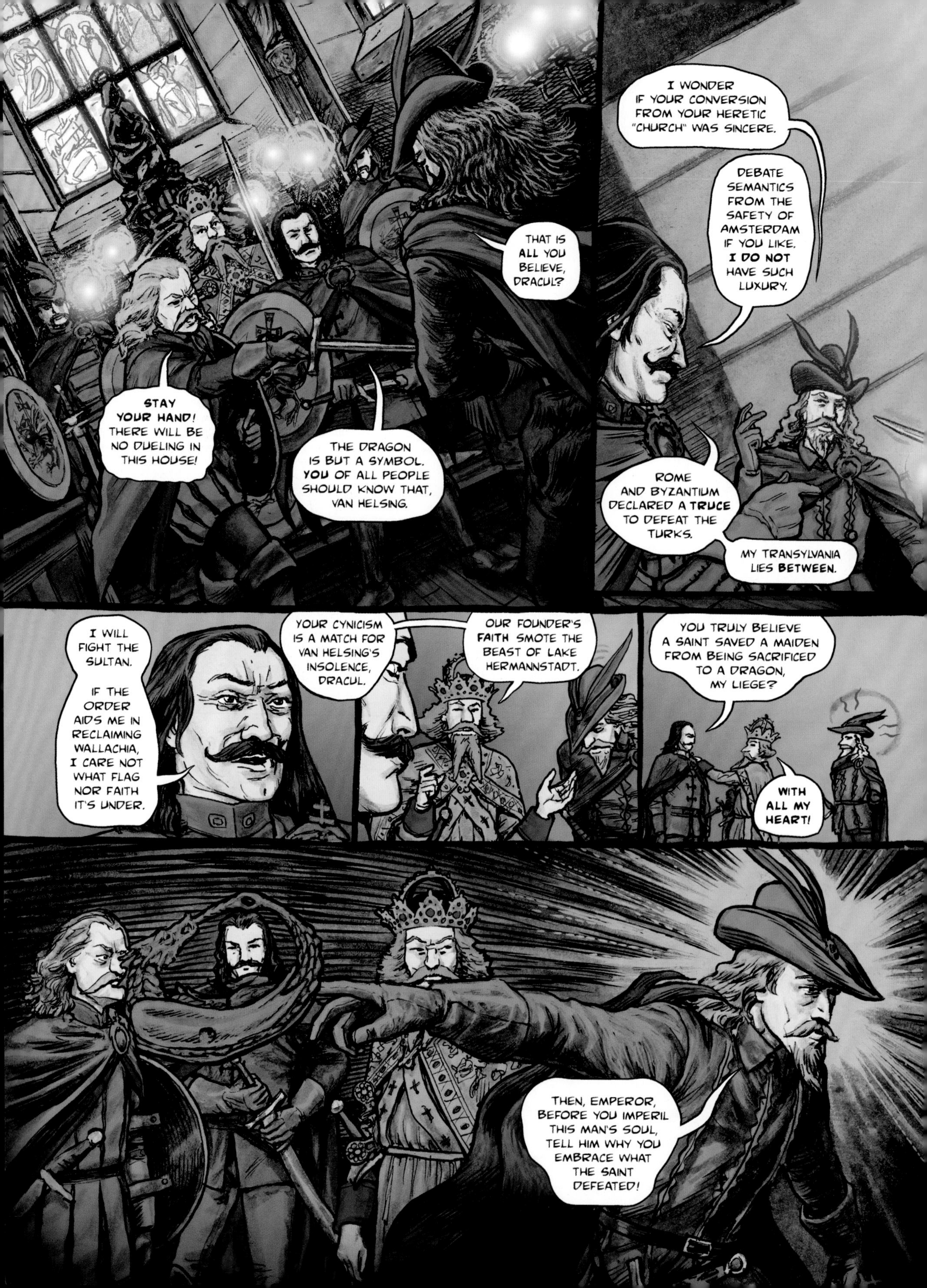
THAT IS ALL YOU BELIEVE, DRACUL?
STAY YOUR HAND! THERE WILL BE NO DUELING IN THIS HOUSE!
THE DRAGON IS BUT A SYMBOL. YOU OF ALL PEOPLE SHOULD KNOW THAT, VAN HELSING.
I WONDER IF YOUR CONVERSION FROM YOUR HERETIC "CHURCH" WAS SINCERE.
DEBATE SEMANTICS FROM THE SAFETY OF AMSTERDAM IF YOU LIKE. I DO NOT HAVE SUCH LUXURY.
ROME AND BYZANTIUM DECLARED A TRUCE TO DEFEAT THE TURKS.
MY TRANSYLVANIA LIES BETWEEN.
I WILL FIGHT THE SULTAN.
IF THE ORDER AIDS ME IN RECLAIMING WALLACHIA, I CARE NOT WHAT FLAG NOR FAITH IT'S UNDER.
YOUR CYNICISM IS A MATCH FOR VAN HELSING'S INSOLENCE, DRACUL.
OUR FOUNDER'S FAITH SMOTE THE BEAST OF LAKE HERMANNSTADT.
YOU TRULY BELIEVE A SAINT SAVED A MAIDEN FROM BEING SACRIFICED TO A DRAGON, MY LIEGE?
WITH ALL MY HEART!
THEN, EMPEROR, BEFORE YOU IMPERIL THIS MAN'S SOUL, TELL HIM WHY YOU EMBRACE WHAT THE SAINT DEFEATED!

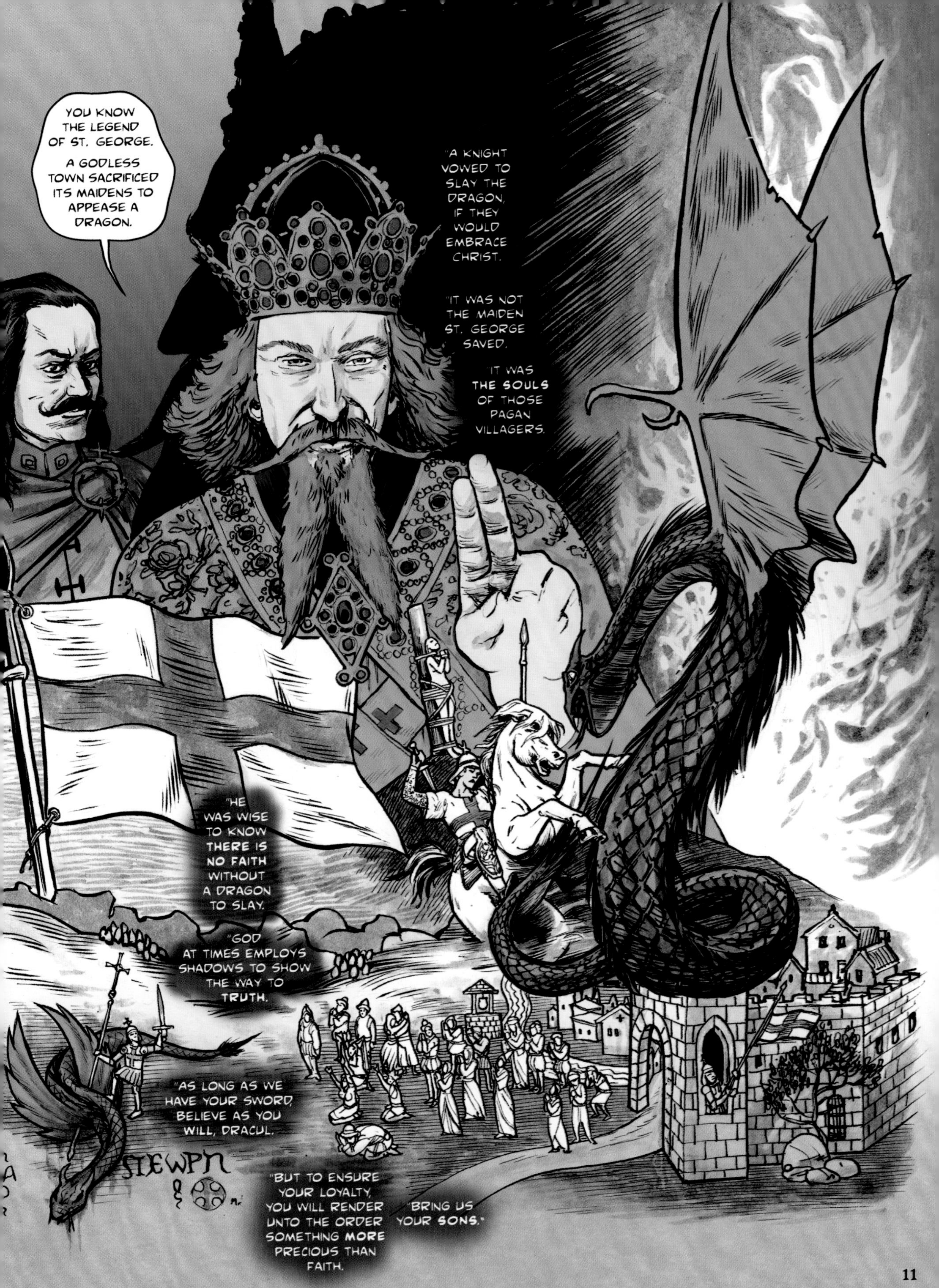
YOU KNOW THE LEGEND OF ST. GEORGE.
A GODLESS TOWN SACRIFICED ITS MAIDENS TO APPEASE A DRAGON.
"A KNIGHT VOWED TO SLAY THE DRAGON, IF THEY WOULD EMBRACE CHRIST.
"IT WAS NOT THE MAIDEN ST. GEORGE SAVED.
"IT WAS **THE SOULS** OF THOSE PAGAN VILLAGERS.
"HE WAS WISE TO KNOW **THERE IS NO FAITH** WITHOUT A DRAGON TO SLAY.
"GOD AT TIMES EMPLOYS SHADOWS TO SHOW THE WAY TO **TRUTH**.
"AS LONG AS WE HAVE YOUR SWORD, BELIEVE AS YOU WILL, DRACUL.
"BUT TO ENSURE YOUR LOYALTY, YOU WILL RENDER UNTO THE ORDER SOMETHING **MORE** PRECIOUS THAN FAITH.
"BRING US YOUR **SONS**."

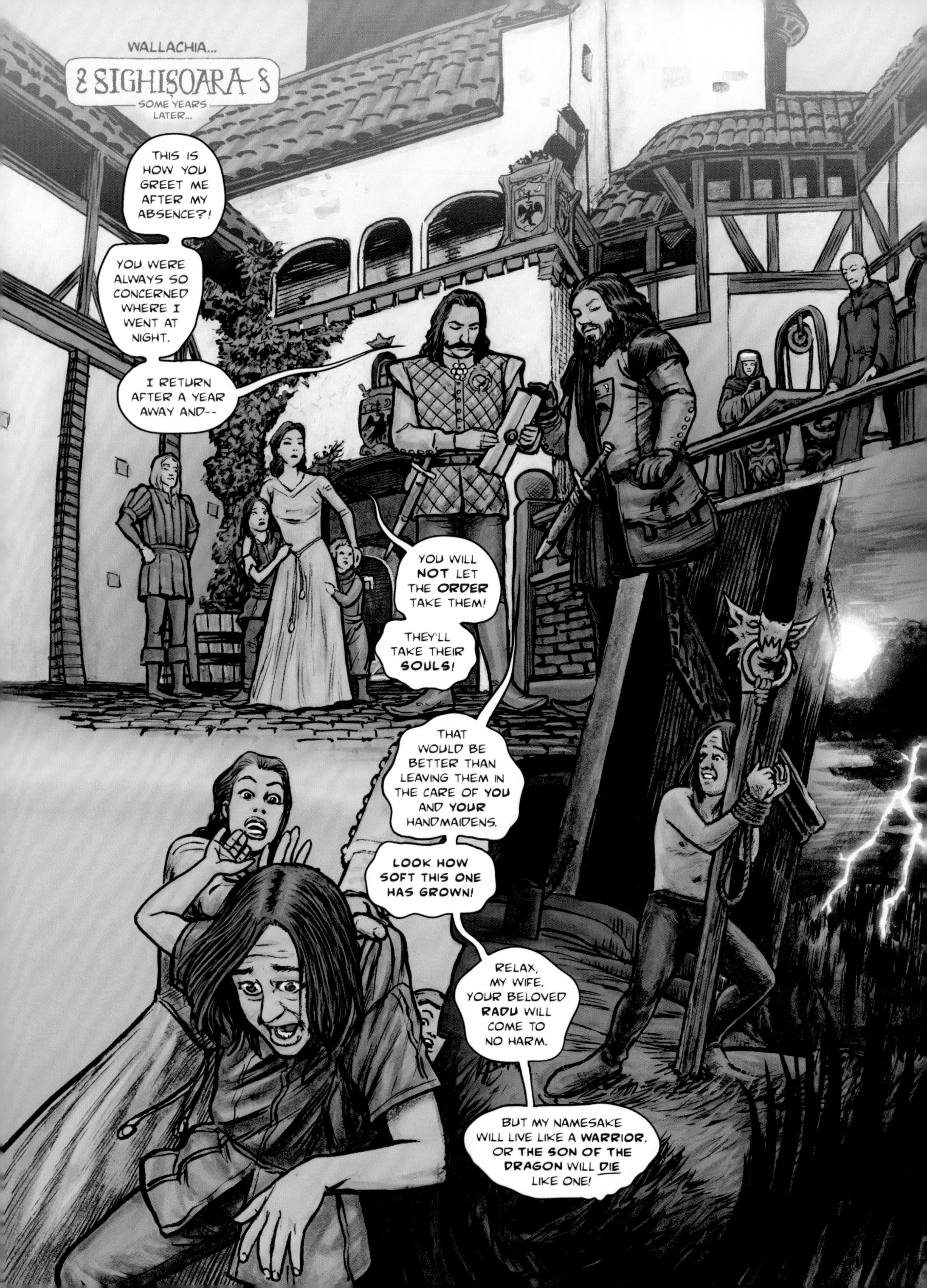
WALLACHIA...
SIGHIŞOARA
SOME YEARS LATER...
THIS IS HOW YOU GREET ME AFTER MY ABSENCE?!
YOU WERE ALWAYS SO CONCERNED WHERE I WENT AT NIGHT.
I RETURN AFTER A YEAR AWAY AND--
YOU WILL NOT LET THE ORDER TAKE THEM!
THEY'LL TAKE THEIR SOULS!
THAT WOULD BE BETTER THAN LEAVING THEM IN THE CARE OF YOU AND YOUR HANDMAIDENS.
LOOK HOW SOFT THIS ONE HAS GROWN!
RELAX, MY WIFE. YOUR BELOVED RADU WILL COME TO NO HARM.
BUT MY NAMESAKE WILL LIVE LIKE A WARRIOR, OR THE SON OF THE DRAGON WILL DIE LIKE ONE!

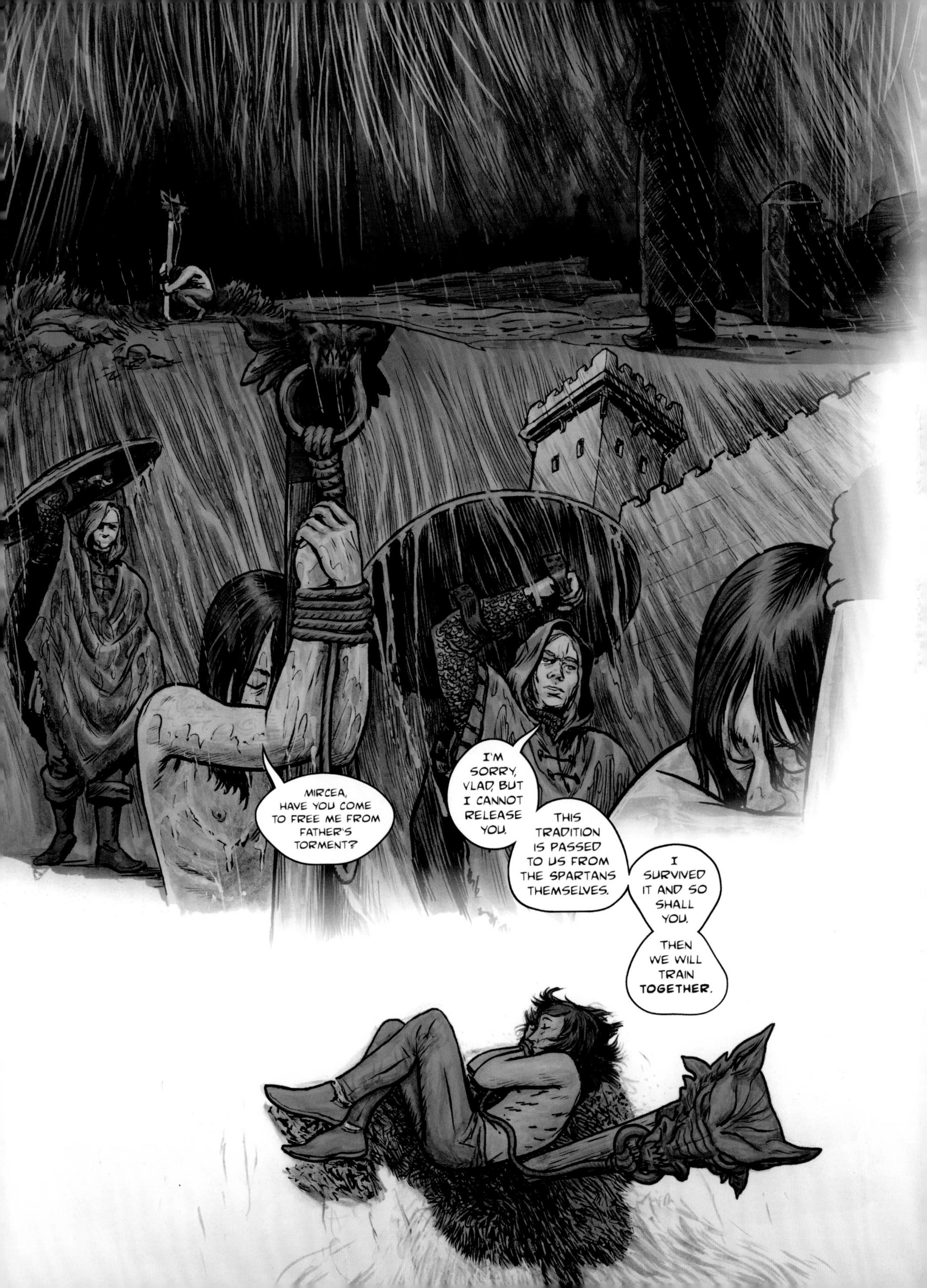
MIRCEA, HAVE YOU COME TO FREE ME FROM FATHER'S TORMENT?
I'M SORRY, VLAD, BUT I CANNOT RELEASE YOU.
THIS TRADITION IS PASSED TO US FROM THE SPARTANS THEMSELVES.
I SURVIVED IT AND SO SHALL YOU.
THEN WE WILL TRAIN TOGETHER.

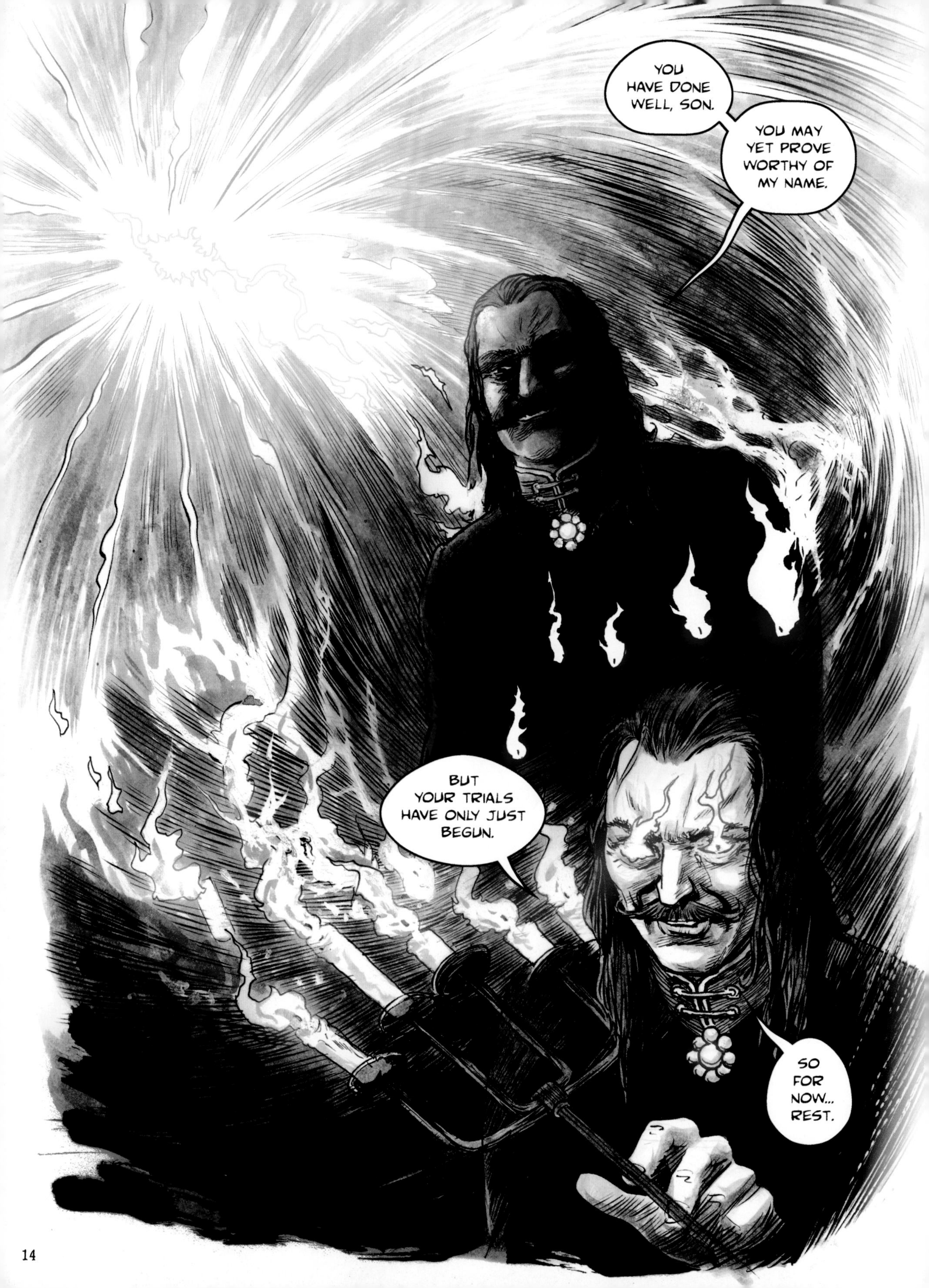
YOU HAVE DONE WELL, SON.
YOU MAY YET PROVE WORTHY OF MY NAME.
BUT YOUR TRIALS HAVE ONLY JUST BEGUN.
SO FOR NOW... REST.

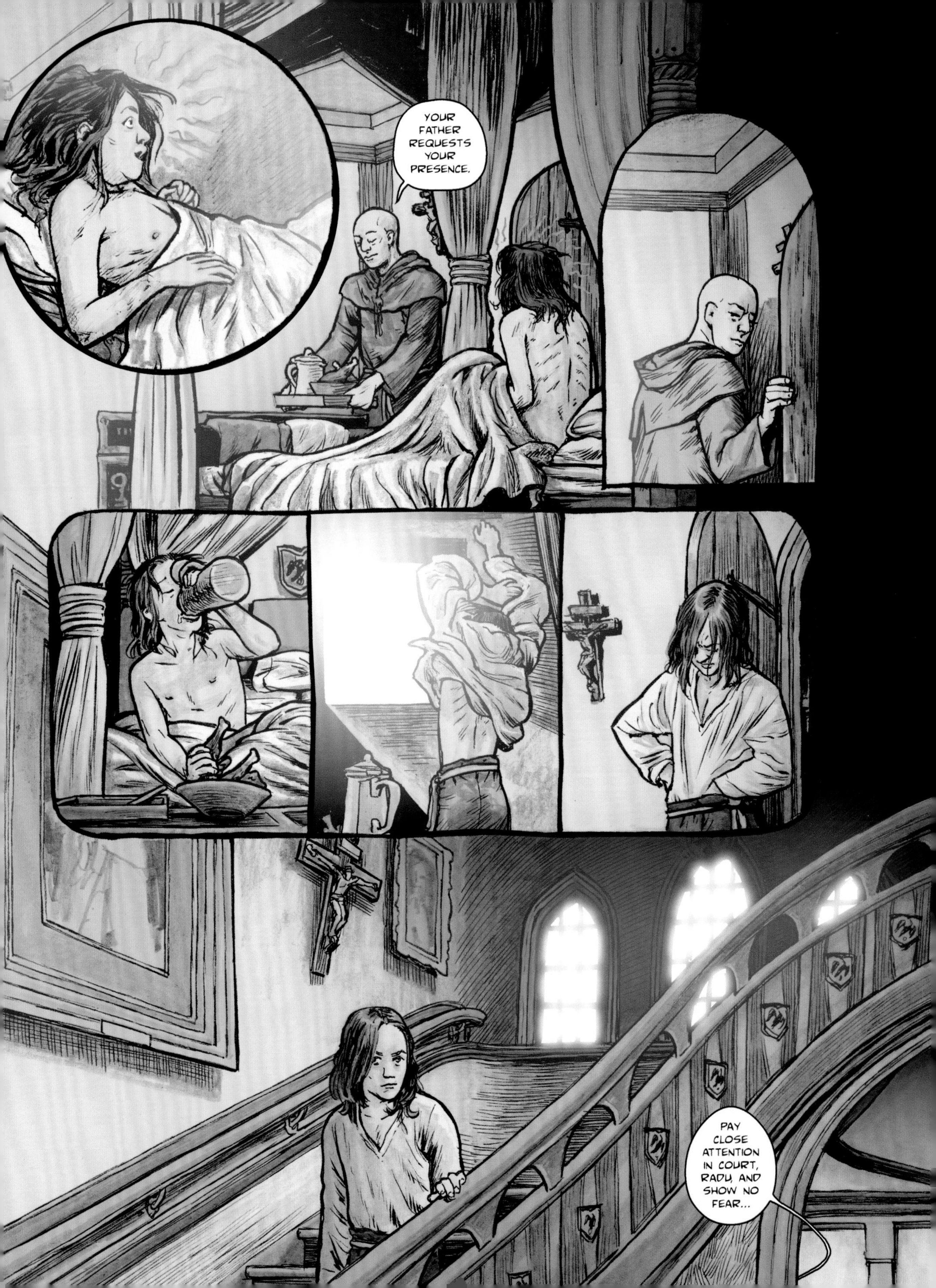

YOUR FATHER REQUESTS YOUR PRESENCE.
PAY CLOSE ATTENTION IN COURT, RADU, AND SHOW NO FEAR...

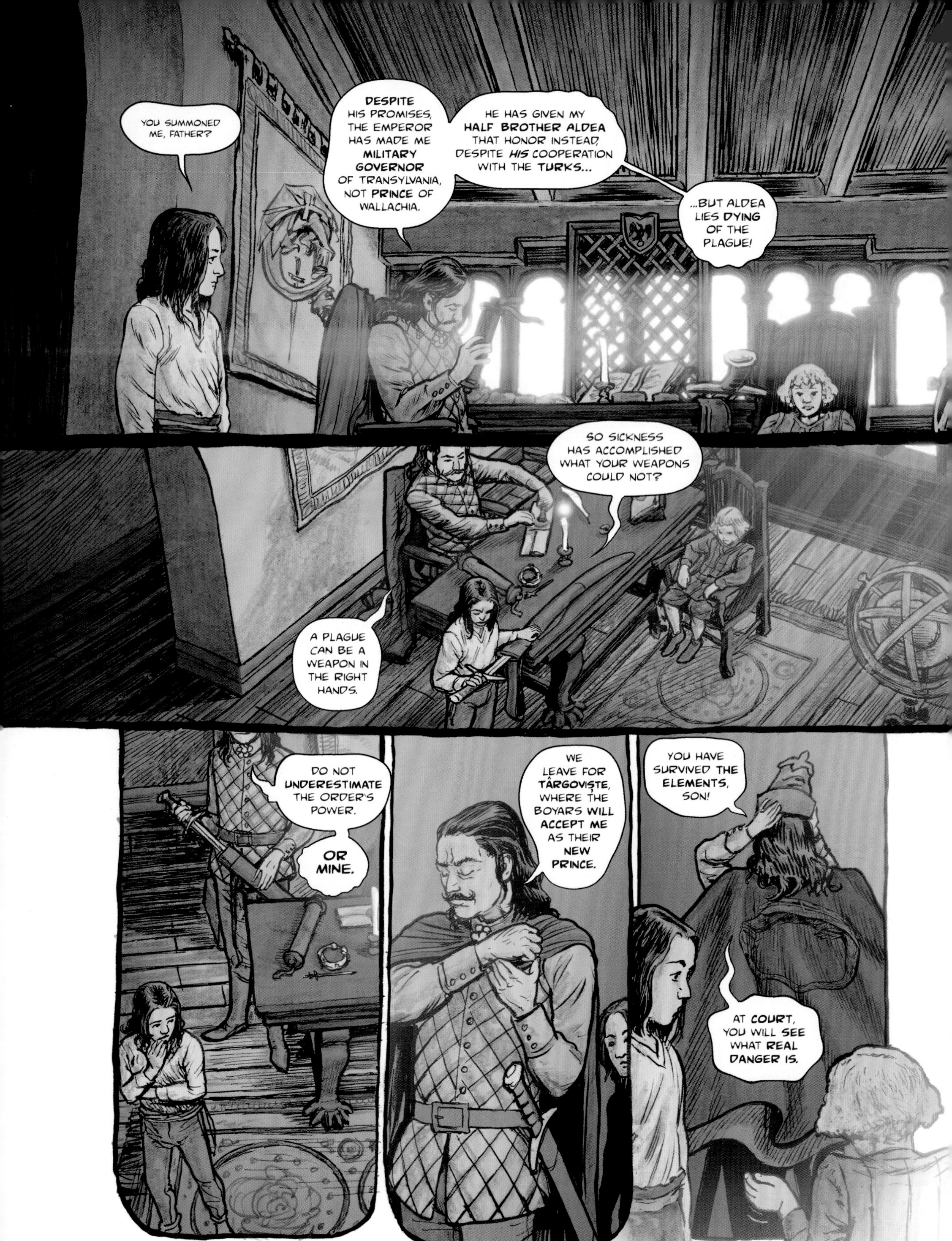
YOU SUMMONED ME, FATHER?
DESPITE HIS PROMISES, THE EMPEROR HAS MADE ME MILITARY GOVERNOR OF TRANSYLVANIA, NOT PRINCE OF WALLACHIA.
HE HAS GIVEN MY HALF BROTHER ALDEA THAT HONOR INSTEAD, DESPITE HIS COOPERATION WITH THE TURKS...
...BUT ALDEA LIES DYING OF THE PLAGUE!
SO SICKNESS HAS ACCOMPLISHED WHAT YOUR WEAPONS COULD NOT?
A PLAGUE CAN BE A WEAPON IN THE RIGHT HANDS.
DO NOT UNDERESTIMATE THE ORDER'S POWER.
OR MINE.
WE LEAVE FOR TÂRGOVIȘTE, WHERE THE BOYARS WILL ACCEPT ME AS THEIR NEW PRINCE.
YOU HAVE SURVIVED THE ELEMENTS, SON!
AT COURT, YOU WILL SEE WHAT REAL DANGER IS.

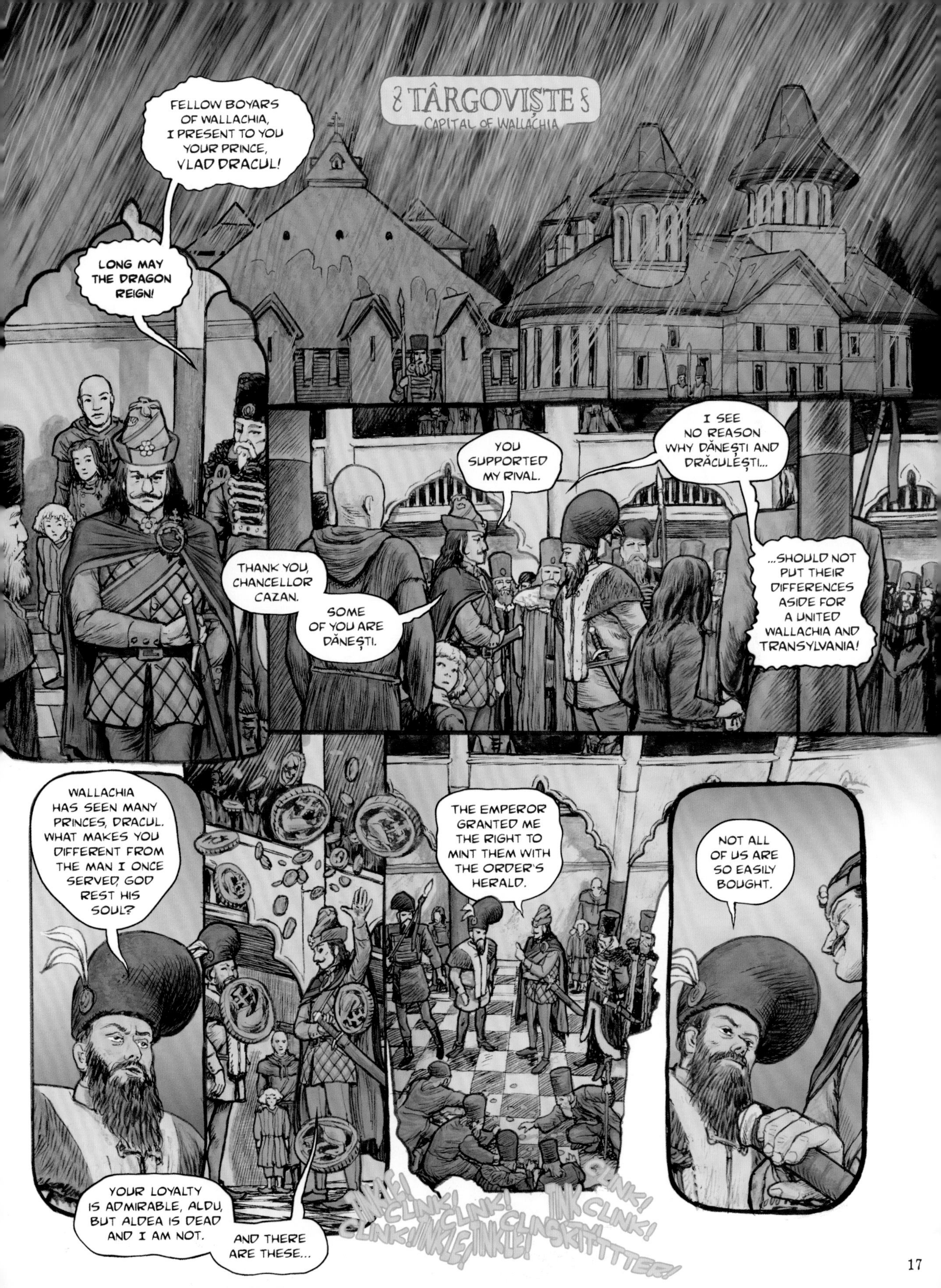
TÂRGOVIȘTE
CAPITAL OF WALLACHIA
FELLOW BOYARS OF WALLACHIA, I PRESENT TO YOU YOUR PRINCE, VLAD DRACUL!
LONG MAY THE DRAGON REIGN!
THANK YOU, CHANCELLOR CAZAN.
SOME OF YOU ARE DĂNEȘTI.
YOU SUPPORTED MY RIVAL.
I SEE NO REASON WHY DĂNEȘTI AND DRĂCULEȘTI...
...SHOULD NOT PUT THEIR DIFFERENCES ASIDE FOR A UNITED WALLACHIA AND TRANSYLVANIA!
WALLACHIA HAS SEEN MANY PRINCES, DRACUL. WHAT MAKES YOU DIFFERENT FROM THE MAN I ONCE SERVED, GOD REST HIS SOUL?
YOUR LOYALTY IS ADMIRABLE, ALDU, BUT ALDEA IS DEAD AND I AM NOT.
AND THERE ARE THESE...
THE EMPEROR GRANTED ME THE RIGHT TO MINT THEM WITH THE ORDER'S HERALD.
NOT ALL OF US ARE SO EASILY BOUGHT.

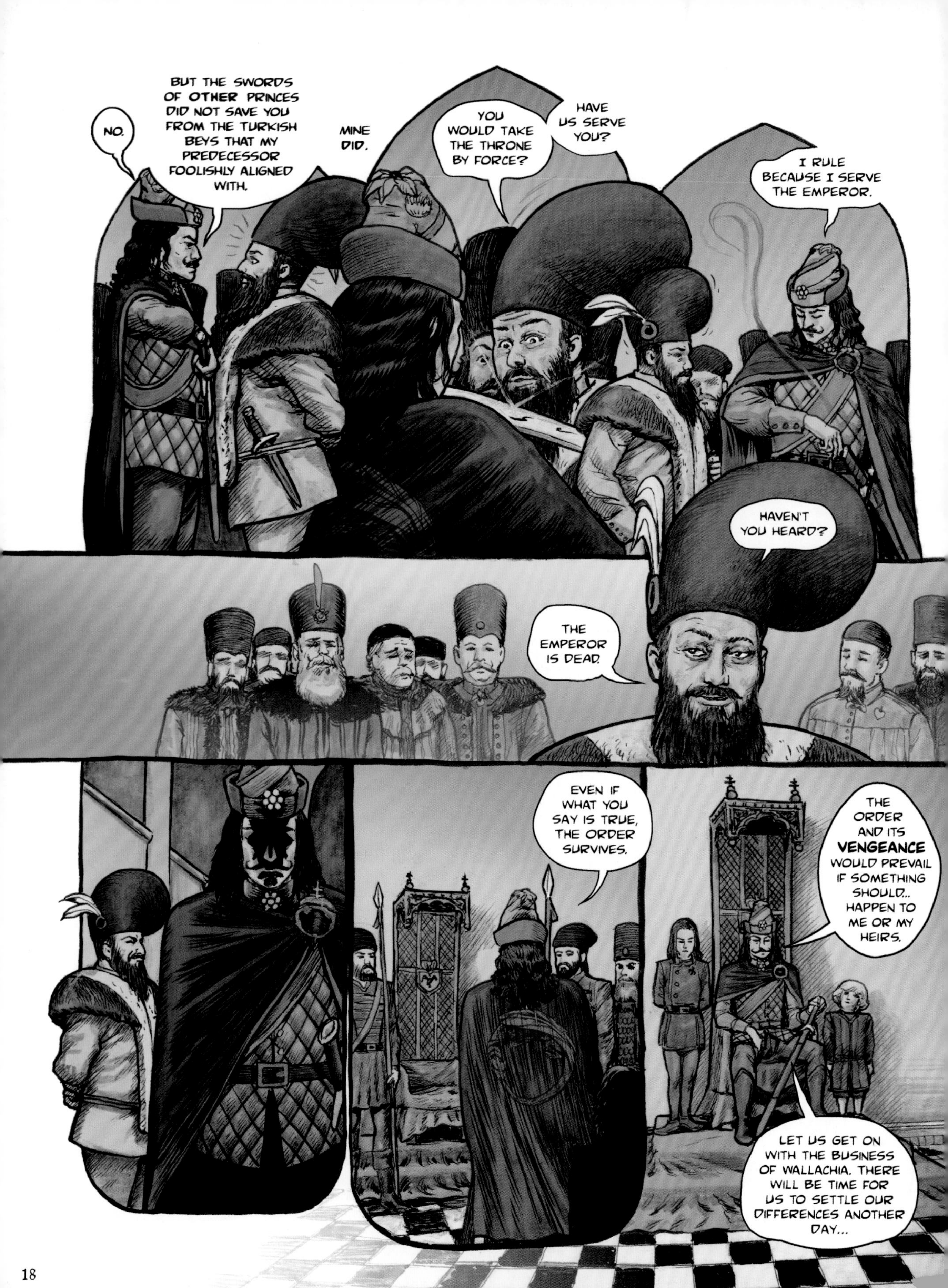
NO.
BUT THE SWORDS OF OTHER PRINCES DID NOT SAVE YOU FROM THE TURKISH BEYS THAT MY PREDECESSOR FOOLISHLY ALIGNED WITH.
MINE DID.
YOU WOULD TAKE THE THRONE BY FORCE?
HAVE US SERVE YOU?
I RULE BECAUSE I SERVE THE EMPEROR.
HAVEN'T YOU HEARD?
THE EMPEROR IS DEAD.
EVEN IF WHAT YOU SAY IS TRUE, THE ORDER SURVIVES.
THE ORDER AND ITS VENGEANCE WOULD PREVAIL IF SOMETHING SHOULD... HAPPEN TO ME OR MY HEIRS.
LET US GET ON WITH THE BUSINESS OF WALLACHIA. THERE WILL BE TIME FOR US TO SETTLE OUR DIFFERENCES ANOTHER DAY...

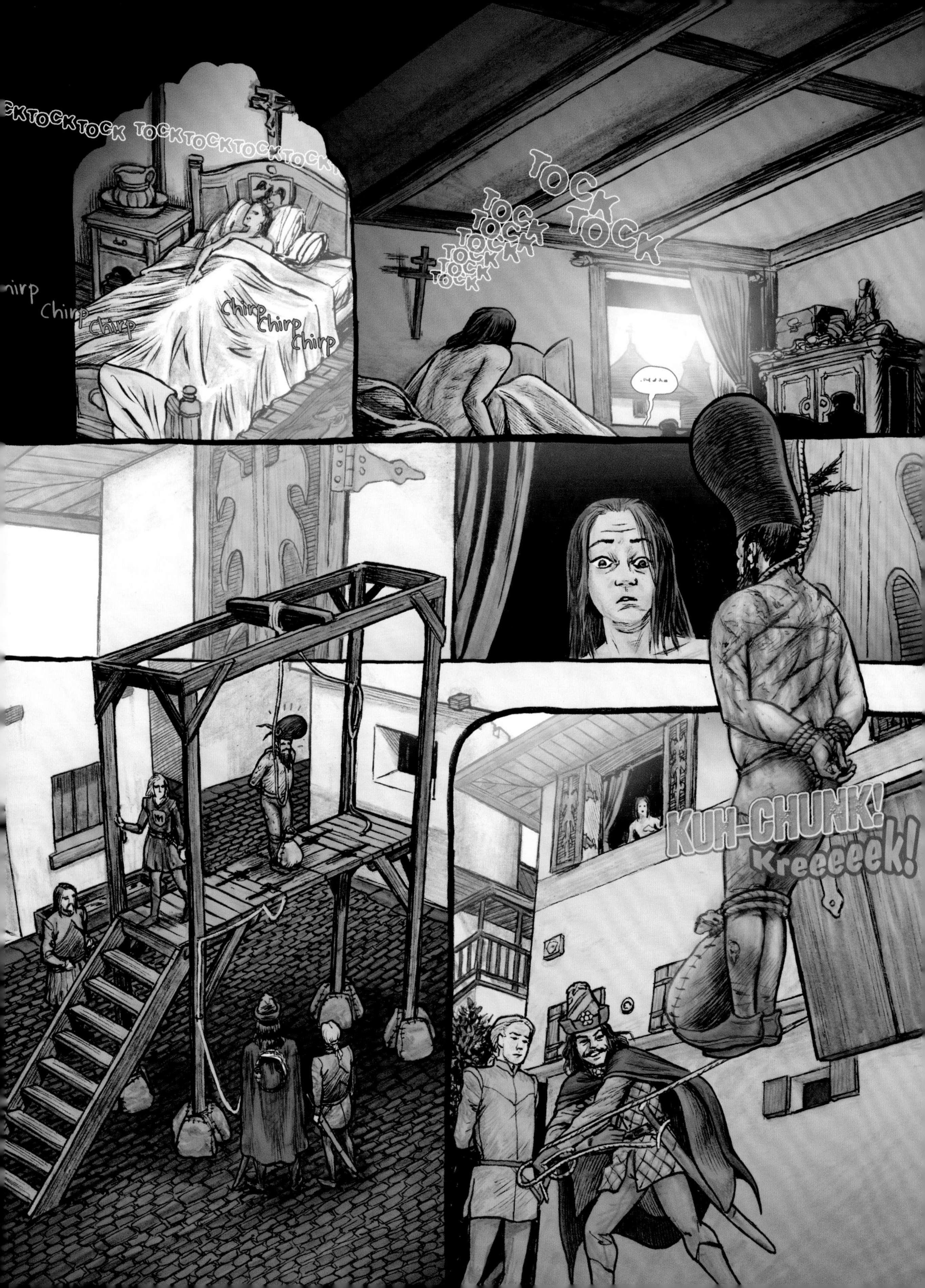
CKTOCKTOCK TOCKTOCKTOCKTOCK
hirp Chirp Chirp
Chirp Chirp Chirp
TOCK TOCK TOCK TOCK TOCK TOCK TOCK
KUH-CHUNK!
Kreeeeek!

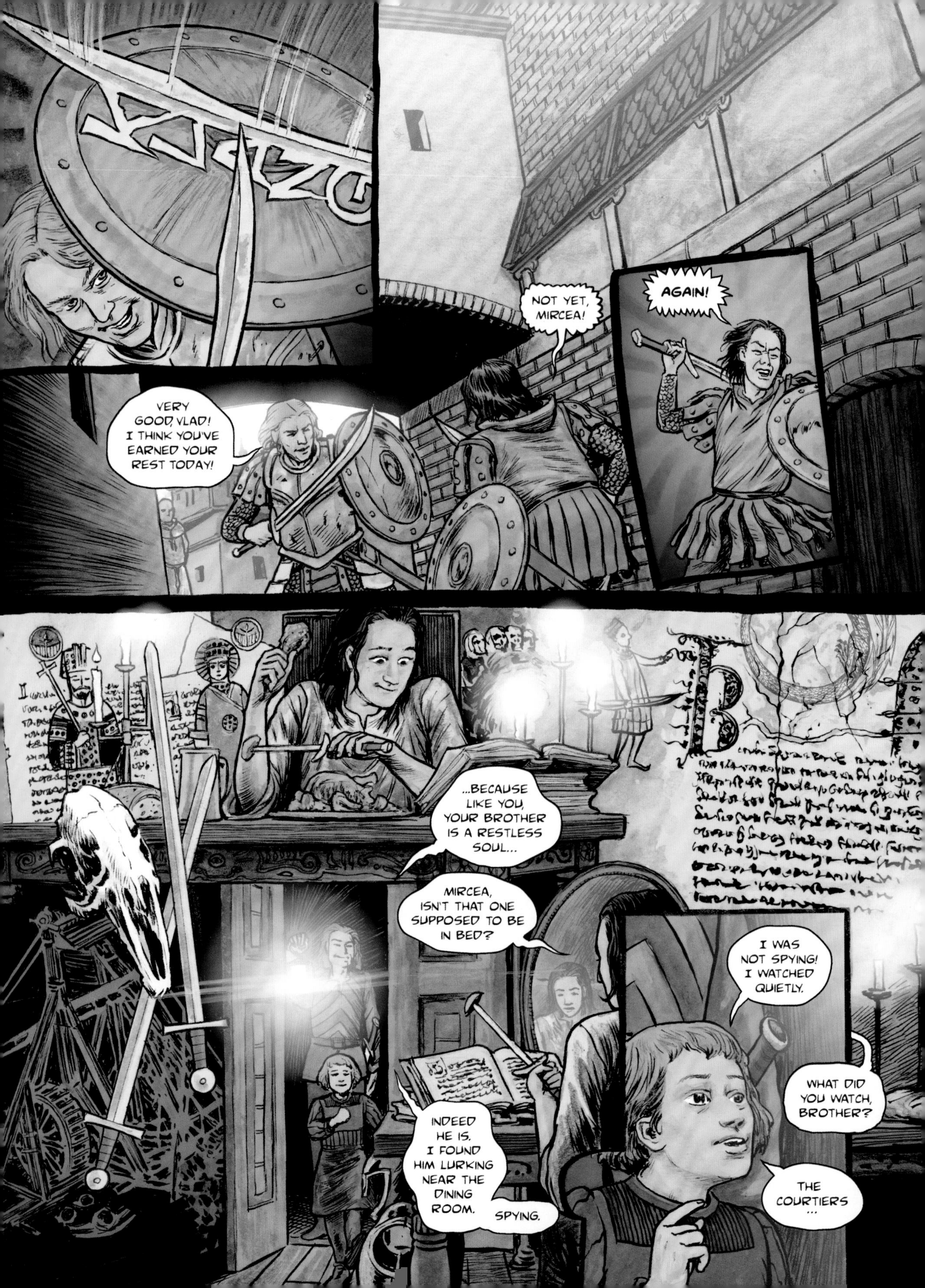

NOT YET, MIRCEA!
AGAIN!
VERY GOOD, VLAD! I THINK YOU'VE EARNED YOUR REST TODAY!
...BECAUSE LIKE YOU, YOUR BROTHER IS A RESTLESS SOUL...
MIRCEA, ISN'T THAT ONE SUPPOSED TO BE IN BED?
INDEED HE IS. I FOUND HIM LURKING NEAR THE DINING ROOM.
SPYING.
I WAS NOT SPYING! I WATCHED QUIETLY.
WHAT DID YOU WATCH, BROTHER?
THE COURTIERS ...

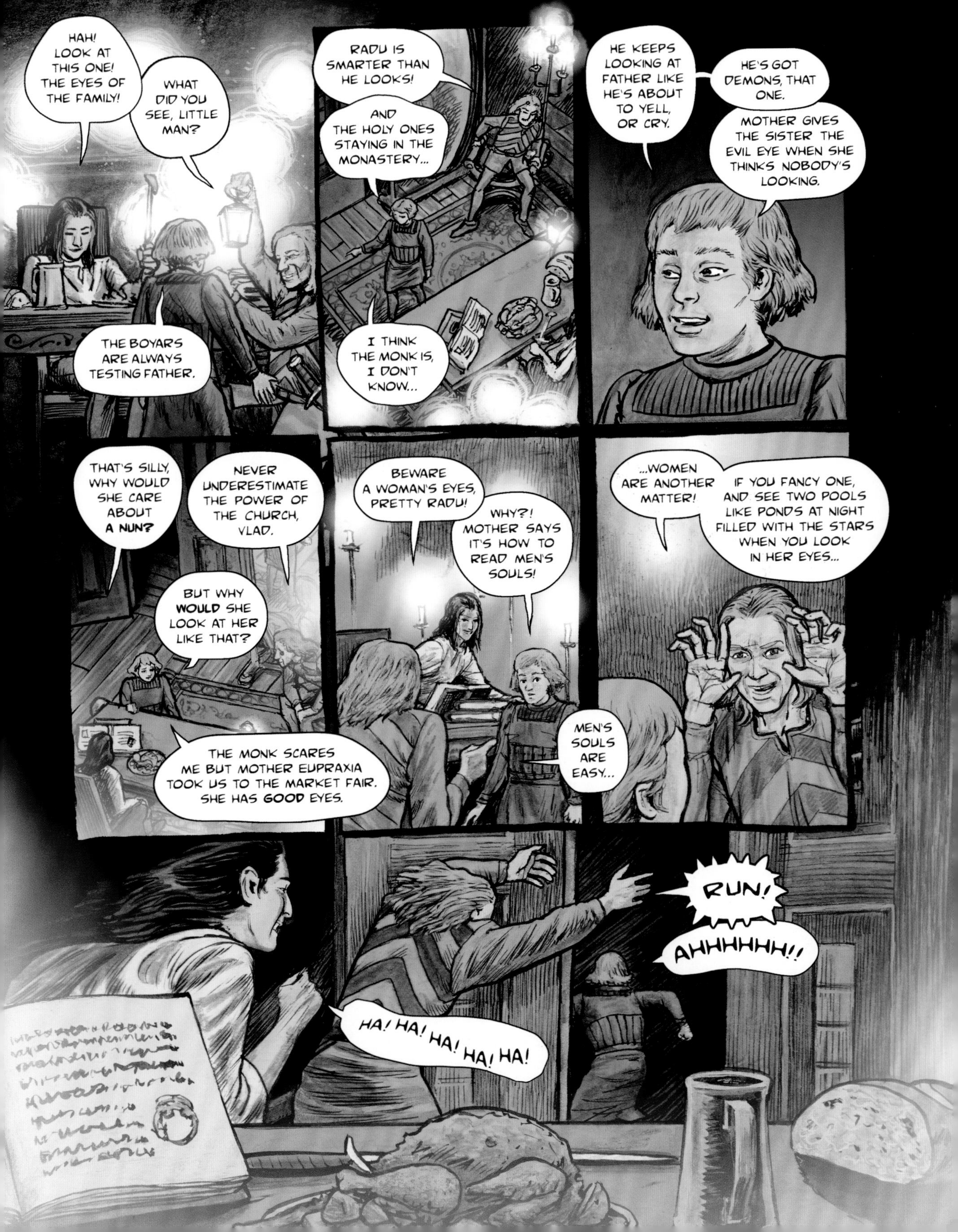
HAH! LOOK AT THIS ONE! THE EYES OF THE FAMILY!
WHAT DID YOU SEE, LITTLE MAN?
THE BOYARS ARE ALWAYS TESTING FATHER.
RADU IS SMARTER THAN HE LOOKS!
AND THE HOLY ONES STAYING IN THE MONASTERY...
I THINK THE MONK IS, I DON'T KNOW...
HE KEEPS LOOKING AT FATHER LIKE HE'S ABOUT TO YELL, OR CRY.
HE'S GOT DEMONS, THAT ONE.
MOTHER GIVES THE SISTER THE EVIL EYE WHEN SHE THINKS NOBODY'S LOOKING.
THAT'S SILLY, WHY WOULD SHE CARE ABOUT A NUN?
NEVER UNDERESTIMATE THE POWER OF THE CHURCH, VLAD.
BUT WHY WOULD SHE LOOK AT HER LIKE THAT?
THE MONK SCARES ME BUT MOTHER EUPRAXIA TOOK US TO THE MARKET FAIR. SHE HAS GOOD EYES.
BEWARE A WOMAN'S EYES, PRETTY RADU!
WHY?! MOTHER SAYS IT'S HOW TO READ MEN'S SOULS!
MEN'S SOULS ARE EASY...
...WOMEN ARE ANOTHER MATTER!
IF YOU FANCY ONE, AND SEE TWO POOLS LIKE PONDS AT NIGHT FILLED WITH THE STARS WHEN YOU LOOK IN HER EYES...
RUN!
AHHHHHH!!
HA! HA! HA! HA! HA!

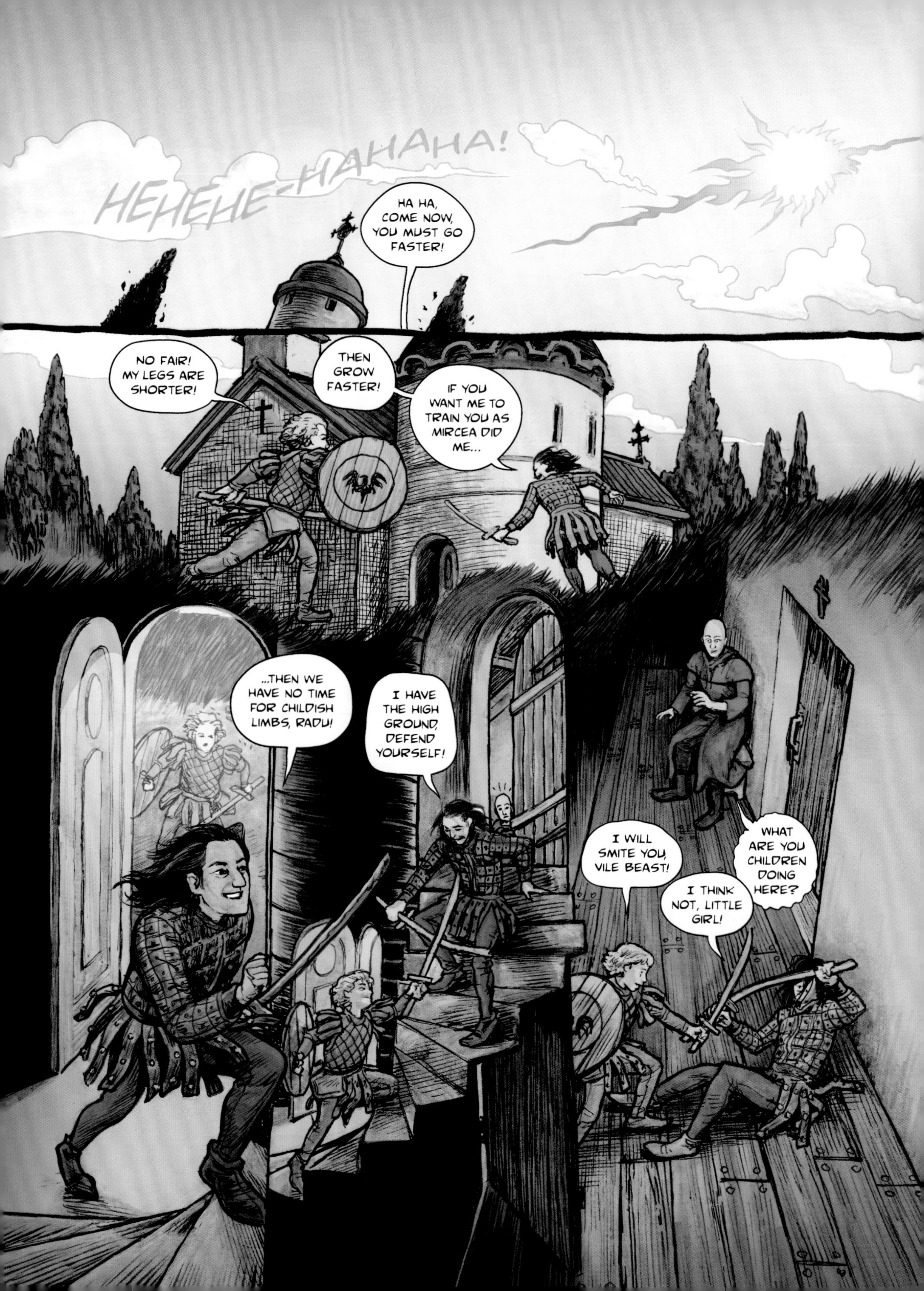
HEHEHE-HAHAHA!
HA HA, COME NOW, YOU MUST GO FASTER!
NO FAIR! MY LEGS ARE SHORTER!
THEN GROW FASTER!
IF YOU WANT ME TO TRAIN YOU AS MIRCEA DID ME...
...THEN WE HAVE NO TIME FOR CHILDISH LIMBS, RADU!
I HAVE THE HIGH GROUND, DEFEND YOURSELF!
I WILL SMITE YOU, VILE BEAST!
I THINK NOT, LITTLE GIRL!
WHAT ARE YOU CHILDREN DOING HERE?

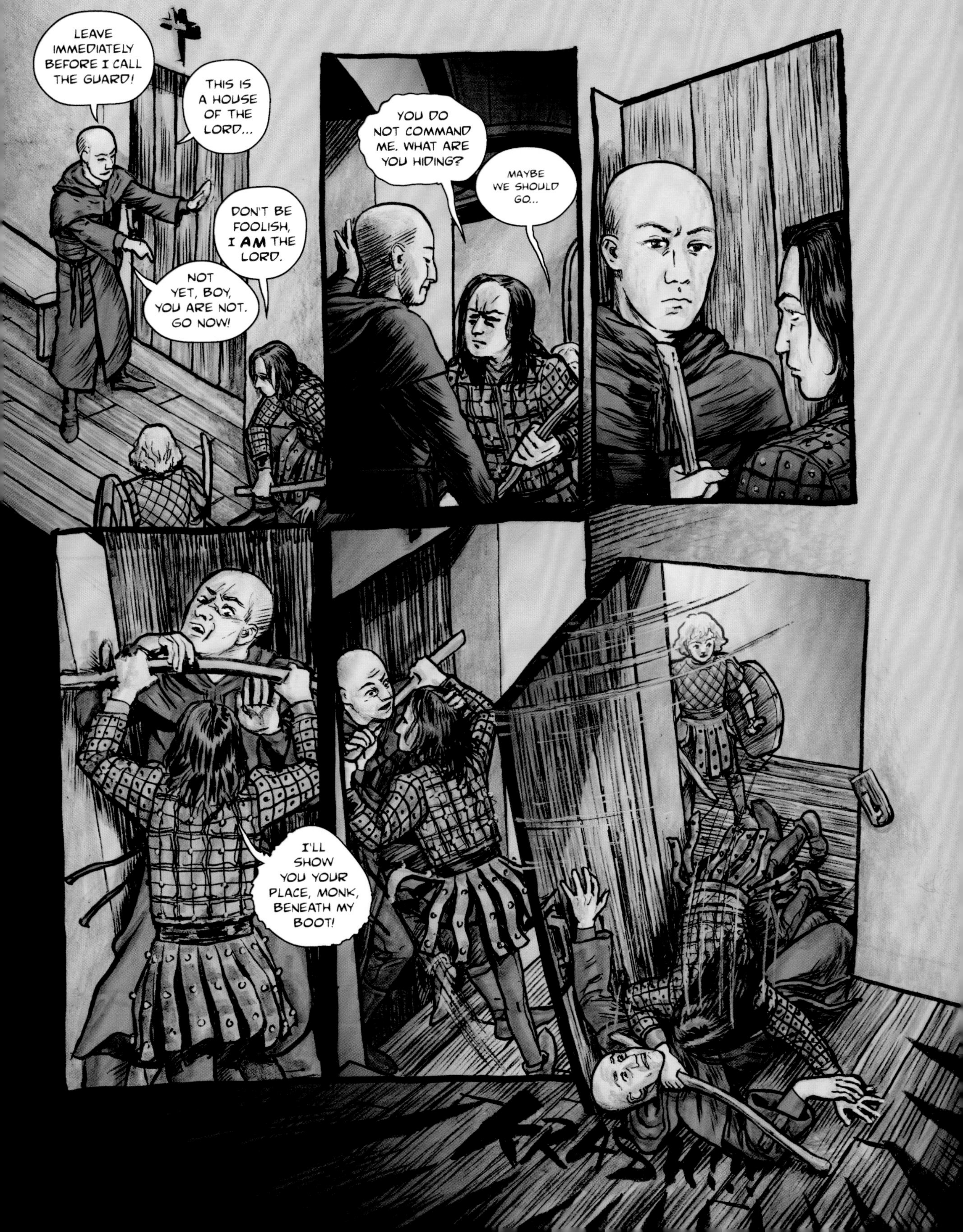
LEAVE IMMEDIATELY BEFORE I CALL THE GUARD!
THIS IS A HOUSE OF THE LORD...
DON'T BE FOOLISH, I **AM** THE LORD.
NOT YET, BOY, YOU ARE NOT. GO NOW!
YOU DO NOT COMMAND ME. WHAT ARE YOU HIDING?
MAYBE WE SHOULD GO...
I'LL SHOW YOU YOUR PLACE, MONK, BENEATH MY BOOT!
KRASH!!

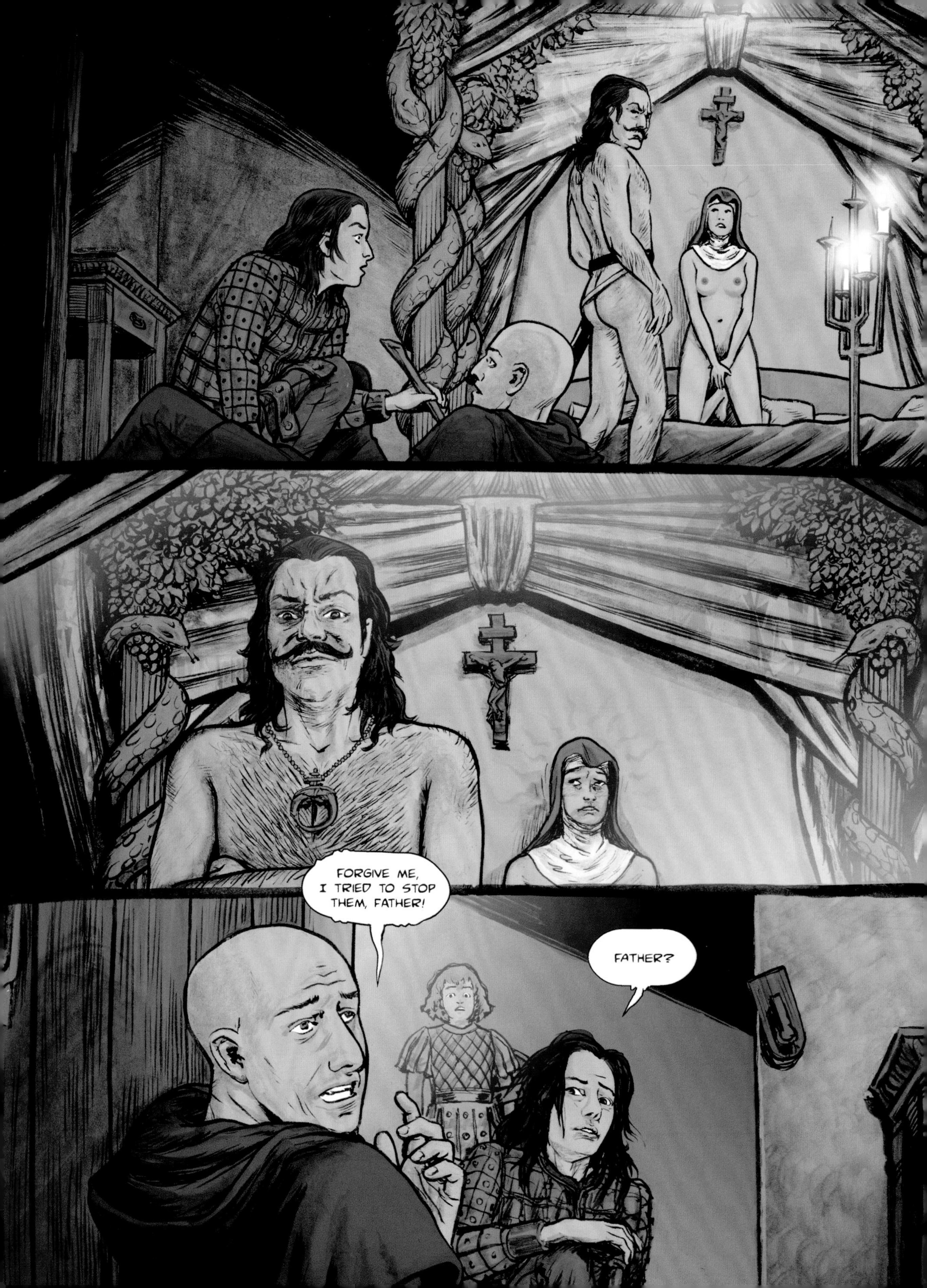
FORGIVE ME, I TRIED TO STOP THEM, FATHER!
FATHER?

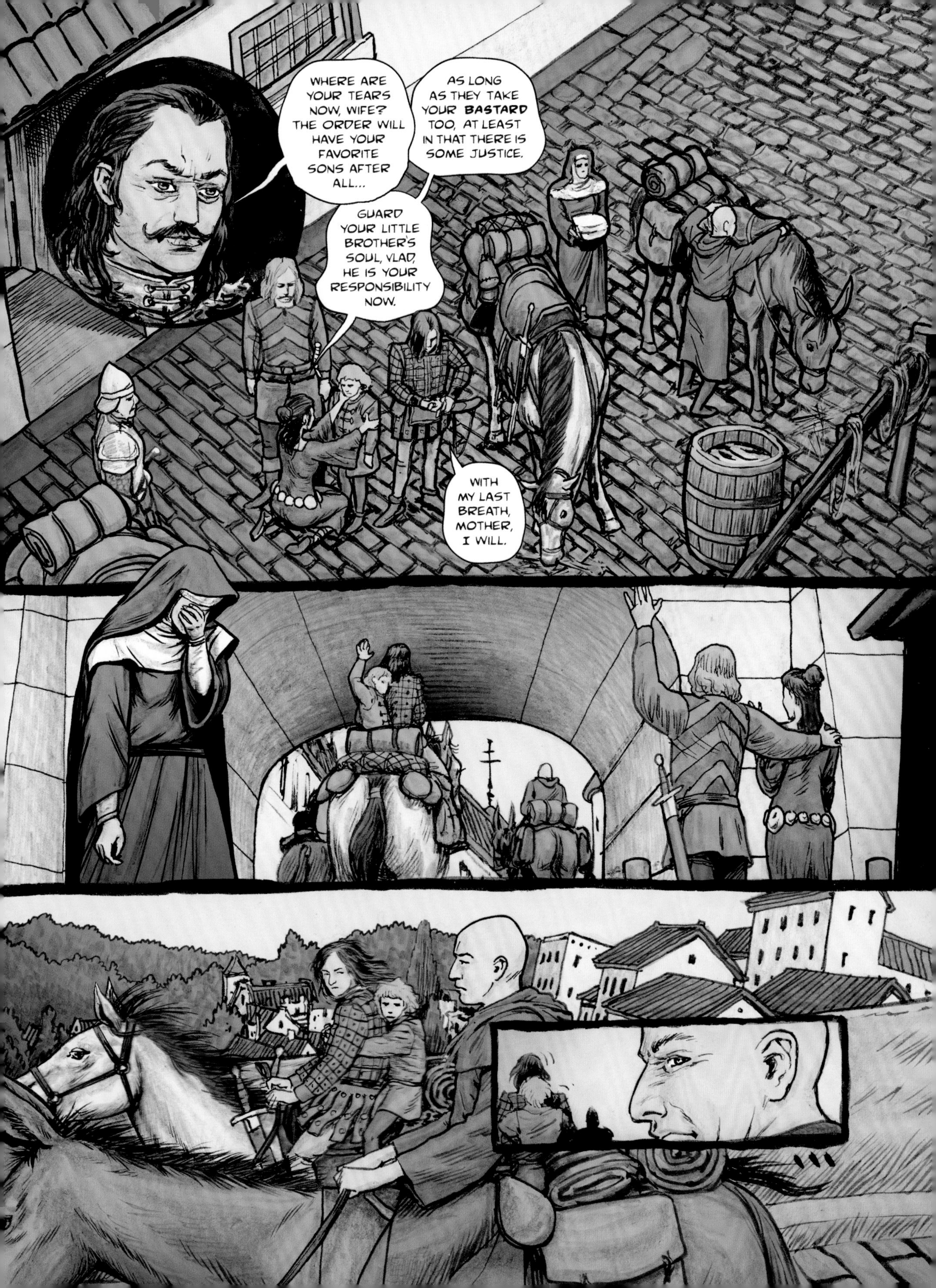
WHERE ARE YOUR TEARS NOW, WIFE? THE ORDER WILL HAVE YOUR FAVORITE SONS AFTER ALL...
AS LONG AS THEY TAKE YOUR **BASTARD** TOO, AT LEAST IN THAT THERE IS SOME JUSTICE.
GUARD YOUR LITTLE BROTHER'S SOUL, VLAD, HE IS YOUR RESPONSIBILITY NOW.
WITH MY LAST BREATH, MOTHER, I WILL.

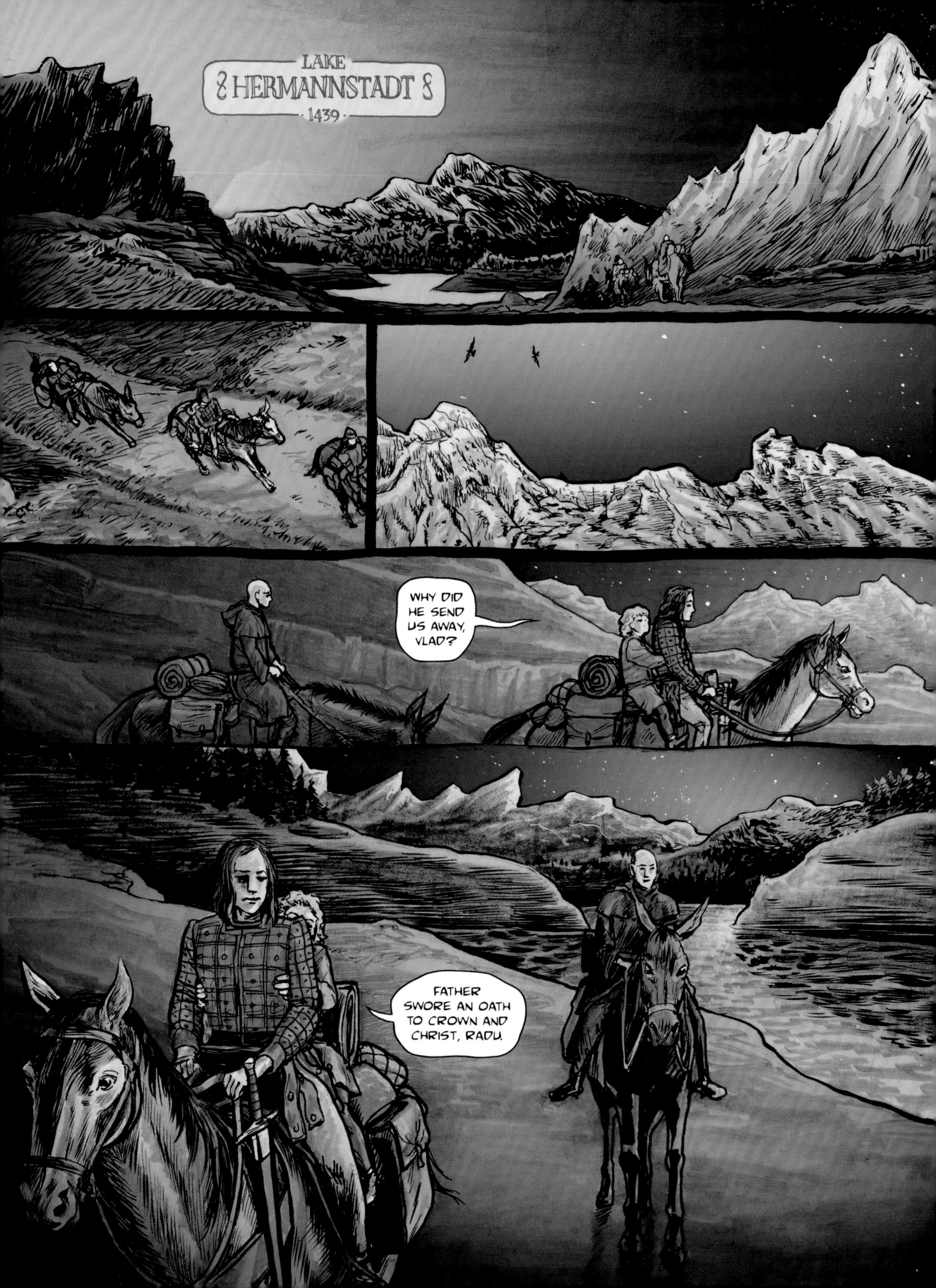
LAKE HERMANNSTADT 1439
WHY DID HE SEND US AWAY, VLAD?
FATHER SWORE AN OATH TO CROWN AND CHRIST, RADU.

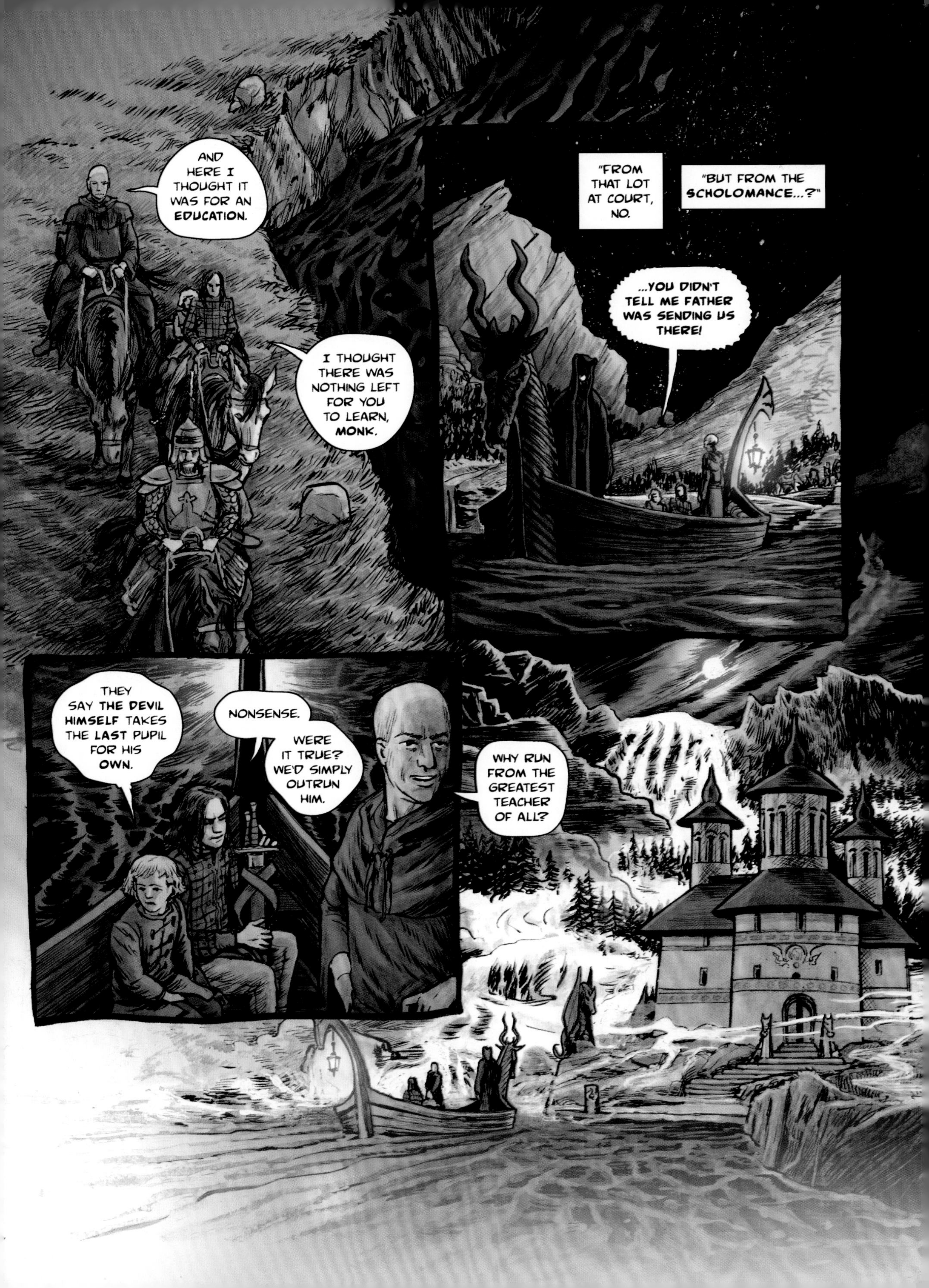
AND HERE I THOUGHT IT WAS FOR AN **EDUCATION.**
I THOUGHT THERE WAS NOTHING LEFT FOR YOU TO LEARN, **MONK.**
"FROM THAT LOT AT COURT, NO.
"BUT FROM THE **SCHOLOMANCE...?"**
...YOU DIDN'T TELL ME FATHER WAS SENDING US THERE!
THEY SAY **THE DEVIL HIMSELF** TAKES THE **LAST** PUPIL FOR HIS **OWN.**
NONSENSE.
WERE IT TRUE? WE'D SIMPLY OUTRUN HIM.
WHY RUN FROM THE GREATEST TEACHER OF ALL?

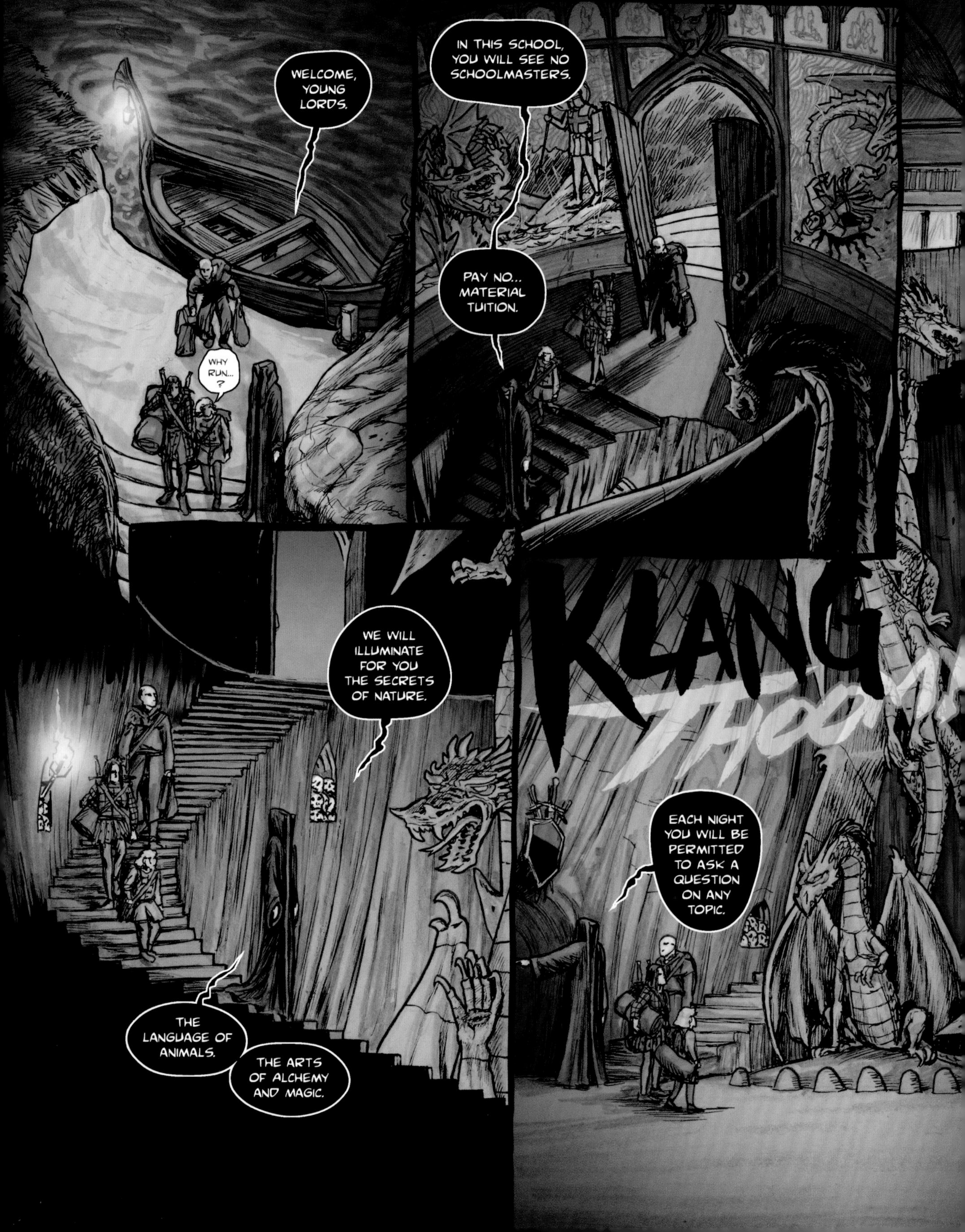
WELCOME, YOUNG LORDS.
WHY RUN...?
IN THIS SCHOOL, YOU WILL SEE NO SCHOOLMASTERS.
PAY NO... MATERIAL TUITION.
WE WILL ILLUMINATE FOR YOU THE SECRETS OF NATURE.
THE LANGUAGE OF ANIMALS.
THE ARTS OF ALCHEMY AND MAGIC.
KLANG
EACH NIGHT YOU WILL BE PERMITTED TO ASK A QUESTION ON ANY TOPIC.

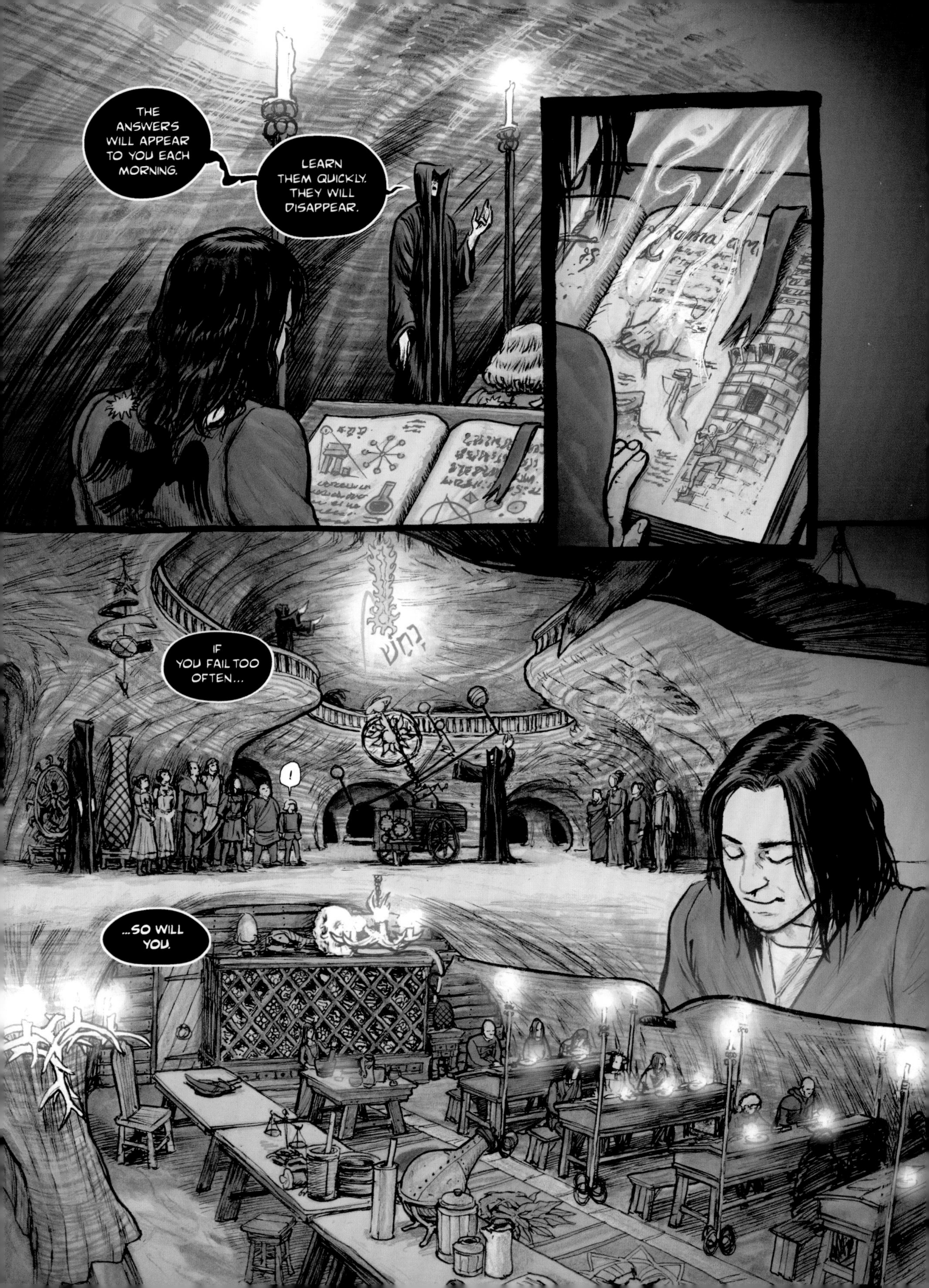
THE ANSWERS WILL APPEAR TO YOU EACH MORNING.
LEARN THEM QUICKLY. THEY WILL DISAPPEAR.
IF YOU FAIL TOO OFTEN...
!
...SO WILL YOU.

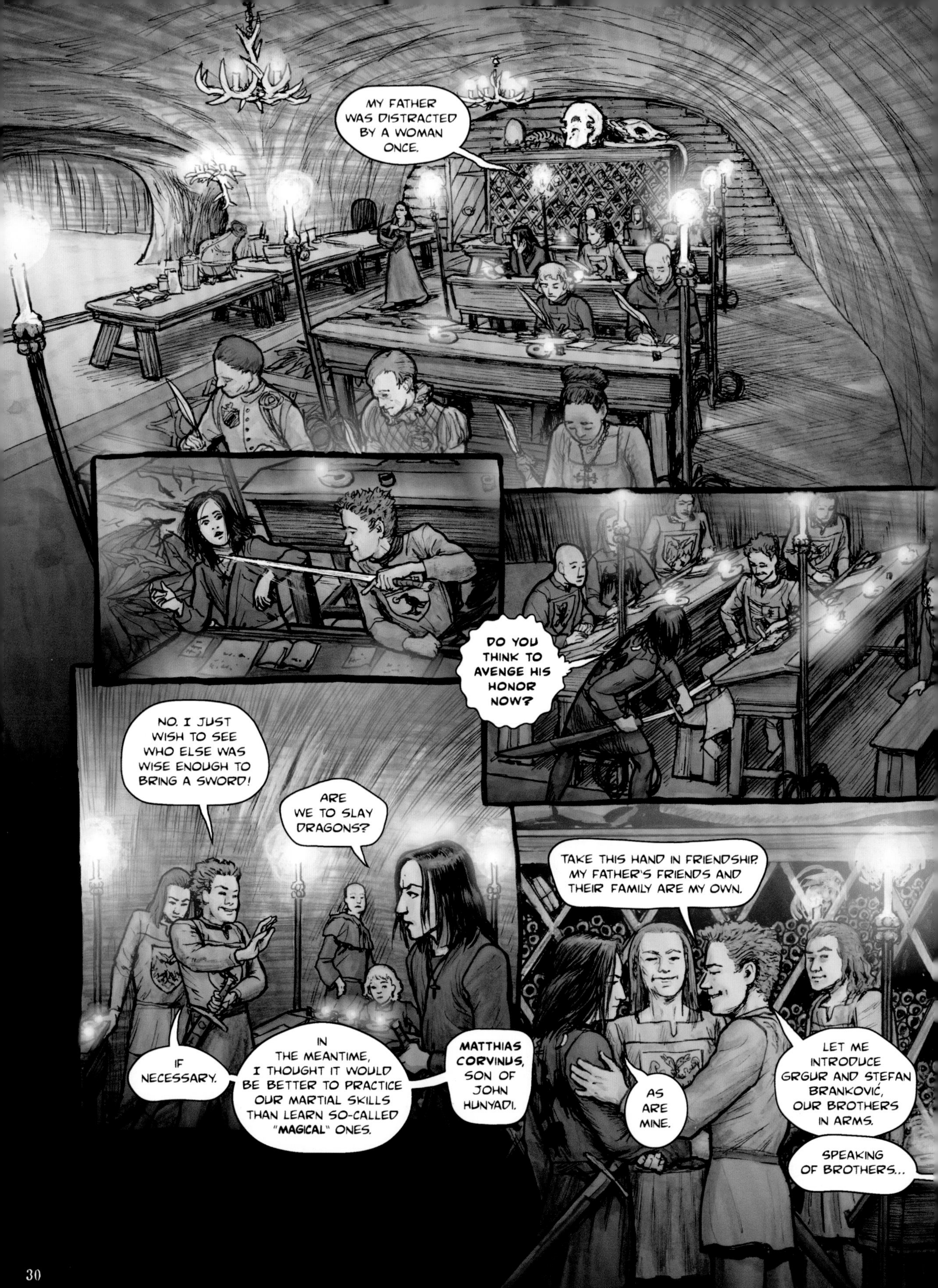

MY FATHER WAS DISTRACTED BY A WOMAN ONCE.
DO YOU THINK TO AVENGE HIS HONOR NOW?
NO. I JUST WISH TO SEE WHO ELSE WAS WISE ENOUGH TO BRING A SWORD!
ARE WE TO SLAY DRAGONS?
IF NECESSARY.
IN THE MEANTIME, I THOUGHT IT WOULD BE BETTER TO PRACTICE OUR MARTIAL SKILLS THAN LEARN SO-CALLED "MAGICAL" ONES.
MATTHIAS CORVINUS, SON OF JOHN HUNYADI.
TAKE THIS HAND IN FRIENDSHIP. MY FATHER'S FRIENDS AND THEIR FAMILY ARE MY OWN.
AS ARE MINE.
LET ME INTRODUCE GRGUR AND STEFAN BRANKOVIĆ, OUR BROTHERS IN ARMS.
SPEAKING OF BROTHERS...

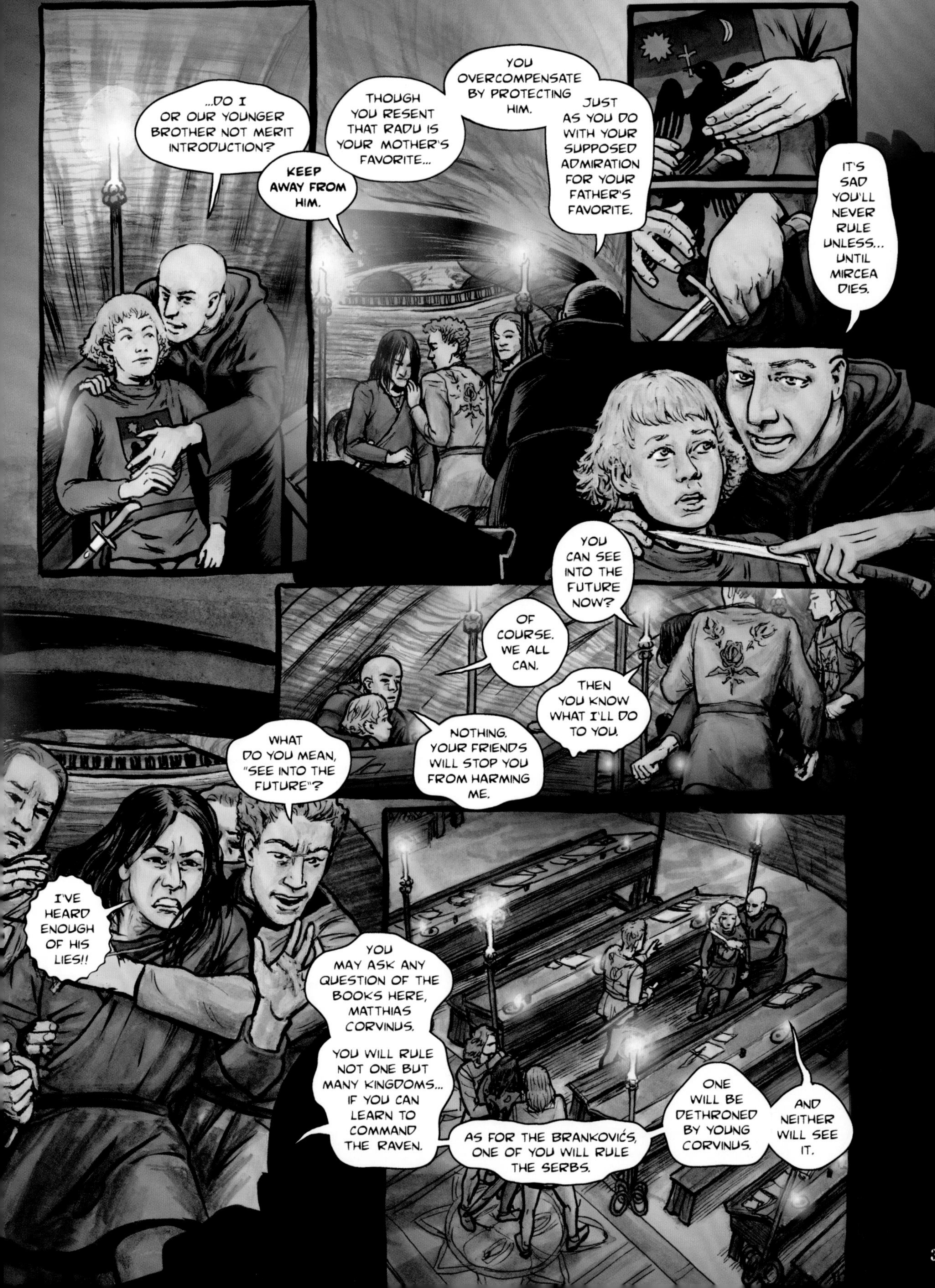
...DO I OR OUR YOUNGER BROTHER NOT MERIT INTRODUCTION?
KEEP AWAY FROM HIM.
THOUGH YOU RESENT THAT RADU IS YOUR MOTHER'S FAVORITE...
YOU OVERCOMPENSATE BY PROTECTING HIM.
JUST AS YOU DO WITH YOUR SUPPOSED ADMIRATION FOR YOUR FATHER'S FAVORITE.
IT'S SAD YOU'LL NEVER RULE UNLESS... UNTIL MIRCEA DIES.
YOU CAN SEE INTO THE FUTURE NOW?
OF COURSE. WE ALL CAN.
THEN YOU KNOW WHAT I'LL DO TO YOU.
NOTHING. YOUR FRIENDS WILL STOP YOU FROM HARMING ME.
WHAT DO YOU MEAN, "SEE INTO THE FUTURE"?
I'VE HEARD ENOUGH OF HIS LIES!!
YOU MAY ASK ANY QUESTION OF THE BOOKS HERE, MATTHIAS CORVINUS.
YOU WILL RULE NOT ONE BUT MANY KINGDOMS... IF YOU CAN LEARN TO COMMAND THE RAVEN.
AS FOR THE BRANKOVIĆS, ONE OF YOU WILL RULE THE SERBS.
ONE WILL BE DETHRONED BY YOUNG CORVINUS.
AND NEITHER WILL SEE IT.

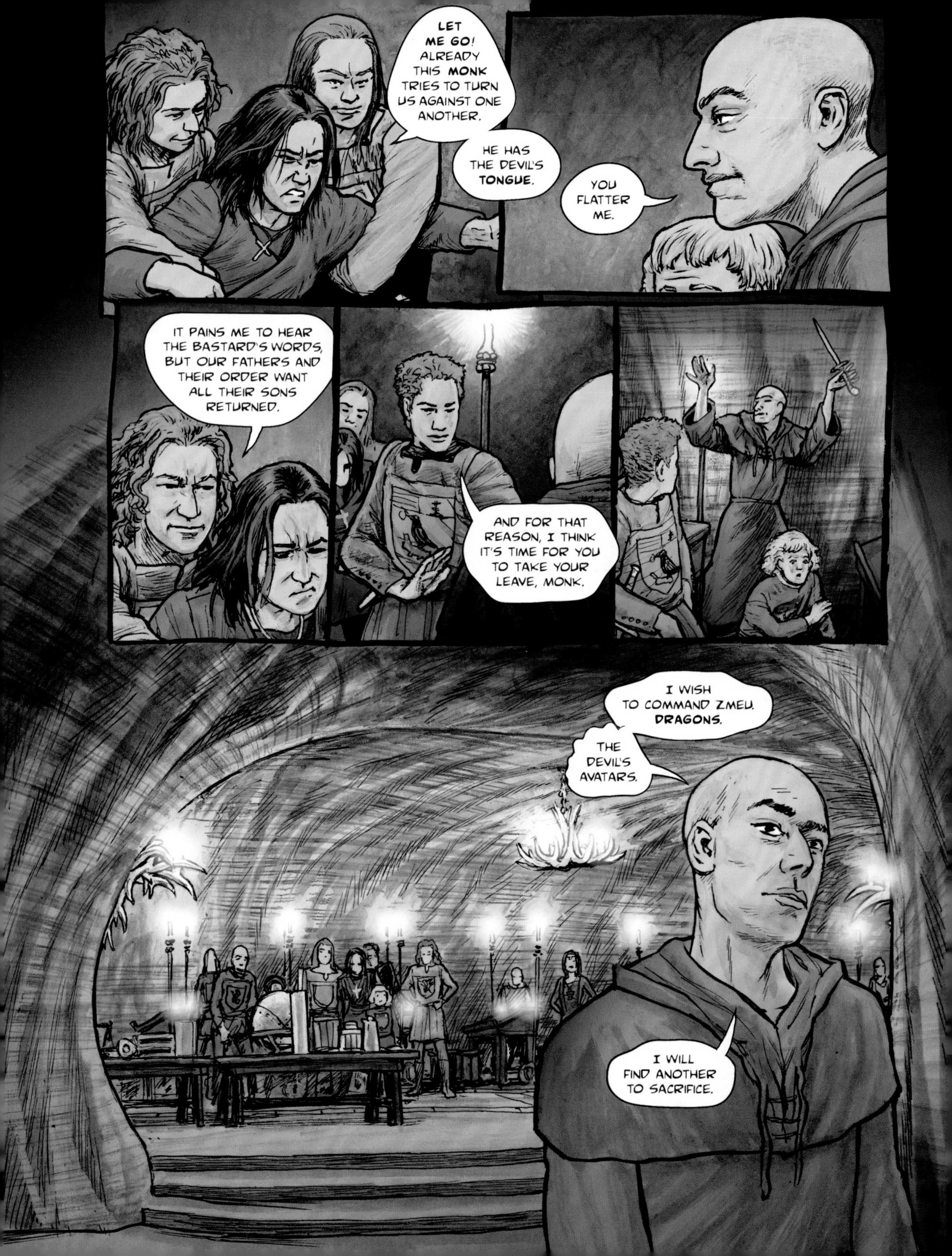
LET ME GO! ALREADY THIS MONK TRIES TO TURN US AGAINST ONE ANOTHER.
HE HAS THE DEVIL'S TONGUE.
YOU FLATTER ME.
IT PAINS ME TO HEAR THE BASTARD'S WORDS, BUT OUR FATHERS AND THEIR ORDER WANT ALL THEIR SONS RETURNED.
AND FOR THAT REASON, I THINK IT'S TIME FOR YOU TO TAKE YOUR LEAVE, MONK.
I WISH TO COMMAND ZMEU. DRAGONS.
THE DEVIL'S AVATARS.
I WILL FIND ANOTHER TO SACRIFICE.

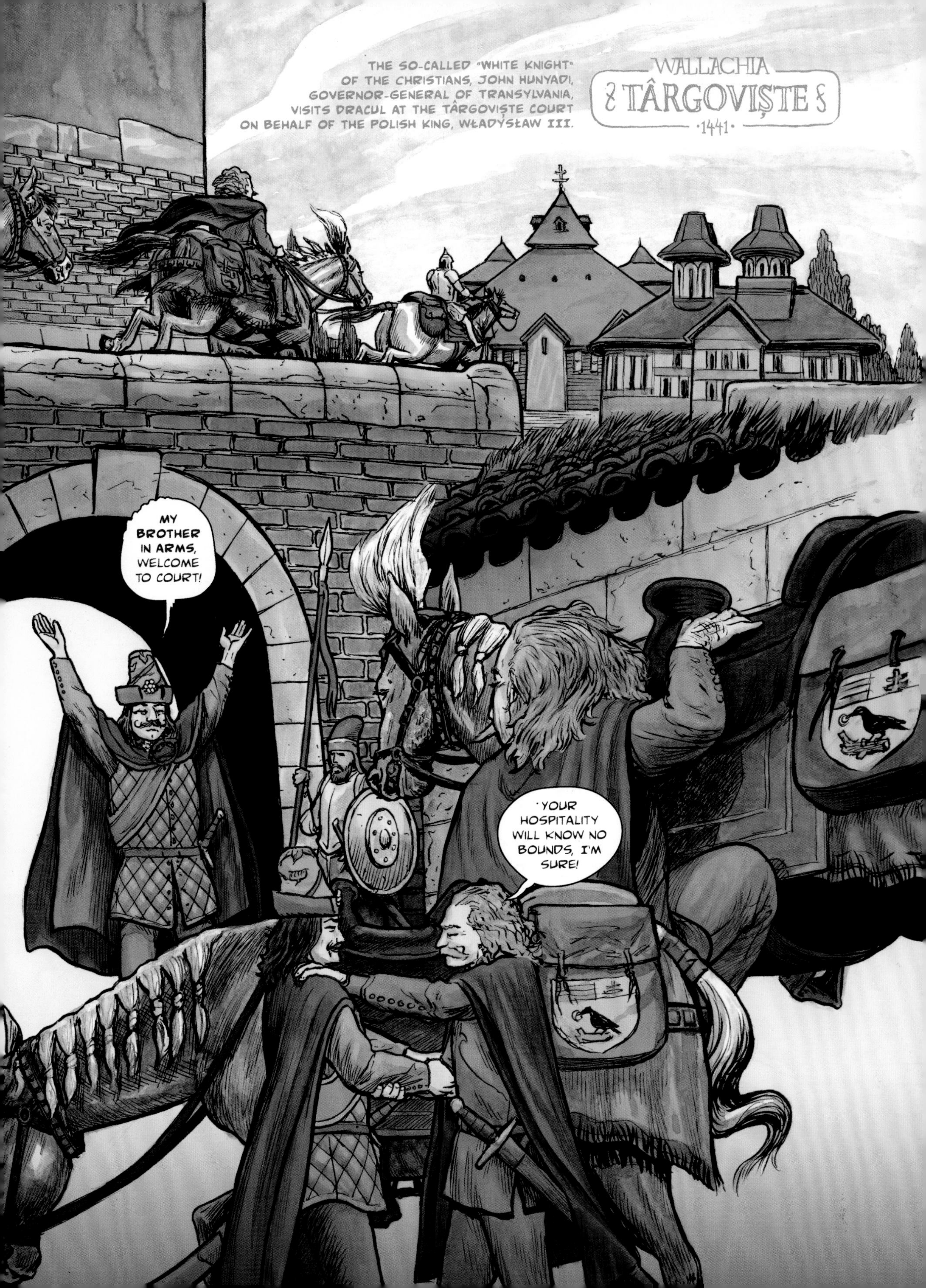

THE SO-CALLED "WHITE KNIGHT" OF THE CHRISTIANS, JOHN HUNYADI, GOVERNOR-GENERAL OF TRANSYLVANIA, VISITS DRACUL AT THE TÂRGOVIȘTE COURT ON BEHALF OF THE POLISH KING, WŁADYSŁAW III.
WALLACHIA
TÂRGOVIȘTE
1441
MY BROTHER IN ARMS, WELCOME TO COURT!
YOUR HOSPITALITY WILL KNOW NO BOUNDS, I'M SURE!

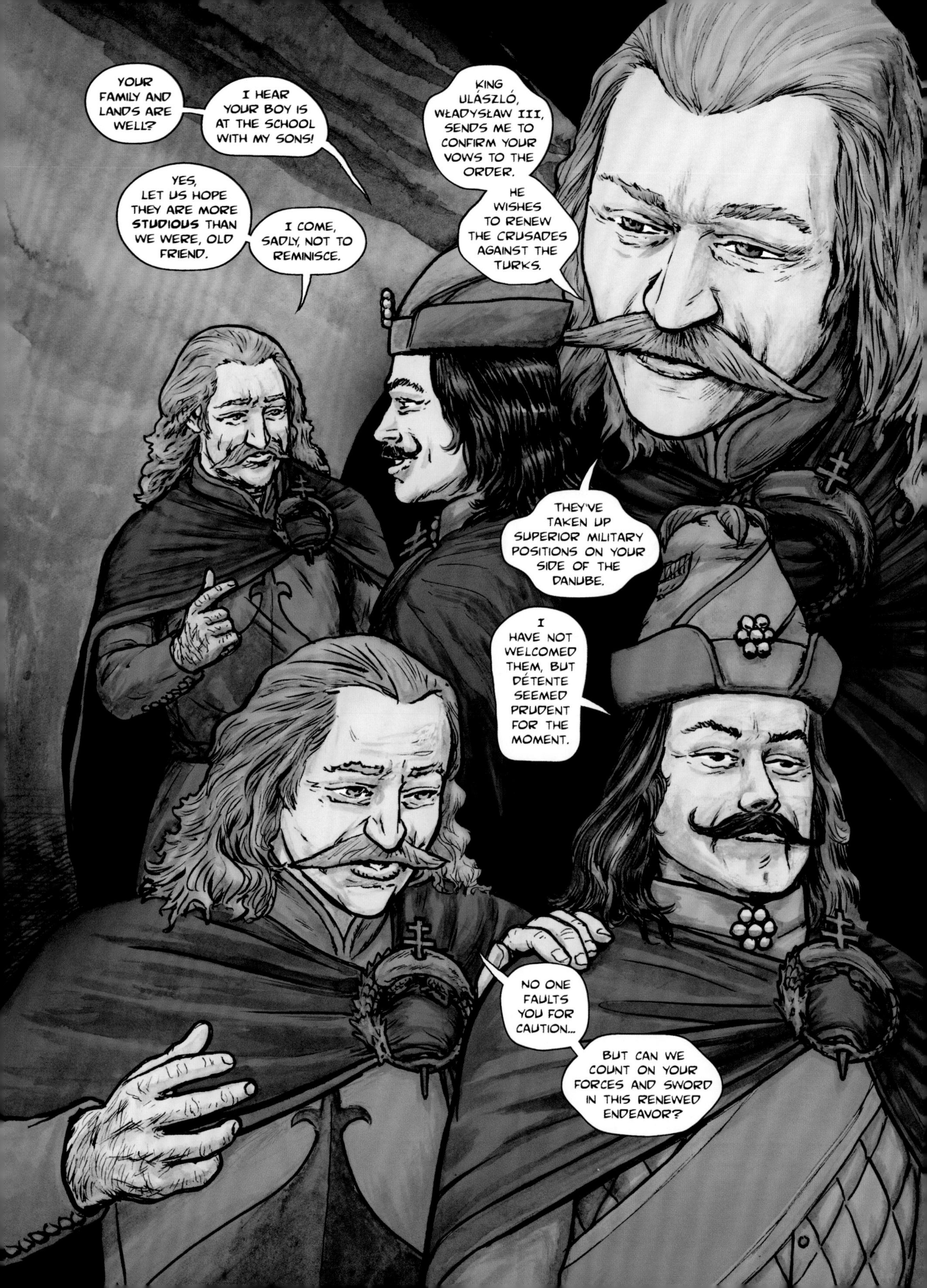
YOUR FAMILY AND LANDS ARE WELL?
I HEAR YOUR BOY IS AT THE SCHOOL WITH MY SONS!
YES, LET US HOPE THEY ARE MORE **STUDIOUS** THAN WE WERE, OLD FRIEND.
I COME, SADLY, NOT TO REMINISCE.
KING ULÁSZLÓ, WŁADYSŁAW III, SENDS ME TO CONFIRM YOUR VOWS TO THE ORDER.
HE WISHES TO RENEW THE CRUSADES AGAINST THE TURKS.
THEY'VE TAKEN UP SUPERIOR MILITARY POSITIONS ON YOUR SIDE OF THE DANUBE.
I HAVE NOT WELCOMED THEM, BUT DÉTENTE SEEMED PRUDENT FOR THE MOMENT.
NO ONE FAULTS YOU FOR CAUTION...
BUT CAN WE COUNT ON YOUR FORCES AND SWORD IN THIS RENEWED ENDEAVOR?

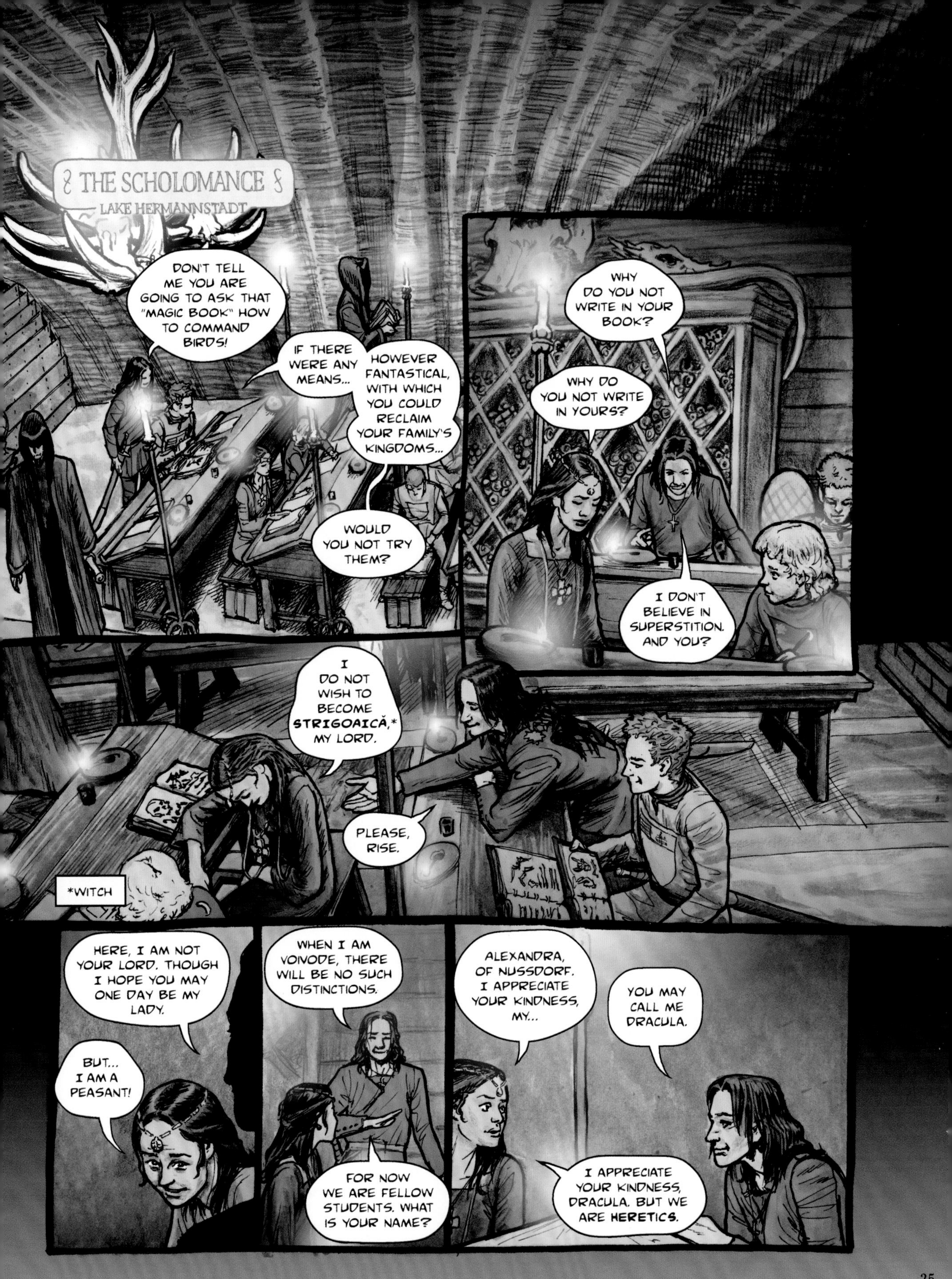
THE SCHOLOMANCE
LAKE HERMANNSTADT
DON'T TELL ME YOU ARE GOING TO ASK THAT "MAGIC BOOK" HOW TO COMMAND BIRDS!
IF THERE WERE ANY MEANS...
HOWEVER FANTASTICAL, WITH WHICH YOU COULD RECLAIM YOUR FAMILY'S KINGDOMS...
WOULD YOU NOT TRY THEM?
WHY DO YOU NOT WRITE IN YOUR BOOK?
WHY DO YOU NOT WRITE IN YOURS?
I DON'T BELIEVE IN SUPERSTITION. AND YOU?
I DO NOT WISH TO BECOME STRIGOAICĂ,* MY LORD.
PLEASE, RISE.
*WITCH
HERE, I AM NOT YOUR LORD. THOUGH I HOPE YOU MAY ONE DAY BE MY LADY.
BUT... I AM A PEASANT!
WHEN I AM VOIVODE, THERE WILL BE NO SUCH DISTINCTIONS.
FOR NOW WE ARE FELLOW STUDENTS. WHAT IS YOUR NAME?
ALEXANDRA, OF NUSSDORF. I APPRECIATE YOUR KINDNESS, MY...
YOU MAY CALL ME DRACULA.
I APPRECIATE YOUR KINDNESS, DRACULA. BUT WE ARE HERETICS.

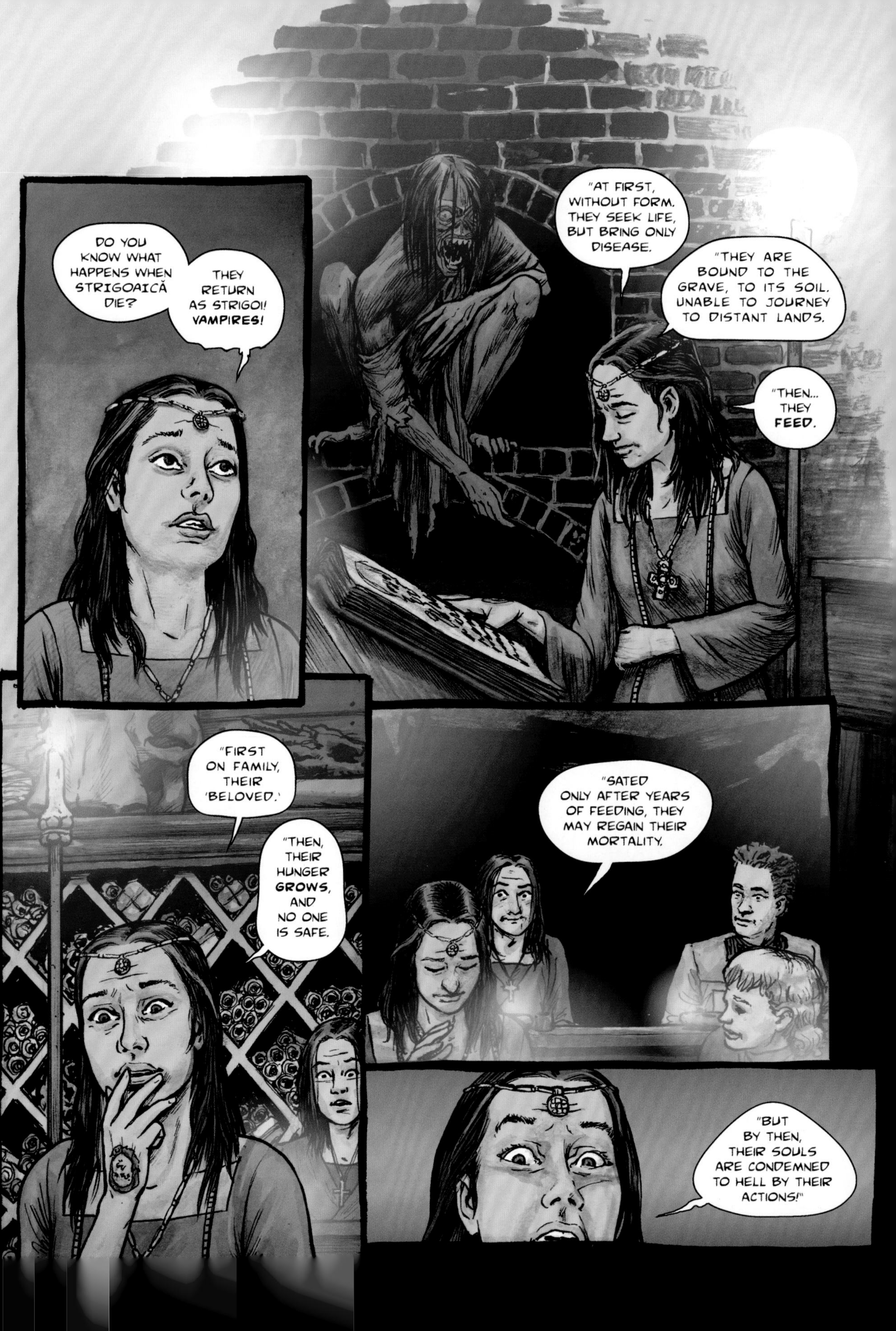
DO YOU KNOW WHAT HAPPENS WHEN STRIGOAICĂ DIE?
THEY RETURN AS STRIGOI! **VAMPIRES!**
"AT FIRST, WITHOUT FORM. THEY SEEK LIFE, BUT BRING ONLY DISEASE.
"THEY ARE BOUND TO THE GRAVE, TO ITS SOIL. UNABLE TO JOURNEY TO DISTANT LANDS.
"THEN... THEY **FEED.**
"FIRST ON FAMILY, THEIR 'BELOVED.'
"THEN, THEIR HUNGER **GROWS,** AND NO ONE IS SAFE.
"SATED ONLY AFTER YEARS OF FEEDING, THEY MAY REGAIN THEIR MORTALITY.
"BUT BY THEN, THEIR SOULS ARE CONDEMNED TO HELL BY THEIR ACTIONS!"

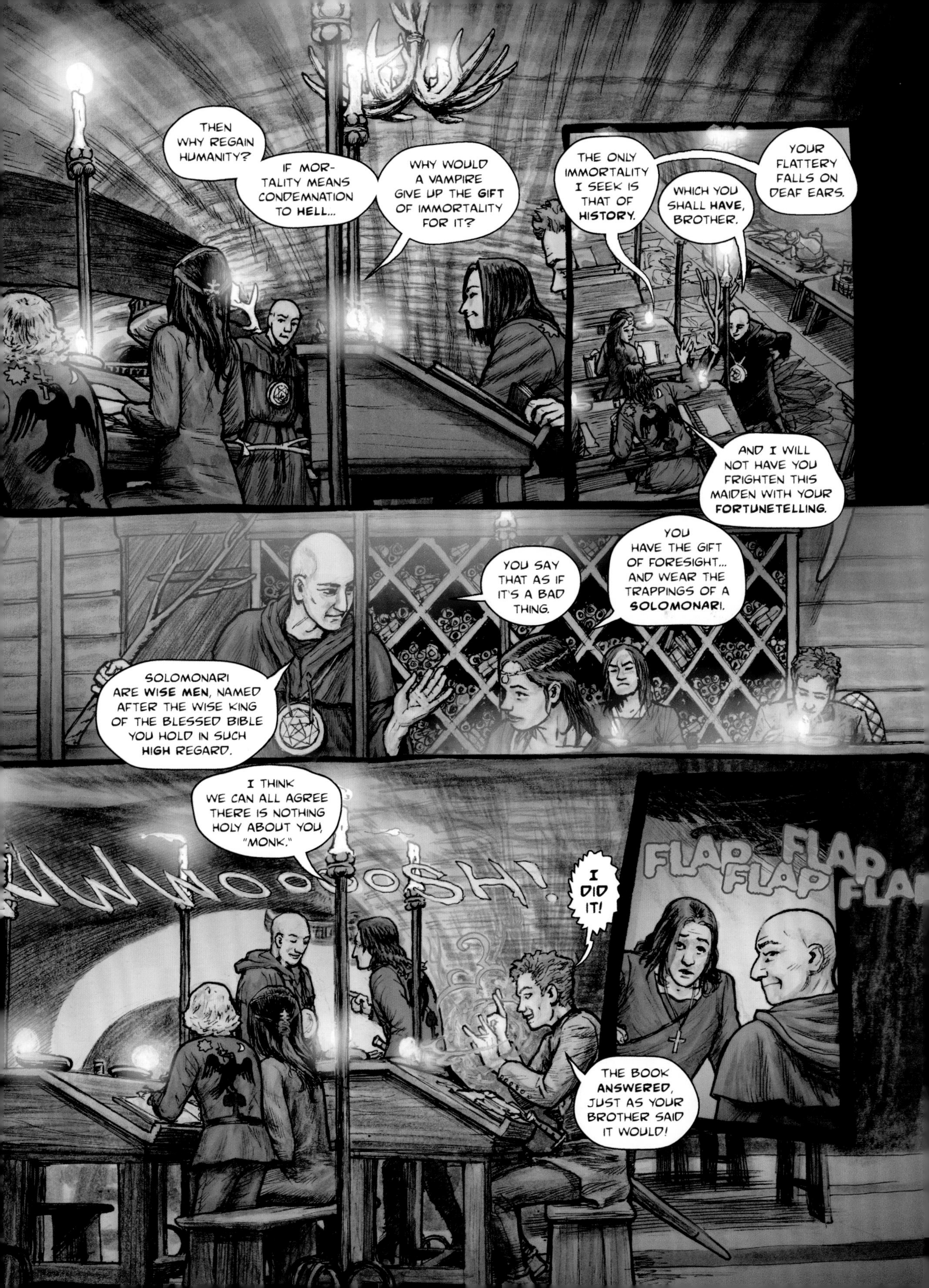
THEN WHY REGAIN HUMANITY?
IF MORTALITY MEANS CONDEMNATION TO HELL...
WHY WOULD A VAMPIRE GIVE UP THE GIFT OF IMMORTALITY FOR IT?
THE ONLY IMMORTALITY I SEEK IS THAT OF HISTORY.
YOUR FLATTERY FALLS ON DEAF EARS.
WHICH YOU SHALL HAVE, BROTHER.
AND I WILL NOT HAVE YOU FRIGHTEN THIS MAIDEN WITH YOUR FORTUNETELLING.
YOU SAY THAT AS IF IT'S A BAD THING.
YOU HAVE THE GIFT OF FORESIGHT... AND WEAR THE TRAPPINGS OF A SOLOMONARI.
SOLOMONARI ARE WISE MEN, NAMED AFTER THE WISE KING OF THE BLESSED BIBLE YOU HOLD IN SUCH HIGH REGARD.
I THINK WE CAN ALL AGREE THERE IS NOTHING HOLY ABOUT YOU, "MONK."
WWINOOOOSH!
I DID IT!
FLAP FLAP FLAP FLAP
THE BOOK ANSWERED, JUST AS YOUR BROTHER SAID IT WOULD!

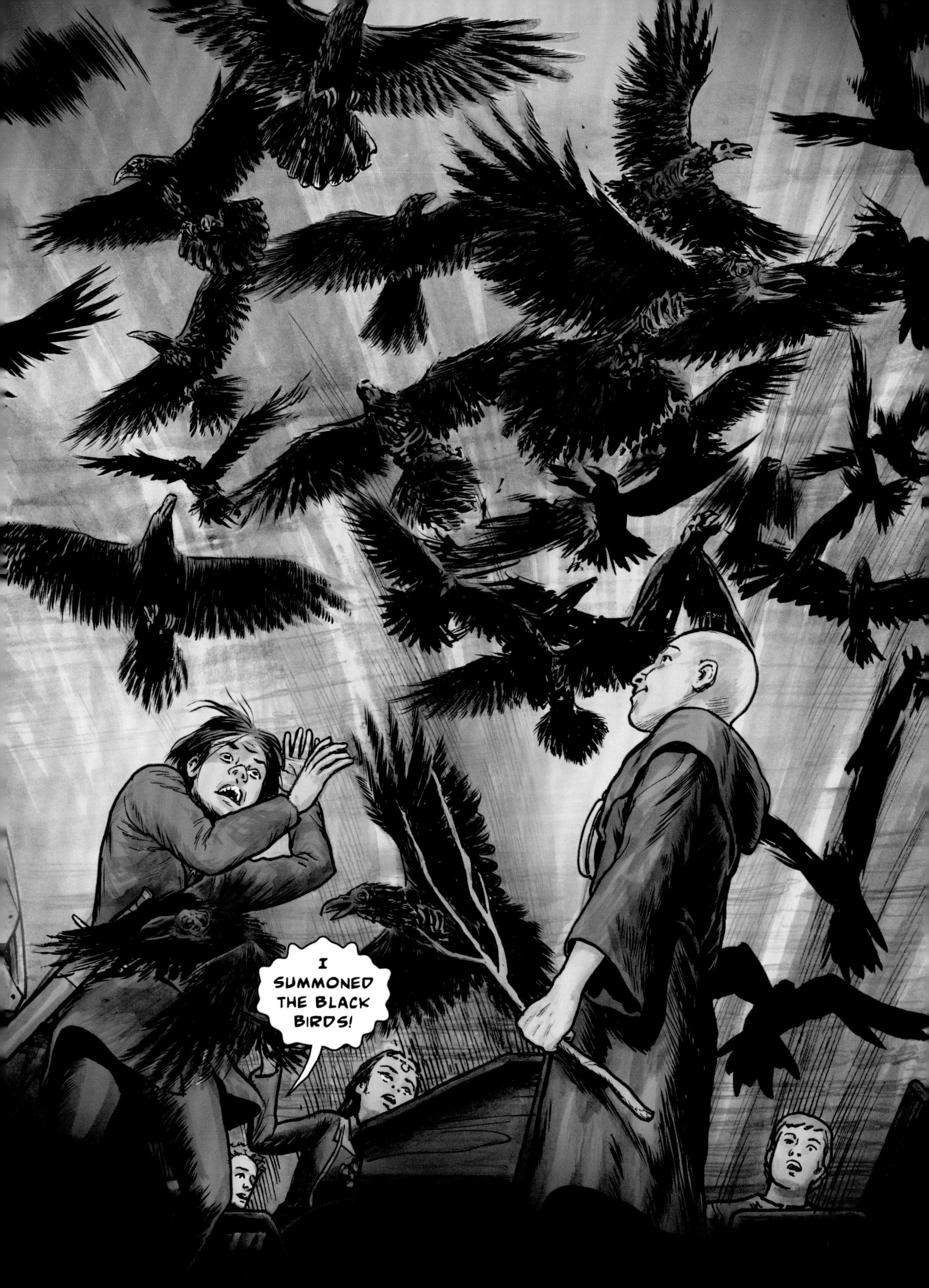
I SUMMONED THE BLACK BIRDS!

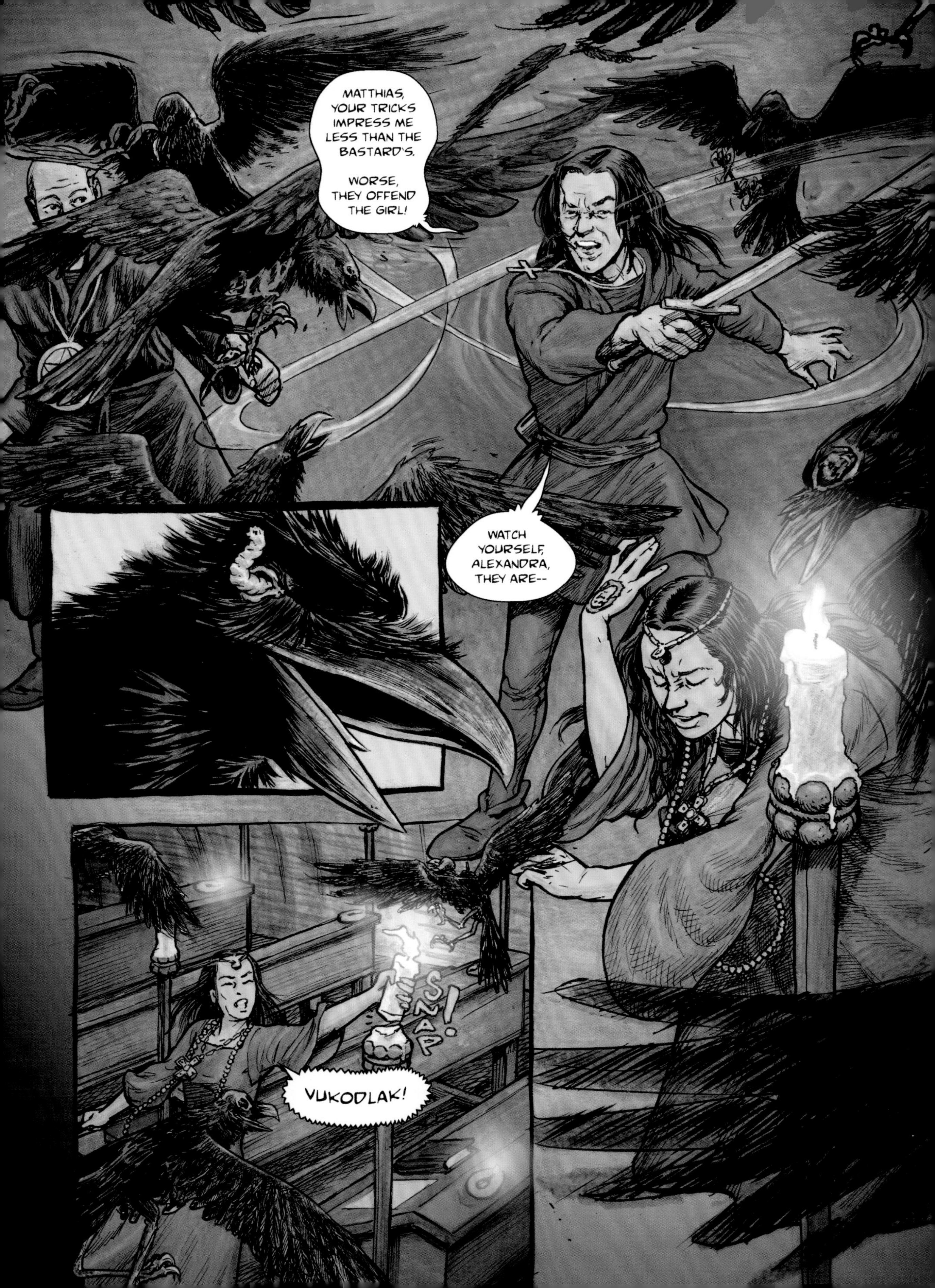
MATTHIAS, YOUR TRICKS IMPRESS ME LESS THAN THE BASTARD'S.
WORSE, THEY OFFEND THE GIRL!
WATCH YOURSELF, ALEXANDRA, THEY ARE--
SNAP!
VUKODLAK!

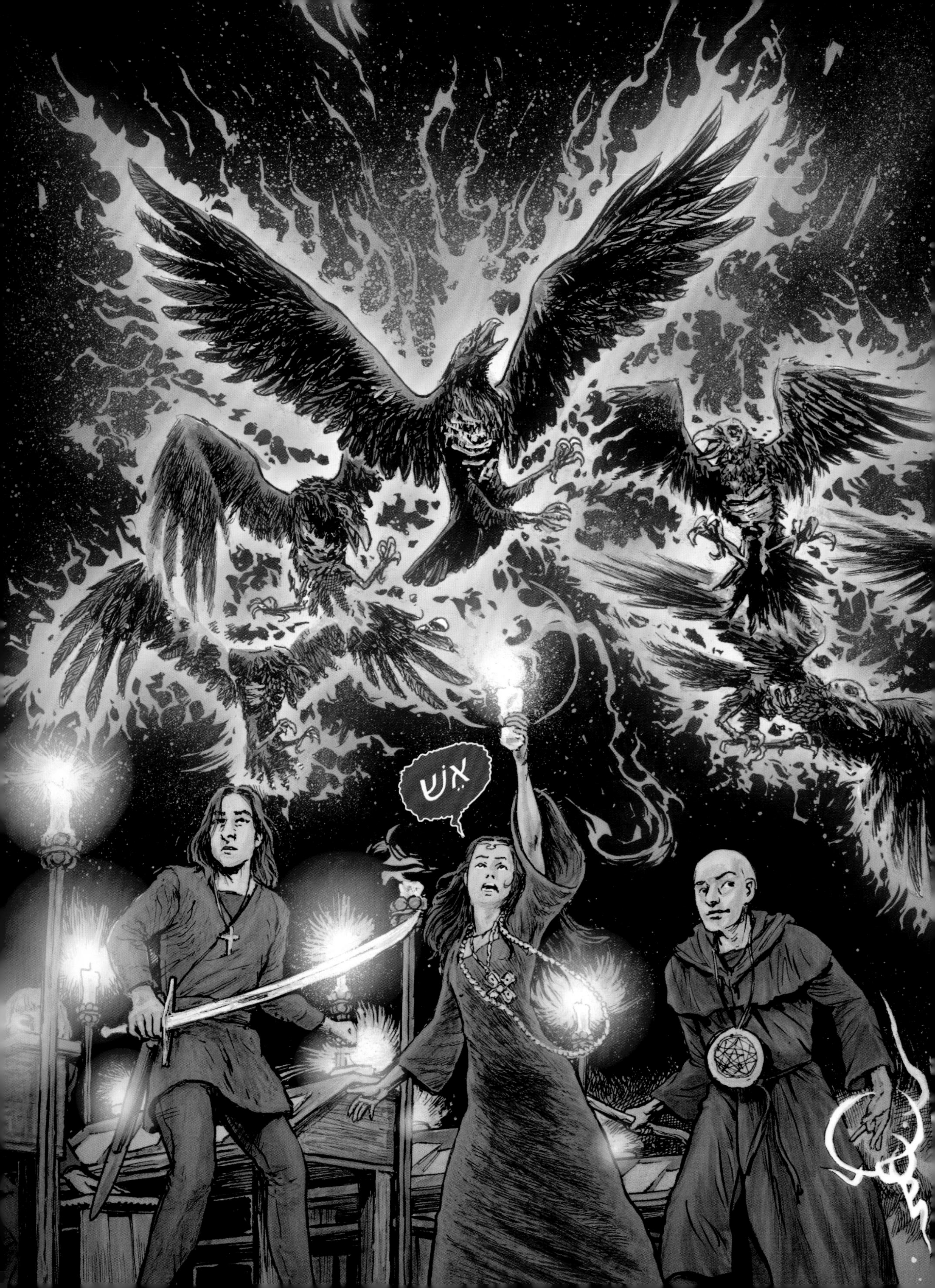
אֵשׁ

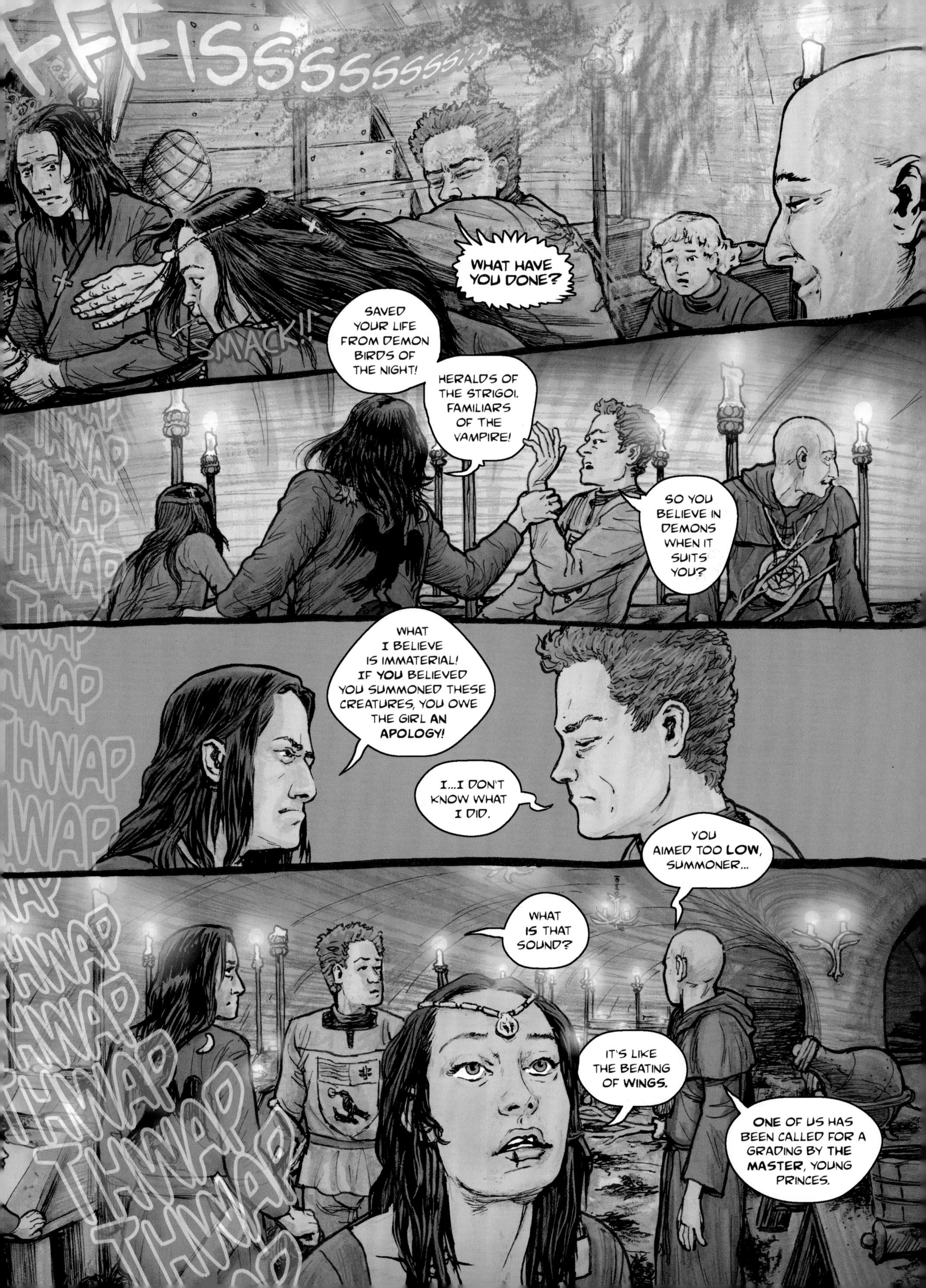

FFFISSSSSSSSS!!!
WHAT HAVE YOU DONE?
SMACK!!
SAVED YOUR LIFE FROM DEMON BIRDS OF THE NIGHT!
HERALDS OF THE STRIGOI. FAMILIARS OF THE VAMPIRE!
SO YOU BELIEVE IN DEMONS WHEN IT SUITS YOU?
THWAP THWAP THWAP THWAP THWAP
WHAT I BELIEVE IS IMMATERIAL! IF YOU BELIEVED YOU SUMMONED THESE CREATURES, YOU OWE THE GIRL AN APOLOGY!
I...I DON'T KNOW WHAT I DID.
YOU AIMED TOO LOW, SUMMONER...
WHAT IS THAT SOUND?
IT'S LIKE THE BEATING OF WINGS.
ONE OF US HAS BEEN CALLED FOR A GRADING BY THE MASTER, YOUNG PRINCES.
THWAP THWAP THWAP THWAP

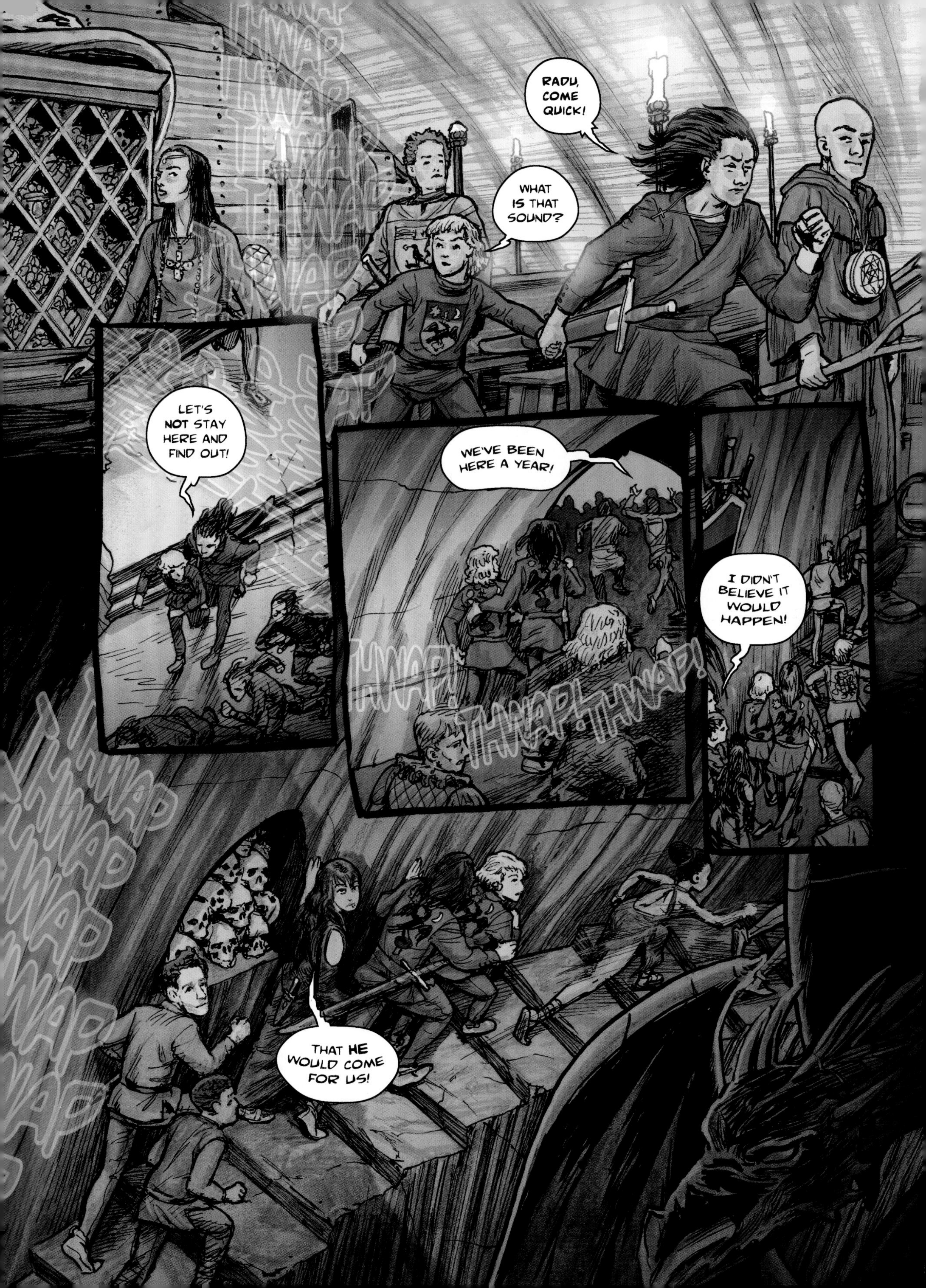
THWAP THWAP THWAP THWAP
RADU, COME QUICK!
WHAT IS THAT SOUND?
LET'S NOT STAY HERE AND FIND OUT!
WE'VE BEEN HERE A YEAR!
THWAP! THWAP! THWAP!
I DIDN'T BELIEVE IT WOULD HAPPEN!
THWAP THWAP THWAP THWAP
THAT HE WOULD COME FOR US!

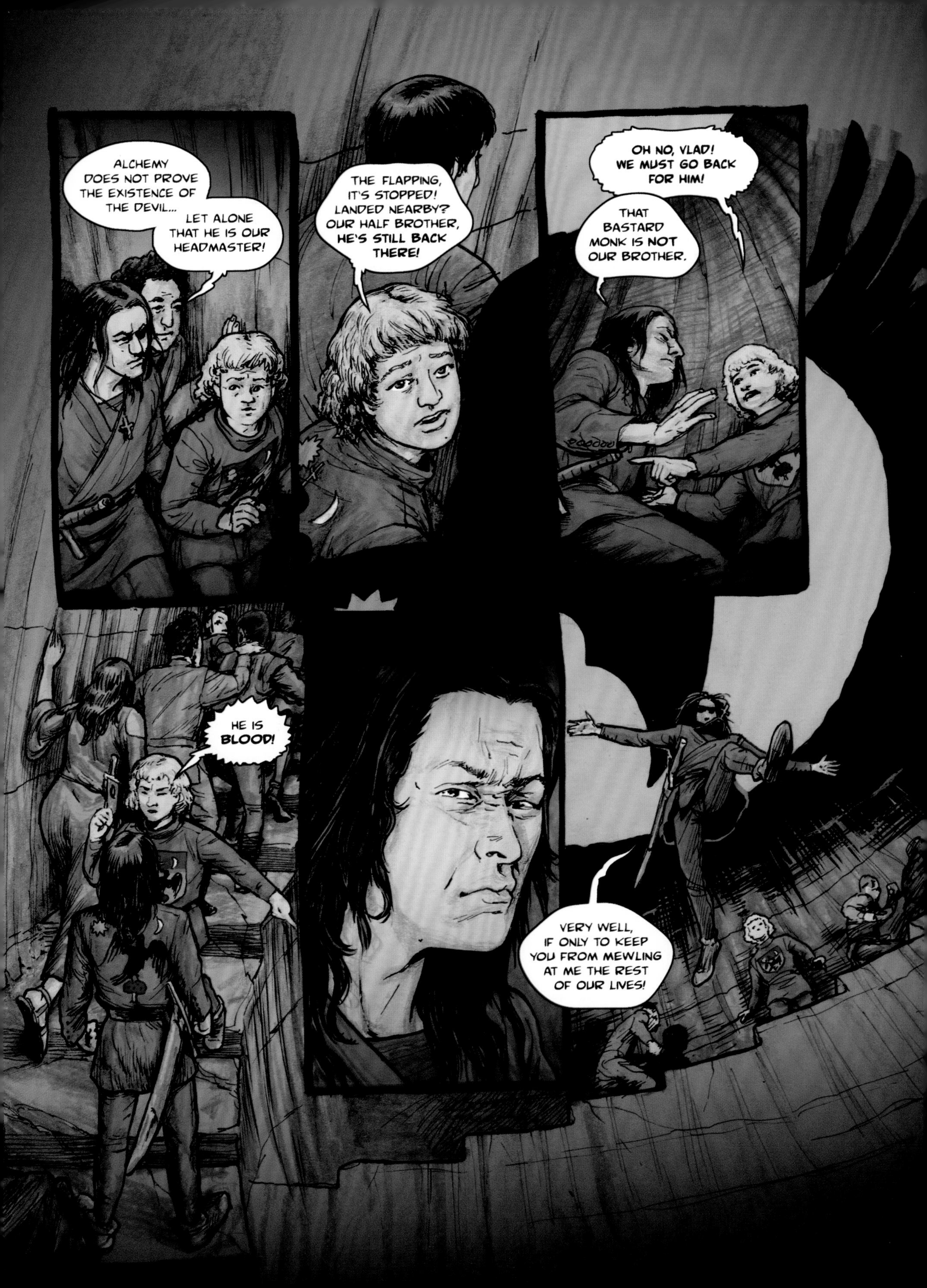
ALCHEMY DOES NOT PROVE THE EXISTENCE OF THE DEVIL...
LET ALONE THAT HE IS OUR HEADMASTER!
THE FLAPPING, IT'S STOPPED! LANDED NEARBY? OUR HALF BROTHER, HE'S STILL BACK THERE!
OH NO, VLAD! WE MUST GO BACK FOR HIM!
THAT BASTARD MONK IS NOT OUR BROTHER.
HE IS BLOOD!
VERY WELL, IF ONLY TO KEEP YOU FROM MEWLING AT ME THE REST OF OUR LIVES!

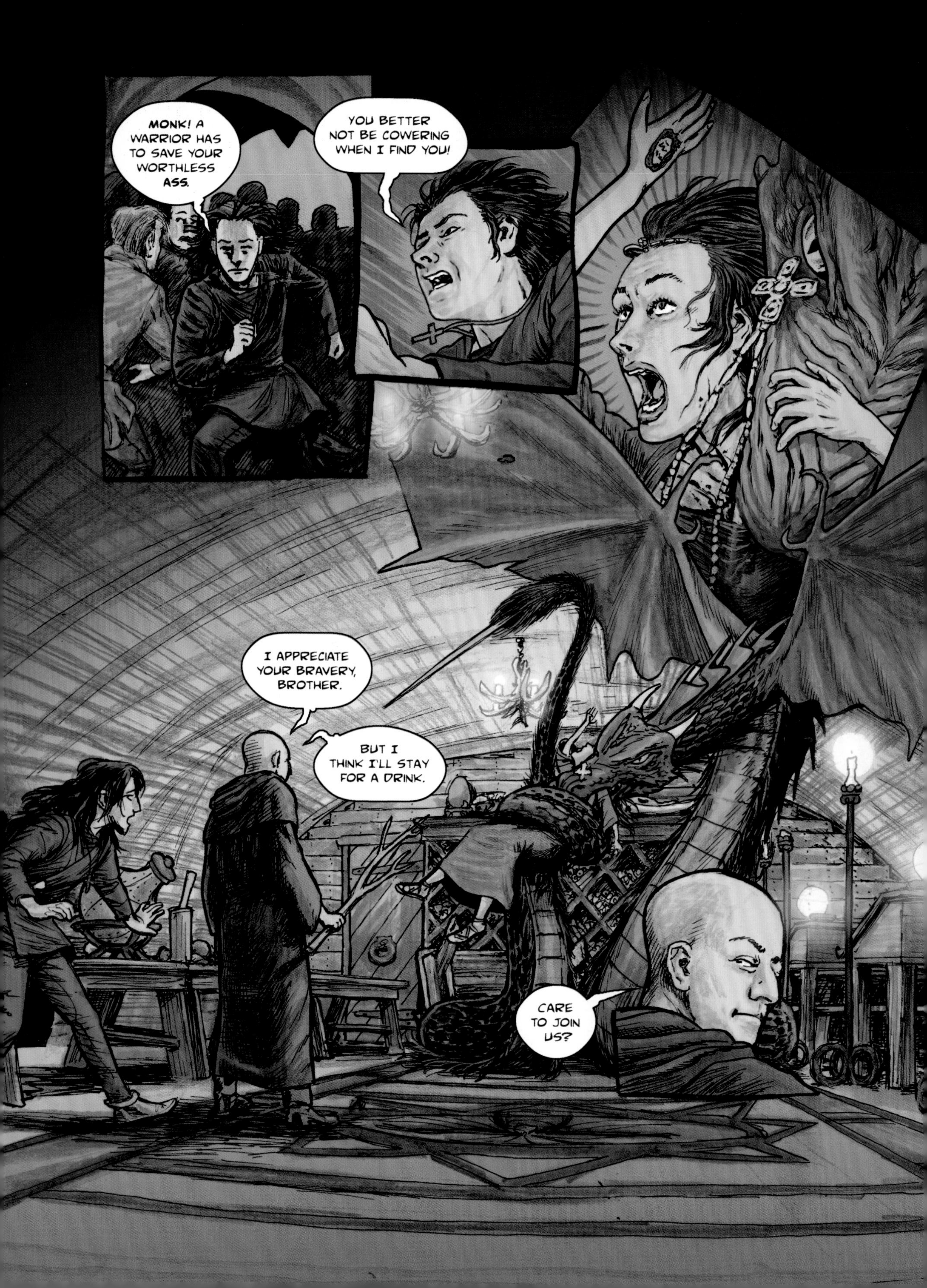
MONK! A WARRIOR HAS TO SAVE YOUR WORTHLESS ASS.
YOU BETTER NOT BE COWERING WHEN I FIND YOU!
I APPRECIATE YOUR BRAVERY, BROTHER.
BUT I THINK I'LL STAY FOR A DRINK.
CARE TO JOIN US?

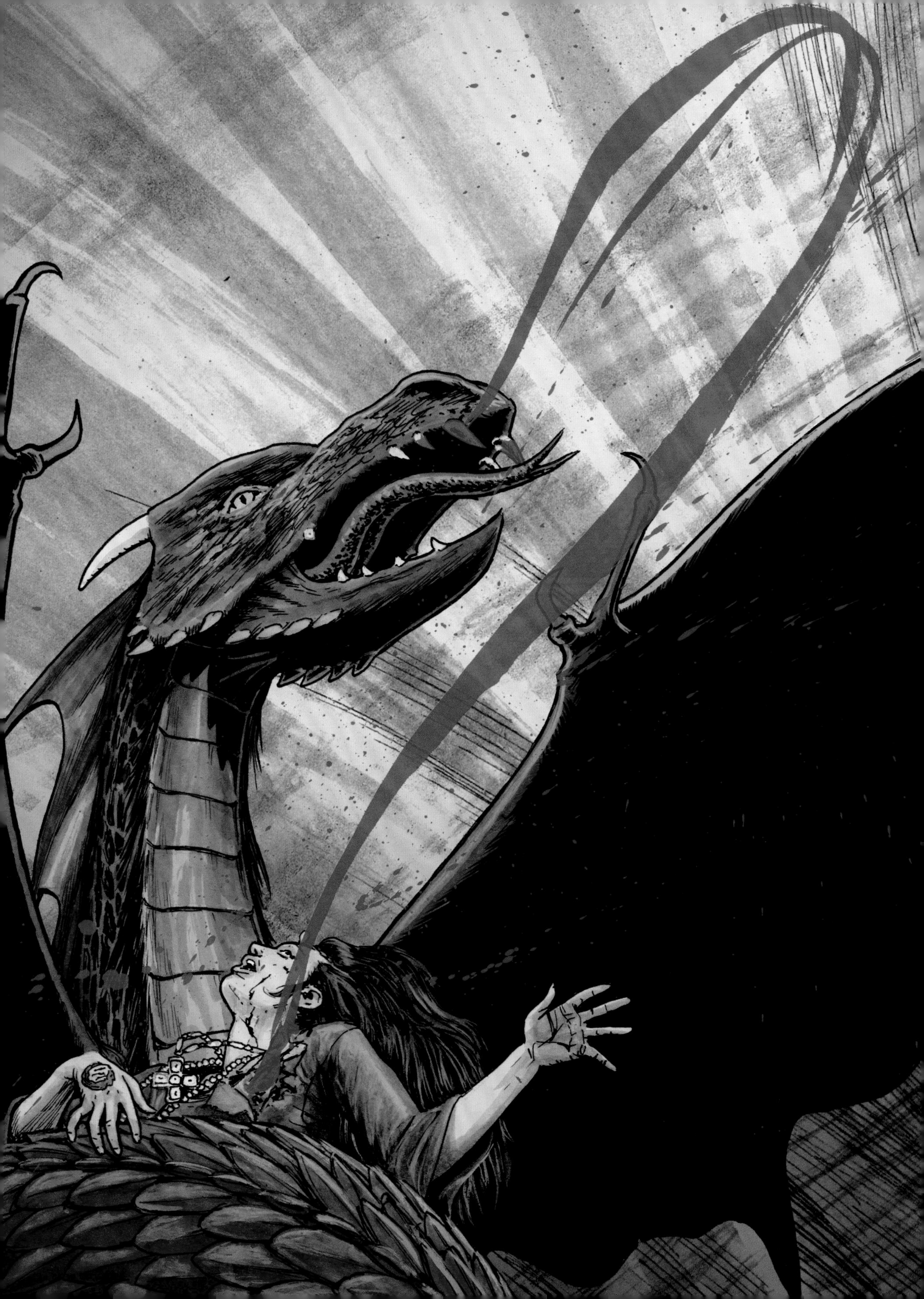

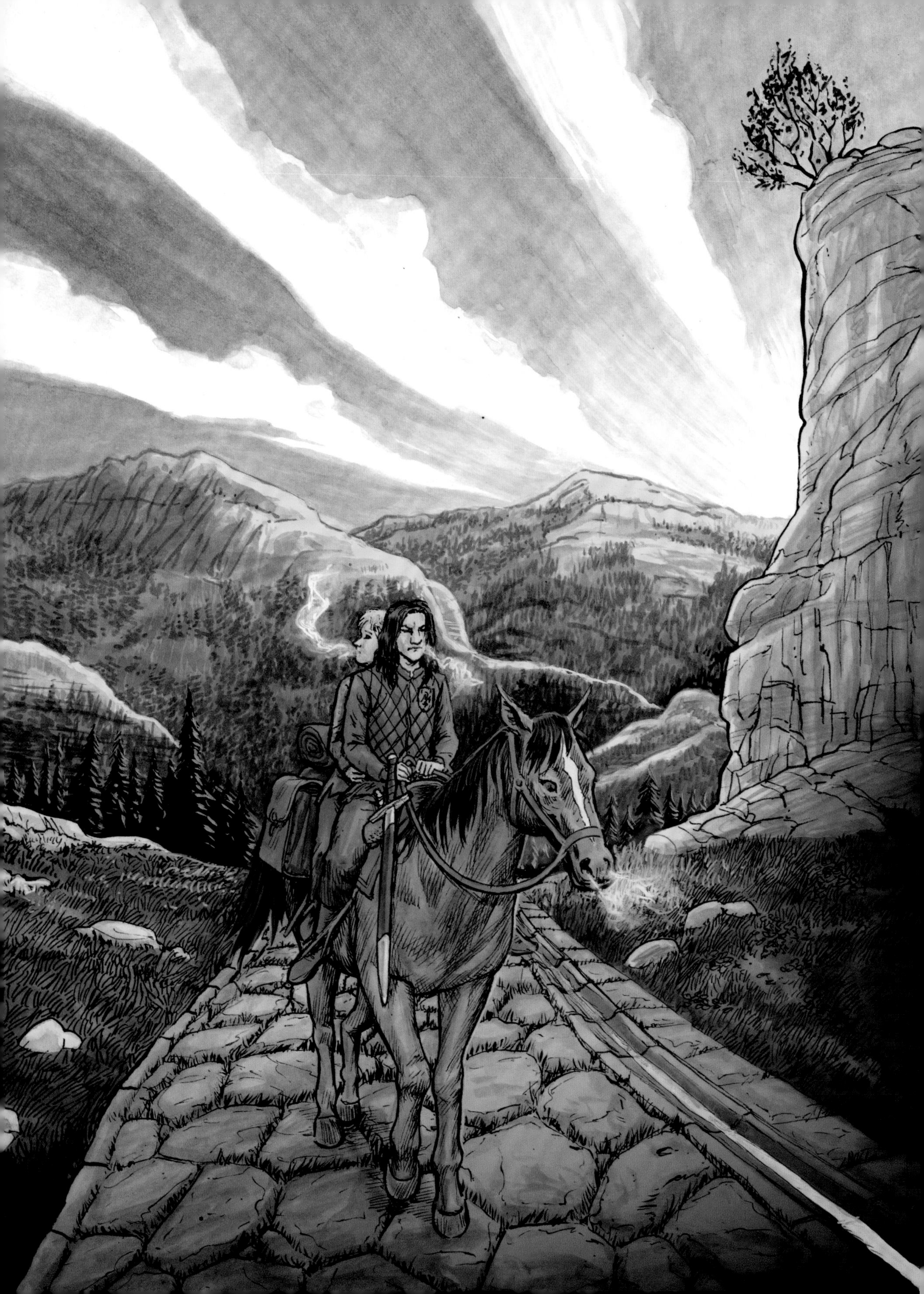

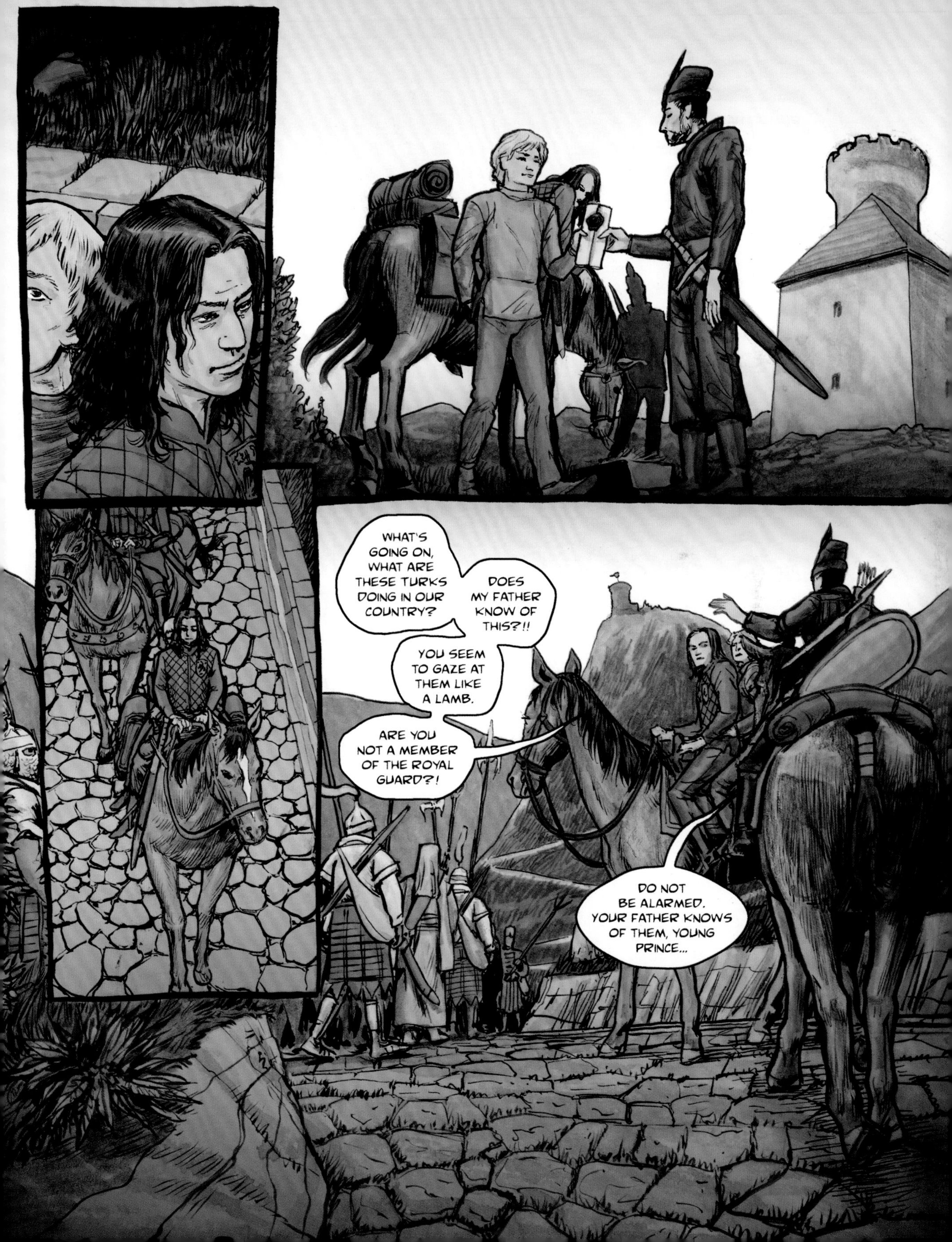
WHAT'S GOING ON, WHAT ARE THESE TURKS DOING IN OUR COUNTRY?
DOES MY FATHER KNOW OF THIS?!!
YOU SEEM TO GAZE AT THEM LIKE A LAMB.
ARE YOU NOT A MEMBER OF THE ROYAL GUARD?!
DO NOT BE ALARMED. YOUR FATHER KNOWS OF THEM, YOUNG PRINCE...

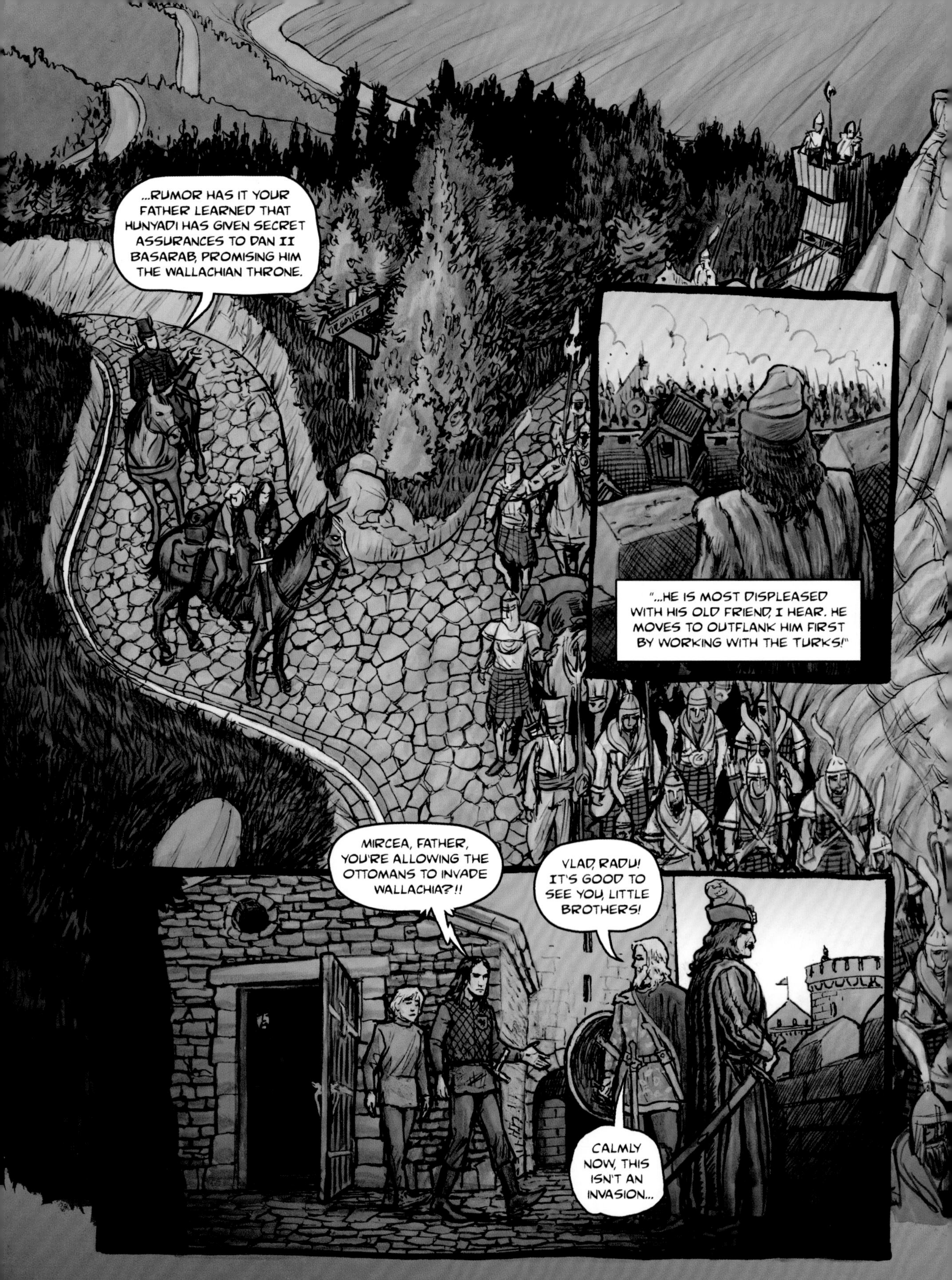
...RUMOR HAS IT YOUR FATHER LEARNED THAT HUNYADI HAS GIVEN SECRET ASSURANCES TO DAN II BASARAB, PROMISING HIM THE WALLACHIAN THRONE.
"...HE IS MOST DISPLEASED WITH HIS OLD FRIEND, I HEAR. HE MOVES TO OUTFLANK HIM FIRST BY WORKING WITH THE TURKS!"
MIRCEA, FATHER, YOU'RE ALLOWING THE OTTOMANS TO INVADE WALLACHIA?!!
VLAD, RADU! IT'S GOOD TO SEE YOU, LITTLE BROTHERS!
CALMLY NOW, THIS ISN'T AN INVASION...

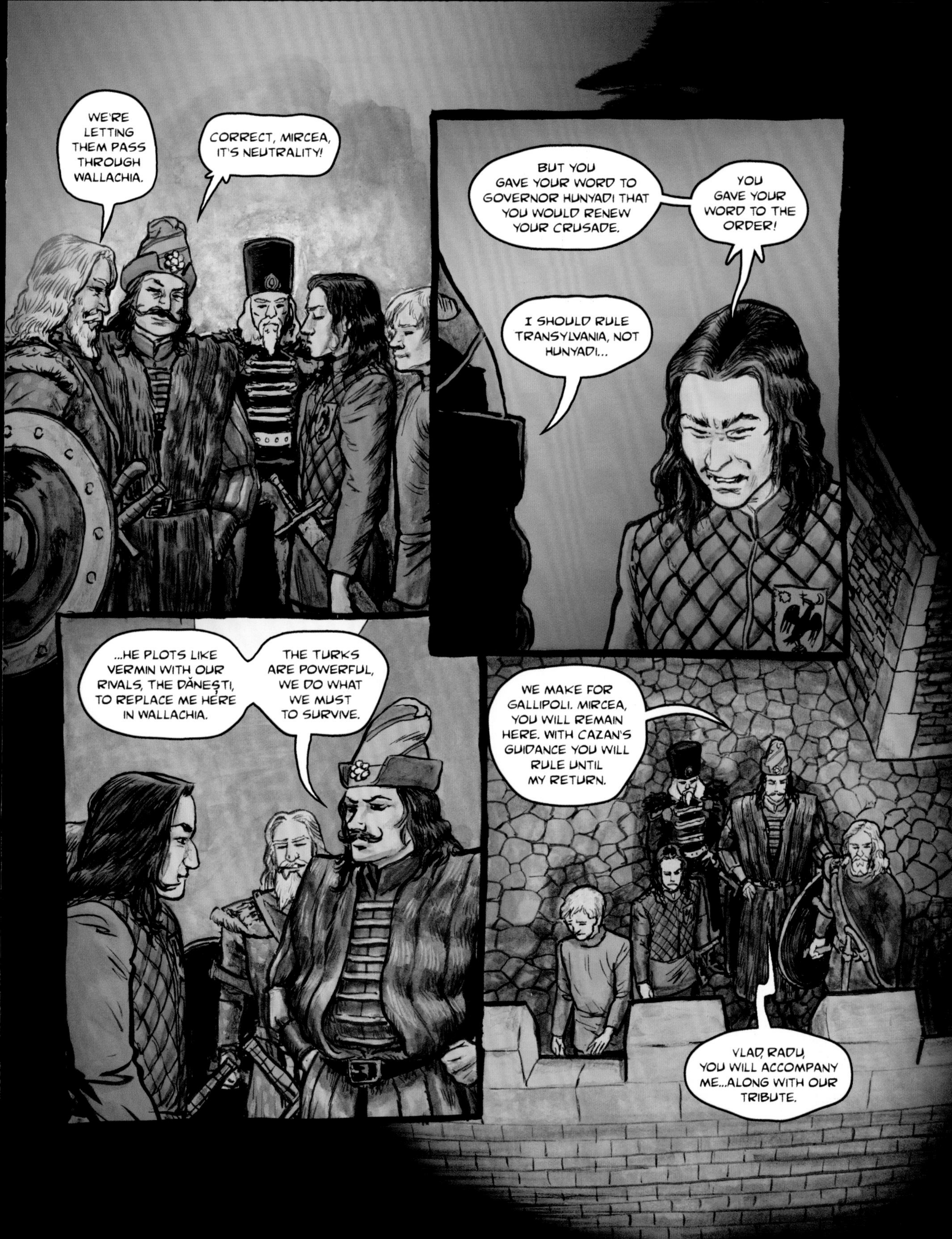
WE'RE LETTING THEM PASS THROUGH WALLACHIA.
CORRECT, MIRCEA, IT'S NEUTRALITY!
BUT YOU GAVE YOUR WORD TO GOVERNOR HUNYADI THAT YOU WOULD RENEW YOUR CRUSADE.
YOU GAVE YOUR WORD TO THE ORDER!
I SHOULD RULE TRANSYLVANIA, NOT HUNYADI...
...HE PLOTS LIKE VERMIN WITH OUR RIVALS, THE DĂNEȘTI, TO REPLACE ME HERE IN WALLACHIA.
THE TURKS ARE POWERFUL, WE DO WHAT WE MUST TO SURVIVE.
WE MAKE FOR GALLIPOLI. MIRCEA, YOU WILL REMAIN HERE. WITH CAZAN'S GUIDANCE YOU WILL RULE UNTIL MY RETURN.
VLAD, RADU, YOU WILL ACCOMPANY ME...ALONG WITH OUR TRIBUTE.

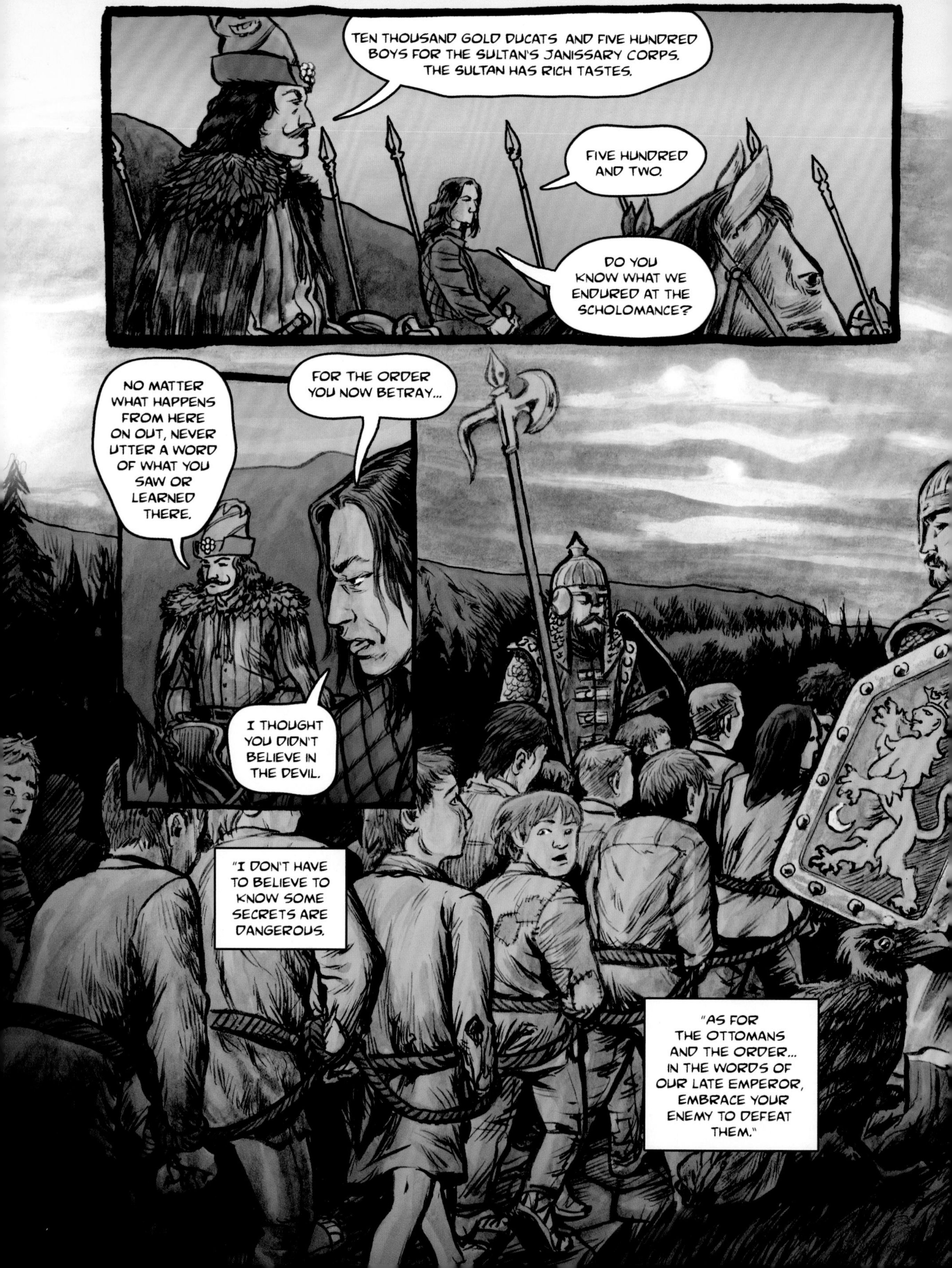

TEN THOUSAND GOLD DUCATS AND FIVE HUNDRED BOYS FOR THE SULTAN'S JANISSARY CORPS. THE SULTAN HAS RICH TASTES.
FIVE HUNDRED AND TWO.
DO YOU KNOW WHAT WE ENDURED AT THE SCHOLOMANCE?
FOR THE ORDER YOU NOW BETRAY...
NO MATTER WHAT HAPPENS FROM HERE ON OUT, NEVER UTTER A WORD OF WHAT YOU SAW OR LEARNED THERE.
I THOUGHT YOU DIDN'T BELIEVE IN THE DEVIL.
"I DON'T HAVE TO BELIEVE TO KNOW SOME SECRETS ARE DANGEROUS.
"AS FOR THE OTTOMANS AND THE ORDER... IN THE WORDS OF OUR LATE EMPEROR, EMBRACE YOUR ENEMY TO DEFEAT THEM."

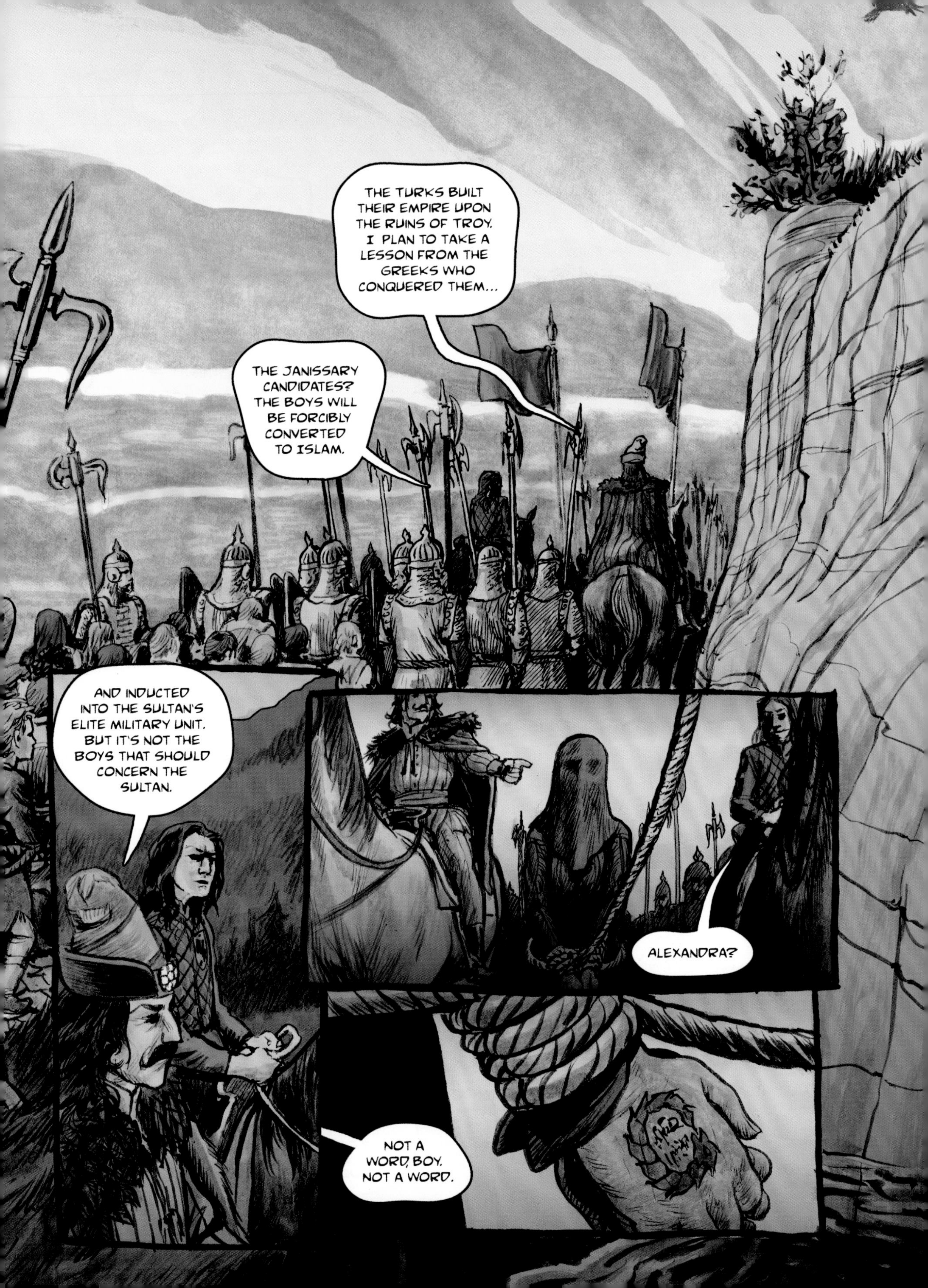
THE TURKS BUILT THEIR EMPIRE UPON THE RUINS OF TROY. I PLAN TO TAKE A LESSON FROM THE GREEKS WHO CONQUERED THEM...
THE JANISSARY CANDIDATES? THE BOYS WILL BE FORCIBLY CONVERTED TO ISLAM.
AND INDUCTED INTO THE SULTAN'S ELITE MILITARY UNIT. BUT IT'S NOT THE BOYS THAT SHOULD CONCERN THE SULTAN.
ALEXANDRA?
NOT A WORD, BOY. NOT A WORD.

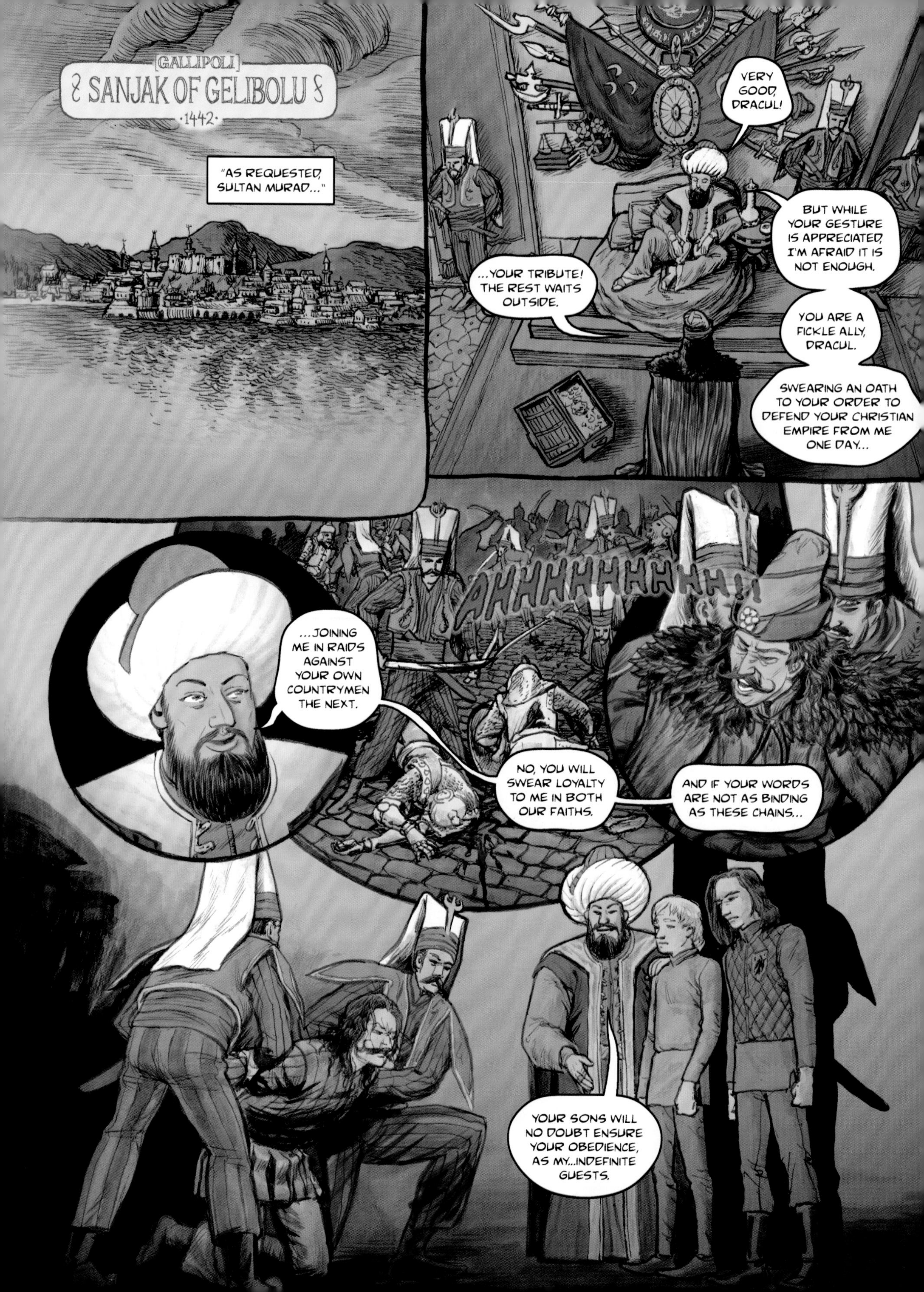
[GALLIPOLI]
SANJAK OF GELIBOLU
·1442·
"AS REQUESTED, SULTAN MURAD..."
...YOUR TRIBUTE! THE REST WAITS OUTSIDE.
VERY GOOD, DRACUL!
BUT WHILE YOUR GESTURE IS APPRECIATED, I'M AFRAID IT IS NOT ENOUGH.
YOU ARE A FICKLE ALLY, DRACUL.
SWEARING AN OATH TO YOUR ORDER TO DEFEND YOUR CHRISTIAN EMPIRE FROM ME ONE DAY...
...JOINING ME IN RAIDS AGAINST YOUR OWN COUNTRYMEN THE NEXT.
AHHHHHHHHHHH!!
NO, YOU WILL SWEAR LOYALTY TO ME IN BOTH OUR FAITHS.
AND IF YOUR WORDS ARE NOT AS BINDING AS THESE CHAINS...
YOUR SONS WILL NO DOUBT ENSURE YOUR OBEDIENCE, AS MY...INDEFINITE GUESTS.

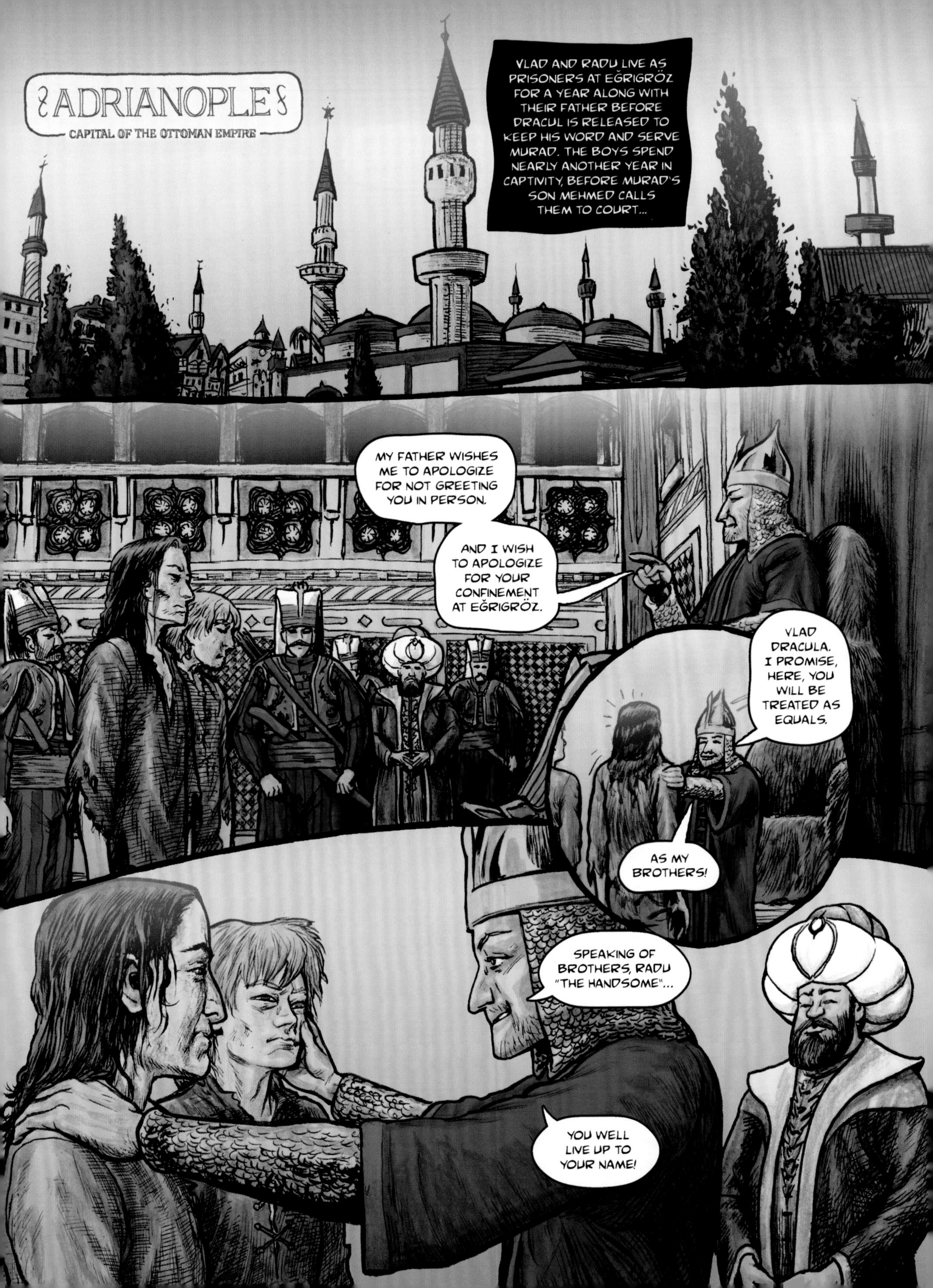
ADRIANOPLE
CAPITAL OF THE OTTOMAN EMPIRE
VLAD AND RADU LIVE AS PRISONERS AT EĞRIGRÖZ FOR A YEAR ALONG WITH THEIR FATHER BEFORE DRACUL IS RELEASED TO KEEP HIS WORD AND SERVE MURAD. THE BOYS SPEND NEARLY ANOTHER YEAR IN CAPTIVITY, BEFORE MURAD'S SON MEHMED CALLS THEM TO COURT...
MY FATHER WISHES ME TO APOLOGIZE FOR NOT GREETING YOU IN PERSON.
AND I WISH TO APOLOGIZE FOR YOUR CONFINEMENT AT EĞRIGRÖZ.
VLAD DRACULA. I PROMISE, HERE, YOU WILL BE TREATED AS EQUALS.
AS MY BROTHERS!
SPEAKING OF BROTHERS, RADU "THE HANDSOME"...
YOU WELL LIVE UP TO YOUR NAME!

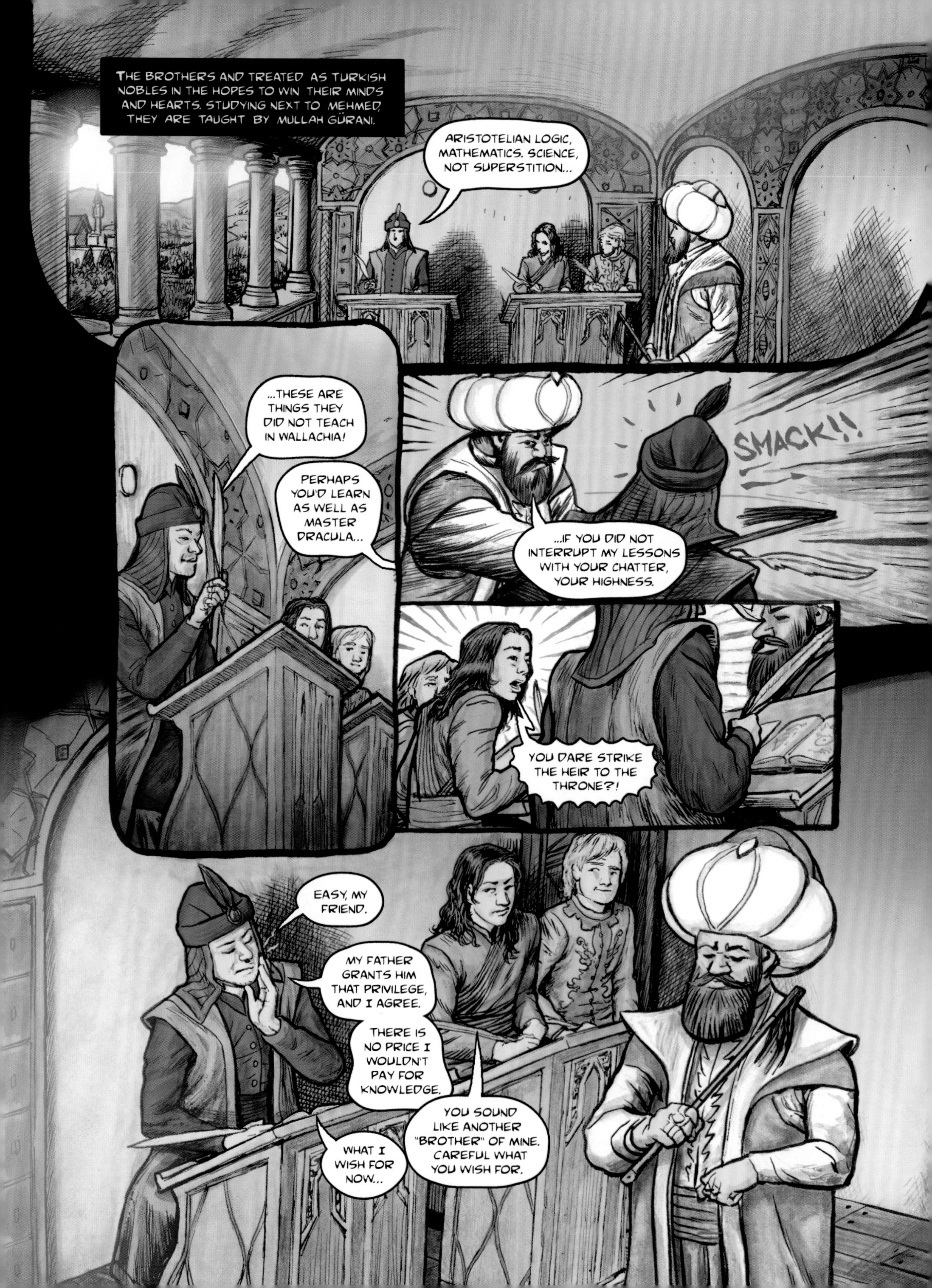
THE BROTHERS AND TREATED AS TURKISH NOBLES IN THE HOPES TO WIN THEIR MINDS AND HEARTS. STUDYING NEXT TO MEHMED, THEY ARE TAUGHT BY MULLAH GÜRANI.
ARISTOTELIAN LOGIC, MATHEMATICS. SCIENCE, NOT SUPERSTITION...
...THESE ARE THINGS THEY DID NOT TEACH IN WALLACHIA!
PERHAPS YOU'D LEARN AS WELL AS MASTER DRACULA...
SMACK!!
...IF YOU DID NOT INTERRUPT MY LESSONS WITH YOUR CHATTER, YOUR HIGHNESS.
YOU DARE STRIKE THE HEIR TO THE THRONE?!
EASY, MY FRIEND.
MY FATHER GRANTS HIM THAT PRIVILEGE, AND I AGREE.
THERE IS NO PRICE I WOULDN'T PAY FOR KNOWLEDGE.
YOU SOUND LIKE ANOTHER "BROTHER" OF MINE. CAREFUL WHAT YOU WISH FOR.
WHAT I WISH FOR NOW...

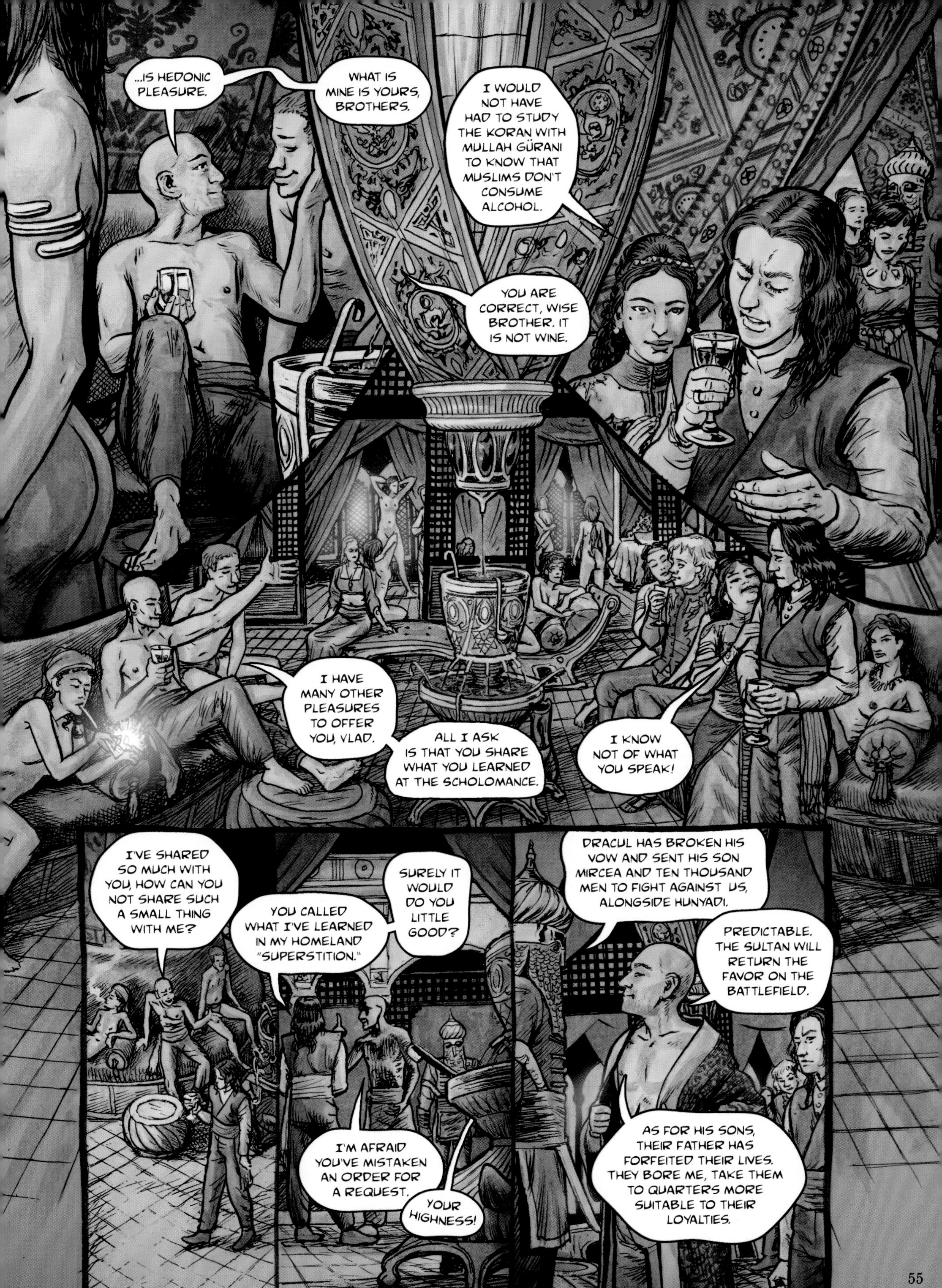
WHAT IS MINE IS YOURS, BROTHERS.
...IS HEDONIC PLEASURE.
I WOULD NOT HAVE HAD TO STUDY THE KORAN WITH MULLAH GÜRANI TO KNOW THAT MUSLIMS DON'T CONSUME ALCOHOL.
YOU ARE CORRECT, WISE BROTHER. IT IS NOT WINE.
I HAVE MANY OTHER PLEASURES TO OFFER YOU, VLAD.
ALL I ASK IS THAT YOU SHARE WHAT YOU LEARNED AT THE SCHOLOMANCE.
I KNOW NOT OF WHAT YOU SPEAK!
I'VE SHARED SO MUCH WITH YOU, HOW CAN YOU NOT SHARE SUCH A SMALL THING WITH ME?
YOU CALLED WHAT I'VE LEARNED IN MY HOMELAND "SUPERSTITION."
SURELY IT WOULD DO YOU LITTLE GOOD?
I'M AFRAID YOU'VE MISTAKEN AN ORDER FOR A REQUEST.
YOUR HIGHNESS!
DRACUL HAS BROKEN HIS VOW AND SENT HIS SON MIRCEA AND TEN THOUSAND MEN TO FIGHT AGAINST US, ALONGSIDE HUNYADI.
PREDICTABLE. THE SULTAN WILL RETURN THE FAVOR ON THE BATTLEFIELD.
AS FOR HIS SONS, THEIR FATHER HAS FORFEITED THEIR LIVES. THEY BORE ME, TAKE THEM TO QUARTERS MORE SUITABLE TO THEIR LOYALTIES.

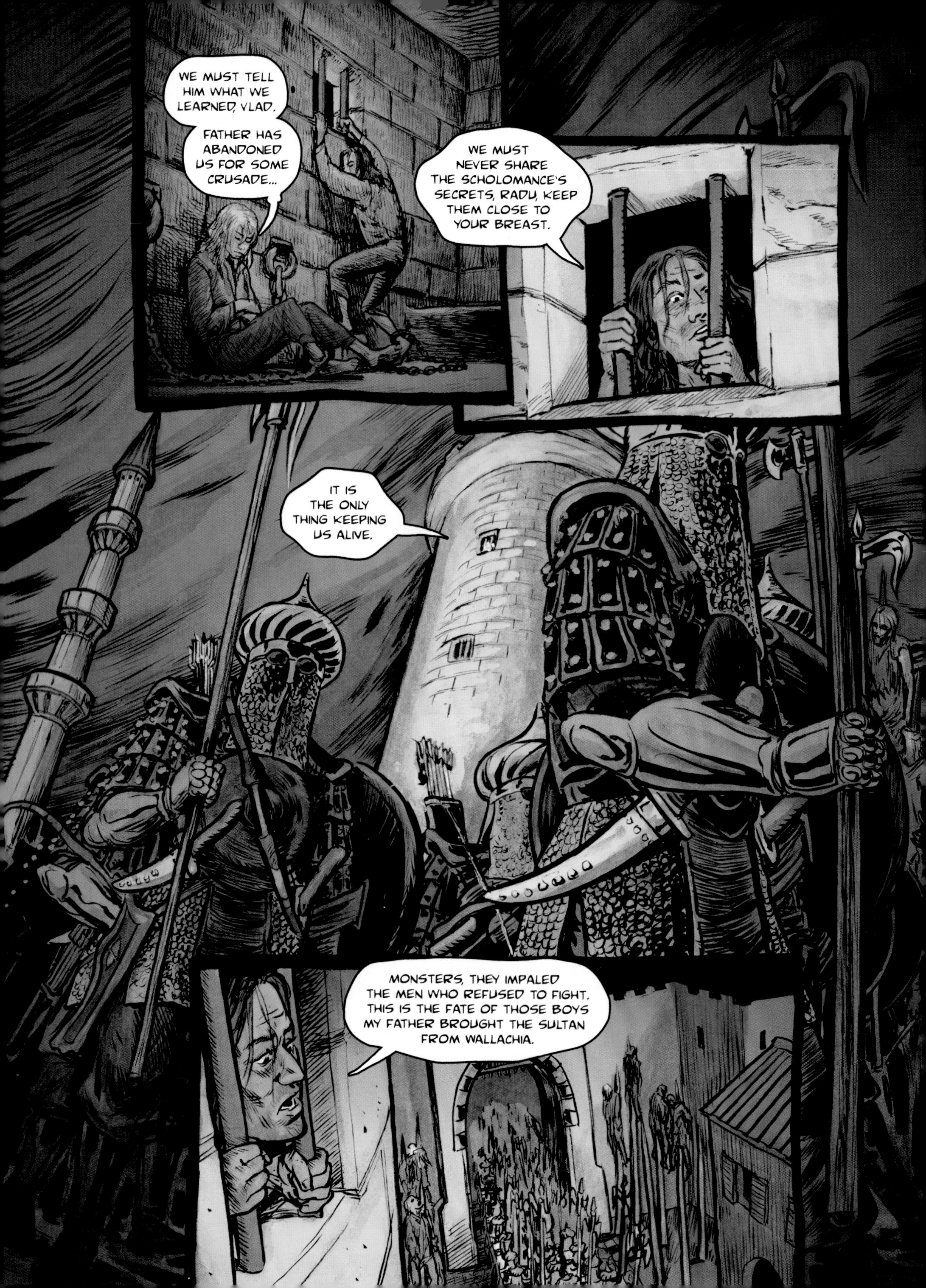
WE MUST TELL HIM WHAT WE LEARNED, VLAD.
FATHER HAS ABANDONED US FOR SOME CRUSADE...
WE MUST NEVER SHARE THE SCHOLOMANCE'S SECRETS, RADU, KEEP THEM CLOSE TO YOUR BREAST.
IT IS THE ONLY THING KEEPING US ALIVE.
MONSTERS, THEY IMPALED THE MEN WHO REFUSED TO FIGHT. THIS IS THE FATE OF THOSE BOYS MY FATHER BROUGHT THE SULTAN FROM WALLACHIA.

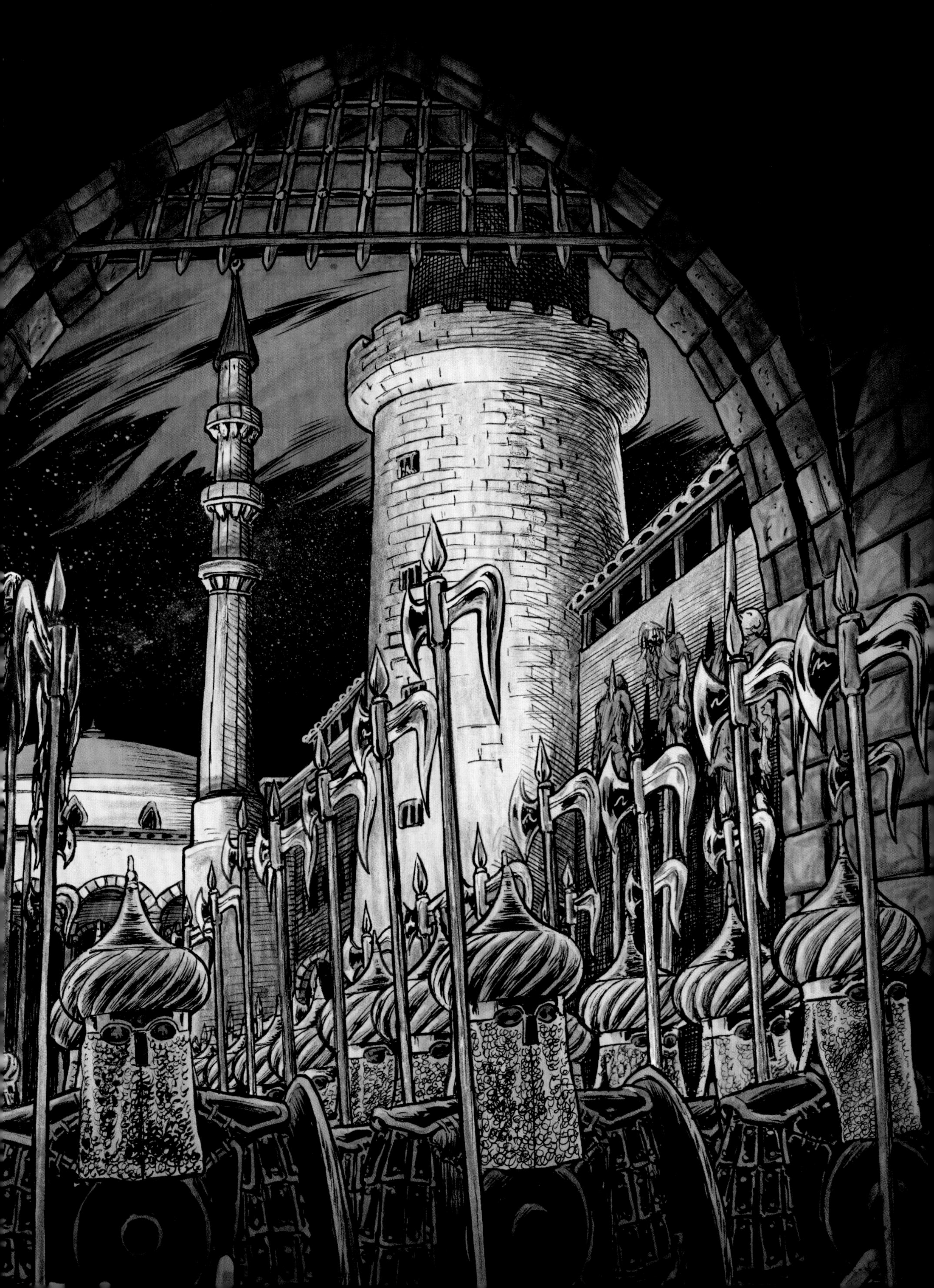

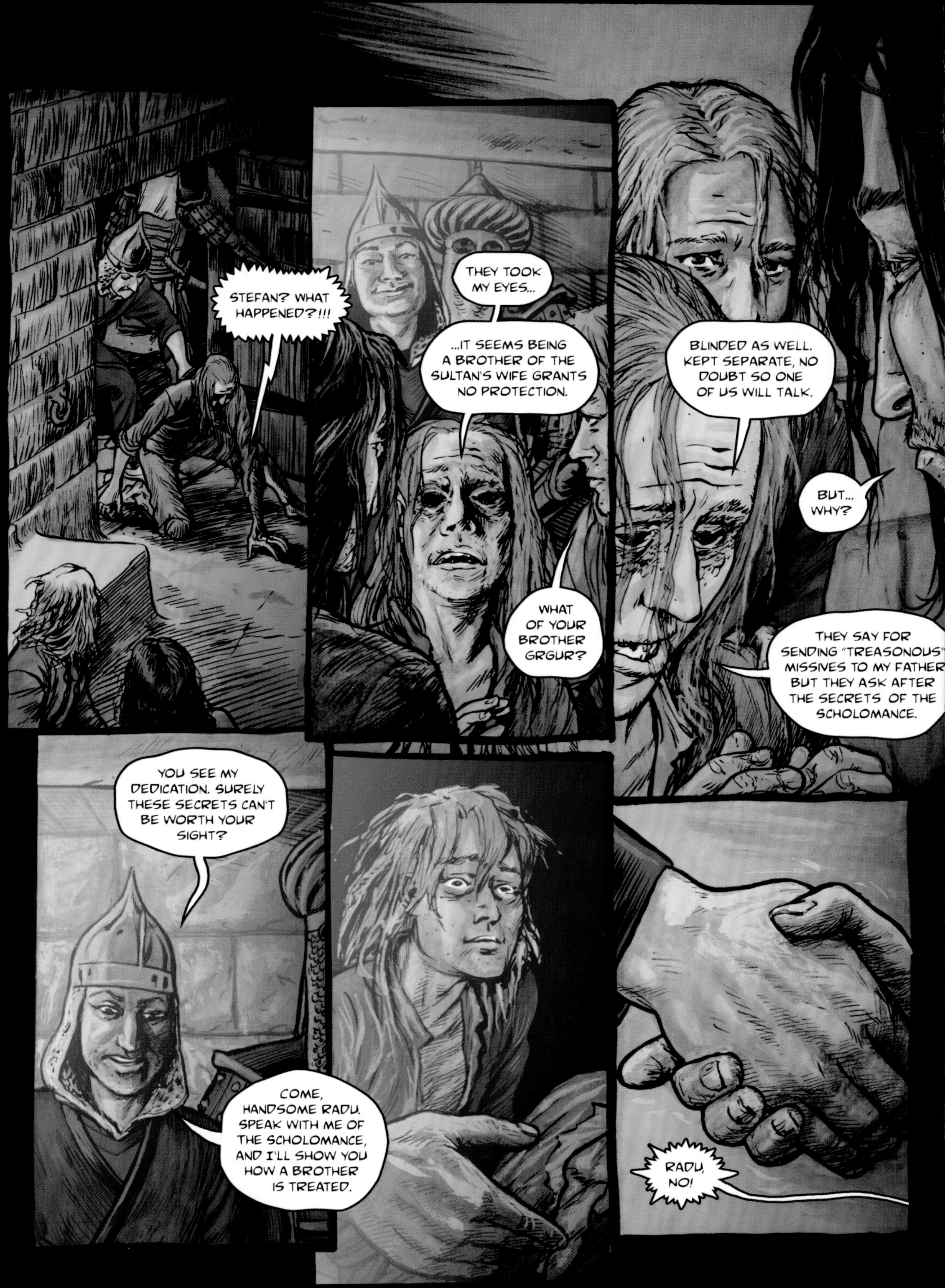
STEFAN? WHAT HAPPENED?!!!
THEY TOOK MY EYES...
...IT SEEMS BEING A BROTHER OF THE SULTAN'S WIFE GRANTS NO PROTECTION.
WHAT OF YOUR BROTHER GRGUR?
BLINDED AS WELL. KEPT SEPARATE, NO DOUBT SO ONE OF US WILL TALK.
BUT... WHY?
THEY SAY FOR SENDING "TREASONOUS" MISSIVES TO MY FATHER BUT THEY ASK AFTER THE SECRETS OF THE SCHOLOMANCE.
YOU SEE MY DEDICATION. SURELY THESE SECRETS CAN'T BE WORTH YOUR SIGHT?
COME, HANDSOME RADU. SPEAK WITH ME OF THE SCHOLOMANCE, AND I'LL SHOW YOU HOW A BROTHER IS TREATED.
RADU, NO!

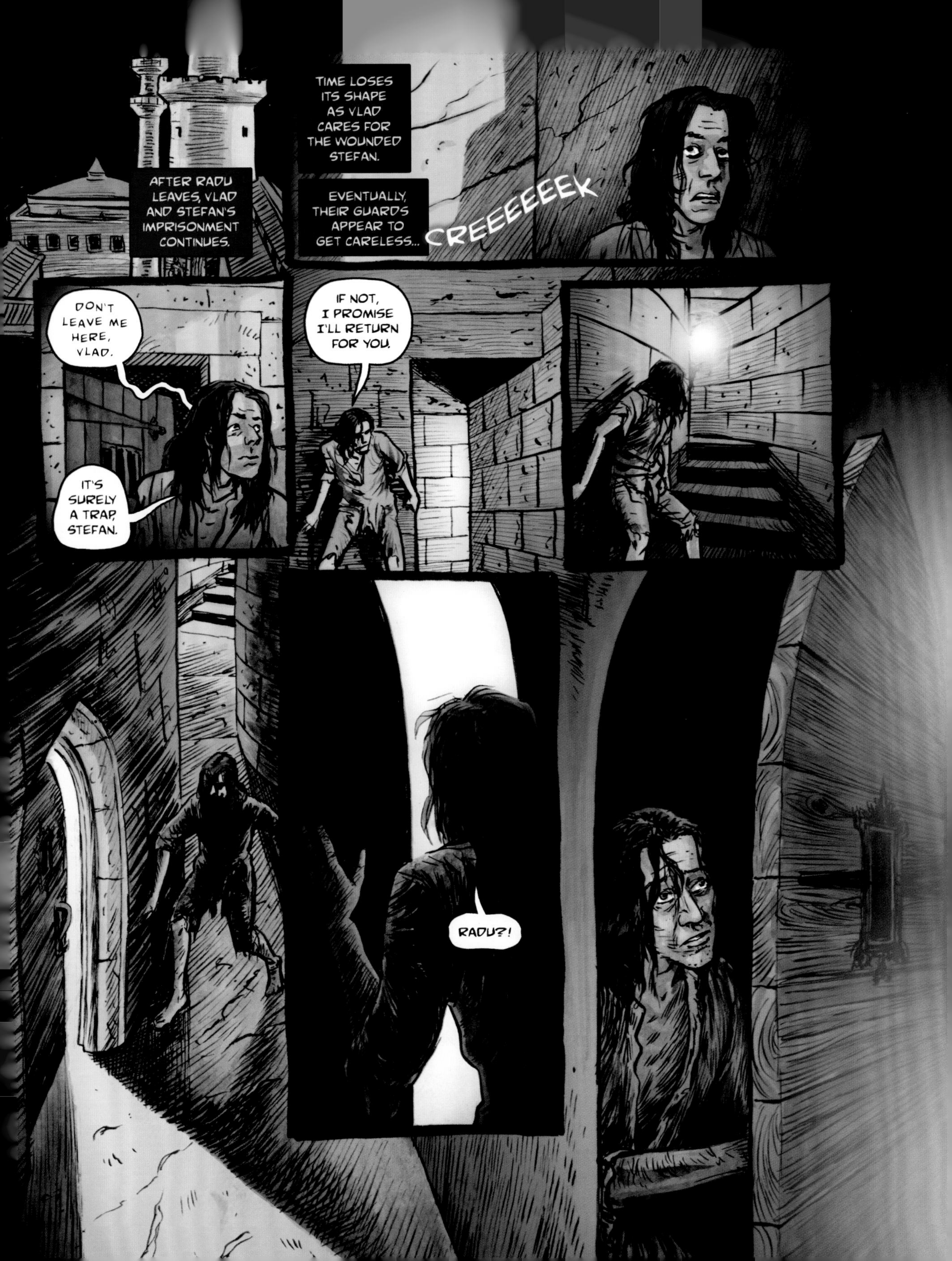
AFTER RADU LEAVES, VLAD AND STEFAN'S IMPRISONMENT CONTINUES.
TIME LOSES ITS SHAPE AS VLAD CARES FOR THE WOUNDED STEFAN.
EVENTUALLY, THEIR GUARDS APPEAR TO GET CARELESS...
CREEEEEEEK
DON'T LEAVE ME HERE, VLAD.
IT'S SURELY A TRAP, STEFAN.
IF NOT, I PROMISE I'LL RETURN FOR YOU.
RADU?!

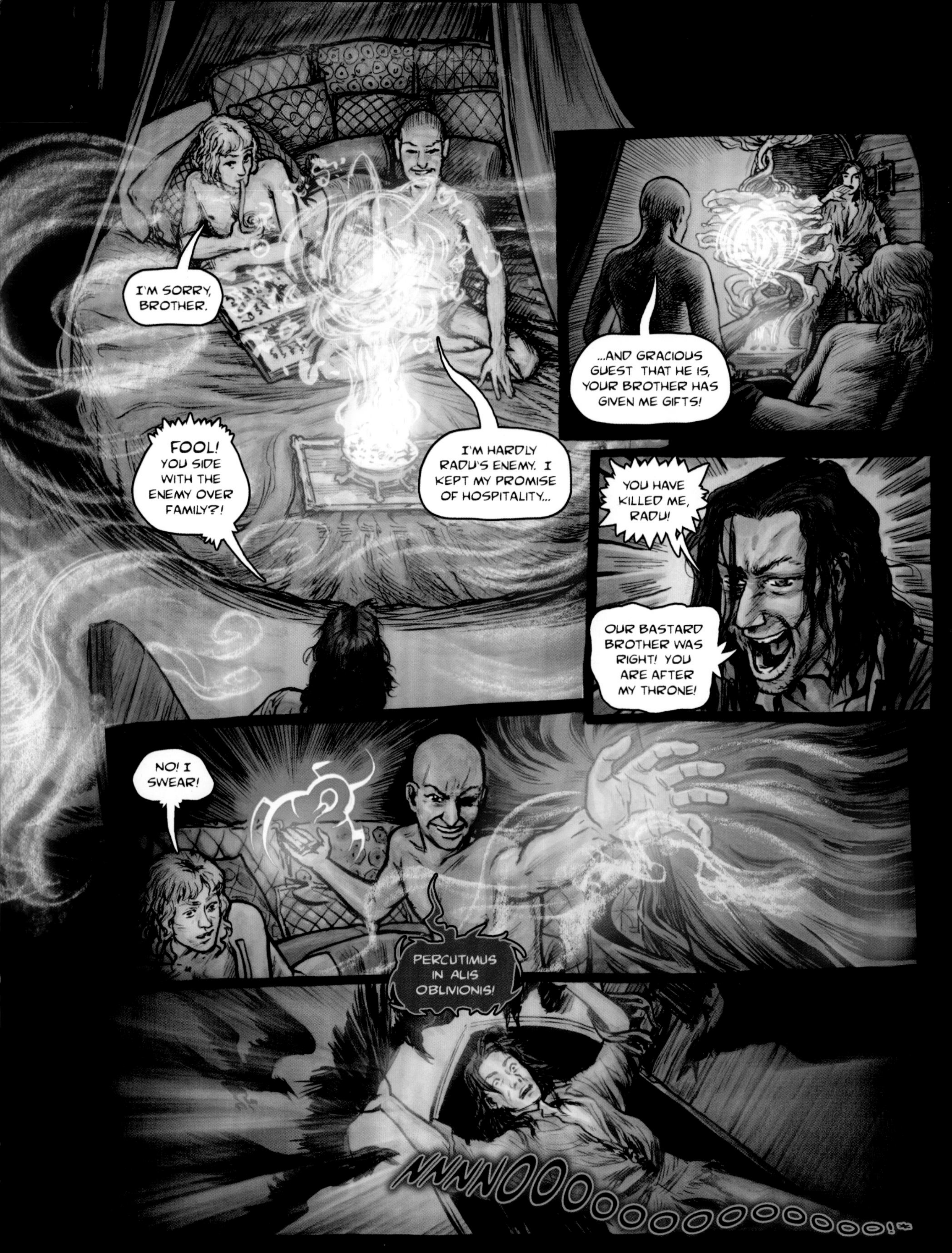

I'M SORRY, BROTHER.
FOOL! YOU SIDE WITH THE ENEMY OVER FAMILY?!
I'M HARDLY RADU'S ENEMY. I KEPT MY PROMISE OF HOSPITALITY...
...AND GRACIOUS GUEST THAT HE IS, YOUR BROTHER HAS GIVEN ME GIFTS!
YOU HAVE KILLED ME, RADU!
OUR BASTARD BROTHER WAS RIGHT! YOU ARE AFTER MY THRONE!
NO! I SWEAR!
PERCUTIMUS IN ALIS OBLIVIONIS!
NNNNOOOOOOOOOOOOOOOOOO!

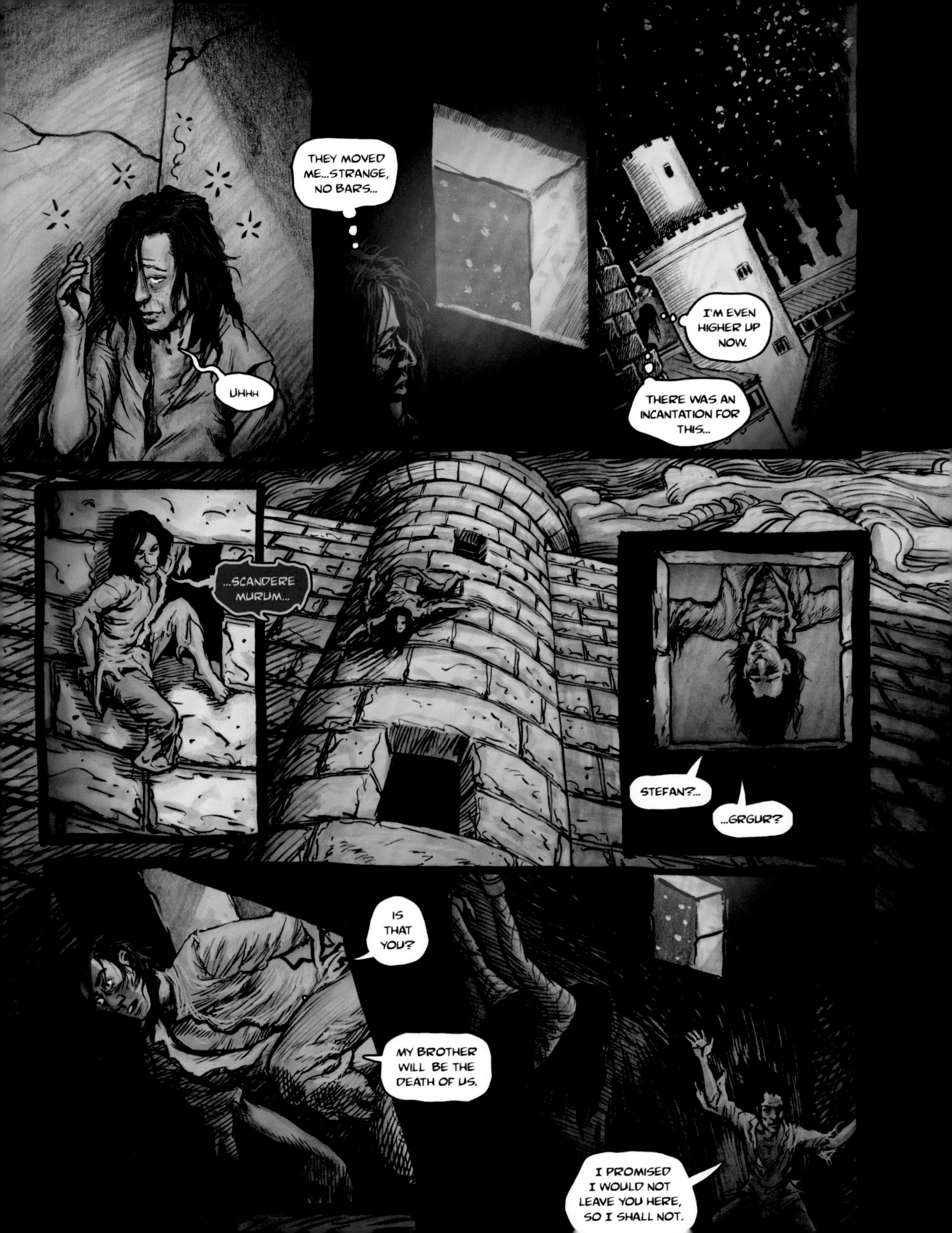
UHHH
THEY MOVED ME...STRANGE, NO BARS...
I'M EVEN HIGHER UP NOW.
THERE WAS AN INCANTATION FOR THIS...
...SCANDERE MURUM...
STEFAN?...
...GRGUR?
IS THAT YOU?
MY BROTHER WILL BE THE DEATH OF US.
I PROMISED I WOULD NOT LEAVE YOU HERE, SO I SHALL NOT.

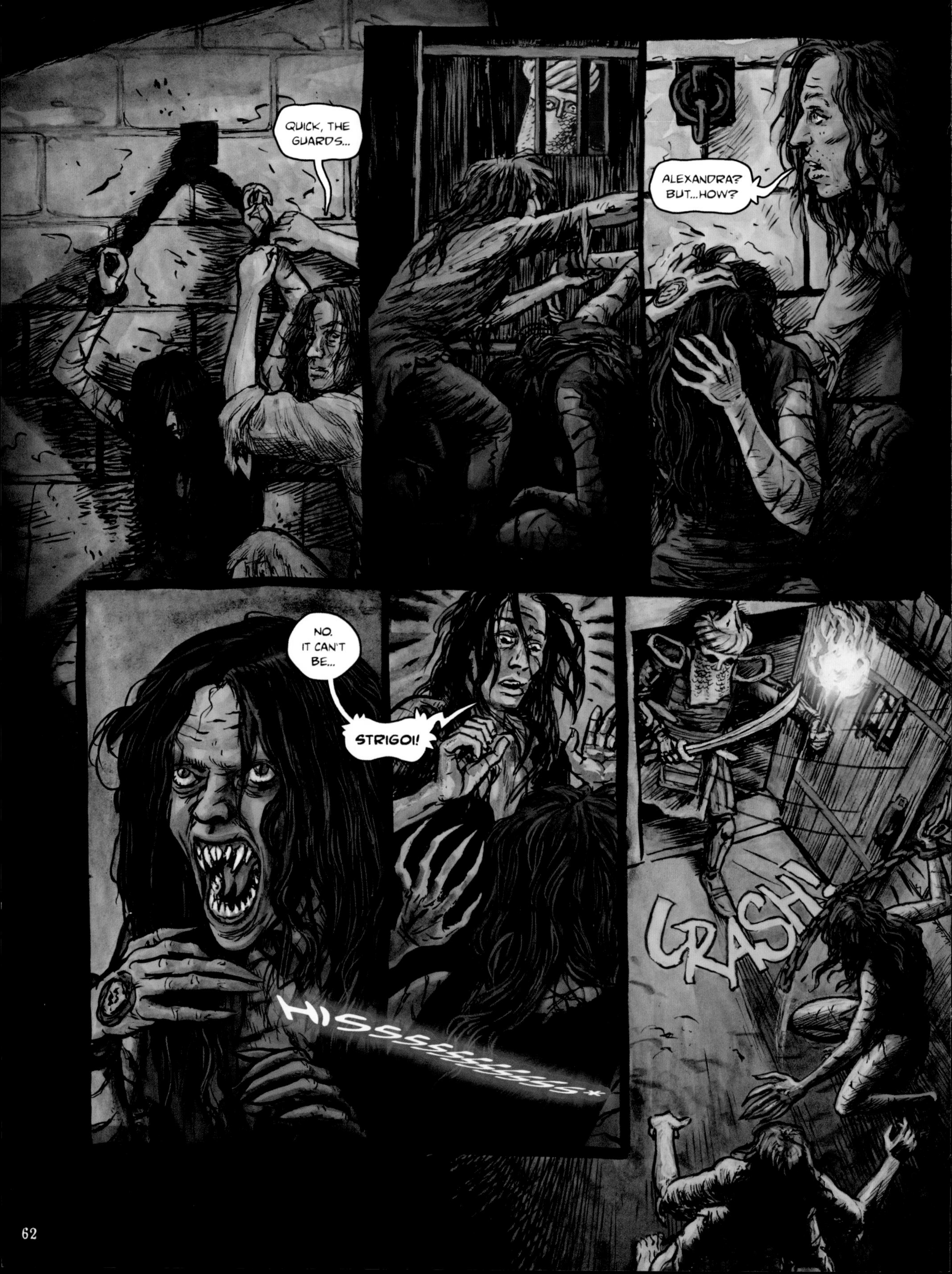
QUICK, THE GUARDS...
ALEXANDRA? BUT...HOW?
NO. IT CAN'T BE...
STRIGOI!
HISSSSSSSSSSS*
CRASH!

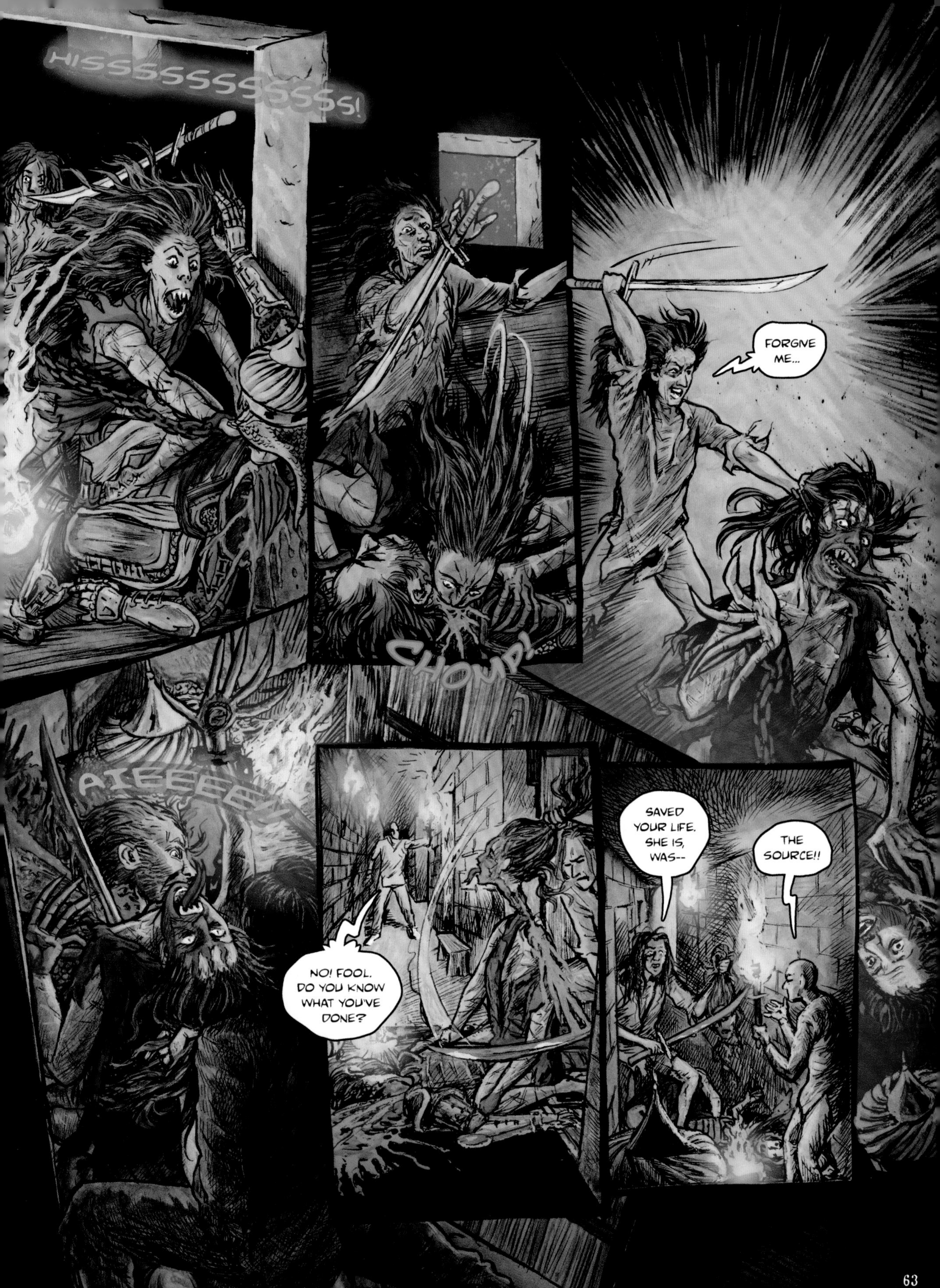
HISSSSSSSSSSSSS!
FORGIVE ME...
CHOMP!
AIEEEE!!
NO! FOOL. DO YOU KNOW WHAT YOU'VE DONE?
SAVED YOUR LIFE. SHE IS, WAS--
THE SOURCE!!

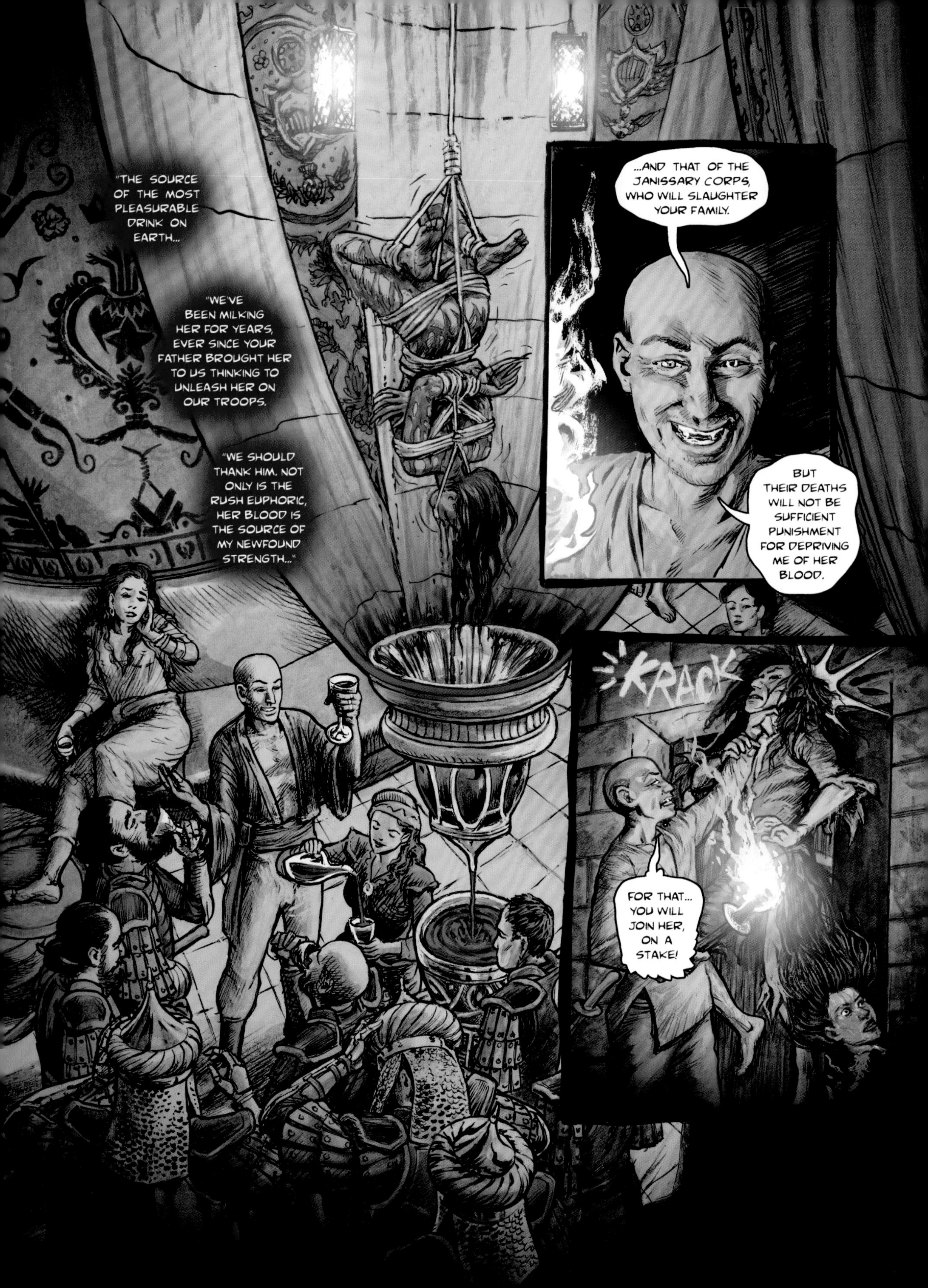
"THE SOURCE OF THE MOST PLEASURABLE DRINK ON EARTH...
"WE'VE BEEN MILKING HER FOR YEARS, EVER SINCE YOUR FATHER BROUGHT HER TO US THINKING TO UNLEASH HER ON OUR TROOPS.
"WE SHOULD THANK HIM. NOT ONLY IS THE RUSH EUPHORIC, HER BLOOD IS THE SOURCE OF MY NEWFOUND STRENGTH..."
...AND THAT OF THE JANISSARY CORPS, WHO WILL SLAUGHTER YOUR FAMILY.
BUT THEIR DEATHS WILL NOT BE SUFFICIENT PUNISHMENT FOR DEPRIVING ME OF HER BLOOD.
KRACK
FOR THAT... YOU WILL JOIN HER, ON A STAKE!

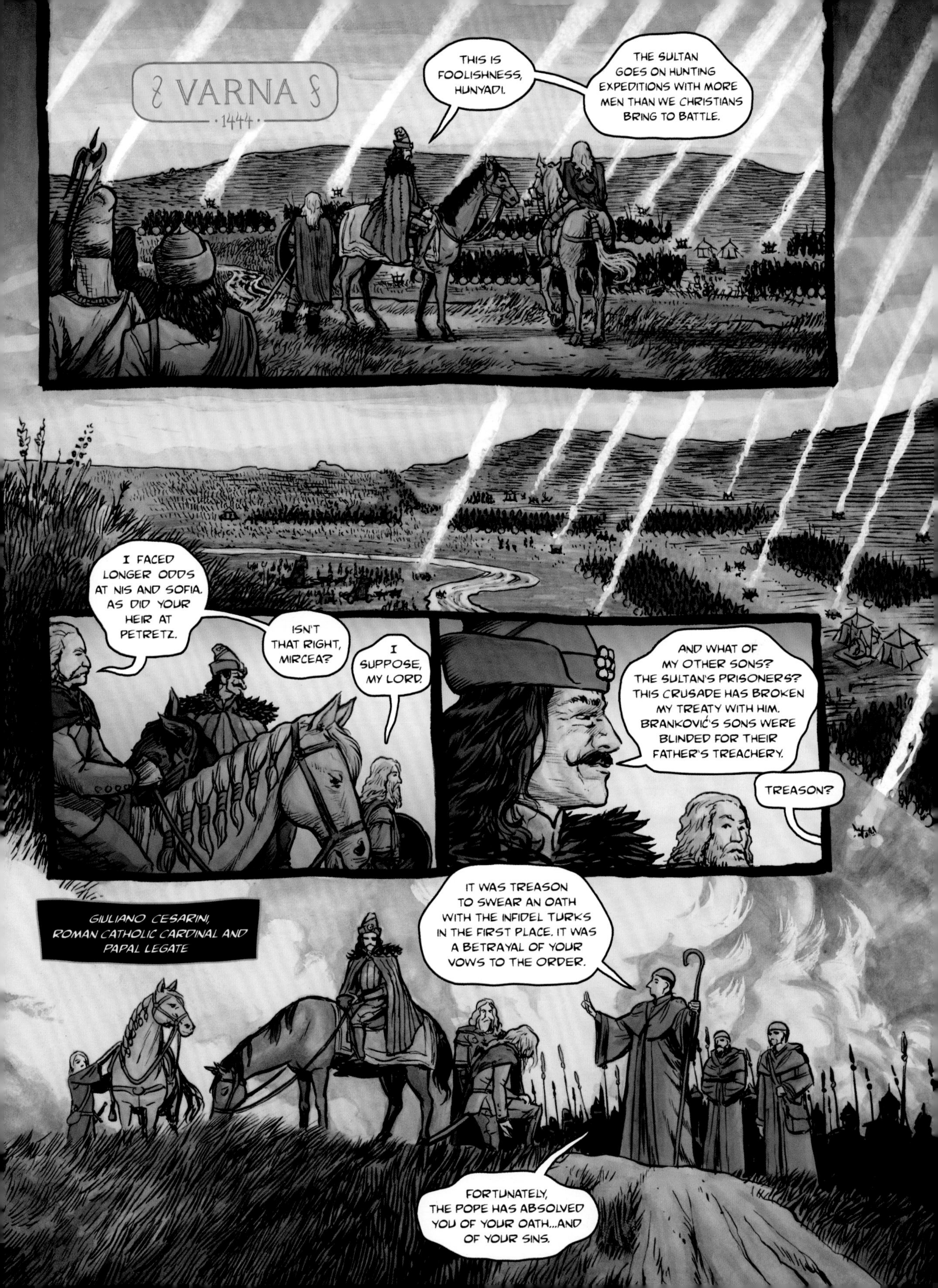
VARNA
1444
THIS IS FOOLISHNESS, HUNYADI.
THE SULTAN GOES ON HUNTING EXPEDITIONS WITH MORE MEN THAN WE CHRISTIANS BRING TO BATTLE.
I FACED LONGER ODDS AT NIS AND SOFIA. AS DID YOUR HEIR AT PETRETZ.
ISN'T THAT RIGHT, MIRCEA?
I SUPPOSE, MY LORD.
AND WHAT OF MY OTHER SONS? THE SULTAN'S PRISONERS? THIS CRUSADE HAS BROKEN MY TREATY WITH HIM. BRANKOVIĆ'S SONS WERE BLINDED FOR THEIR FATHER'S TREACHERY.
TREASON?
GIULIANO CESARINI, ROMAN CATHOLIC CARDINAL AND PAPAL LEGATE
IT WAS TREASON TO SWEAR AN OATH WITH THE INFIDEL TURKS IN THE FIRST PLACE. IT WAS A BETRAYAL OF YOUR VOWS TO THE ORDER.
FORTUNATELY, THE POPE HAS ABSOLVED YOU OF YOUR OATH...AND OF YOUR SINS.

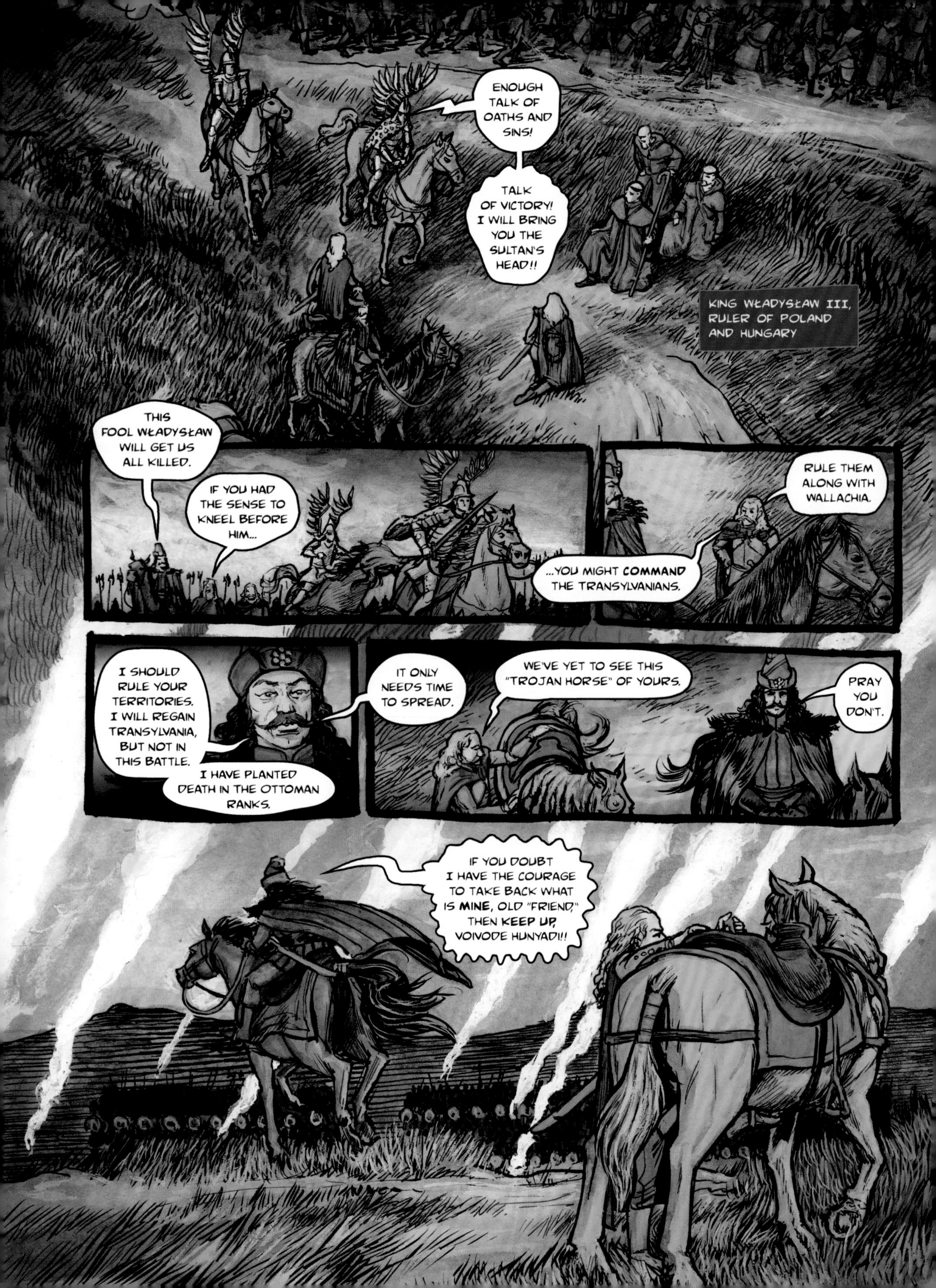
ENOUGH TALK OF OATHS AND SINS!
TALK OF VICTORY! I WILL BRING YOU THE SULTAN'S HEAD!!
KING WŁADYSŁAW III, RULER OF POLAND AND HUNGARY
THIS FOOL WŁADYSŁAW WILL GET US ALL KILLED.
IF YOU HAD THE SENSE TO KNEEL BEFORE HIM...
...YOU MIGHT COMMAND THE TRANSYLVANIANS.
RULE THEM ALONG WITH WALLACHIA.
I SHOULD RULE YOUR TERRITORIES. I WILL REGAIN TRANSYLVANIA, BUT NOT IN THIS BATTLE.
I HAVE PLANTED DEATH IN THE OTTOMAN RANKS.
IT ONLY NEEDS TIME TO SPREAD.
WE'VE YET TO SEE THIS "TROJAN HORSE" OF YOURS.
PRAY YOU DON'T.
IF YOU DOUBT I HAVE THE COURAGE TO TAKE BACK WHAT IS MINE, OLD "FRIEND," THEN KEEP UP, VOIVODE HUNYADI!!

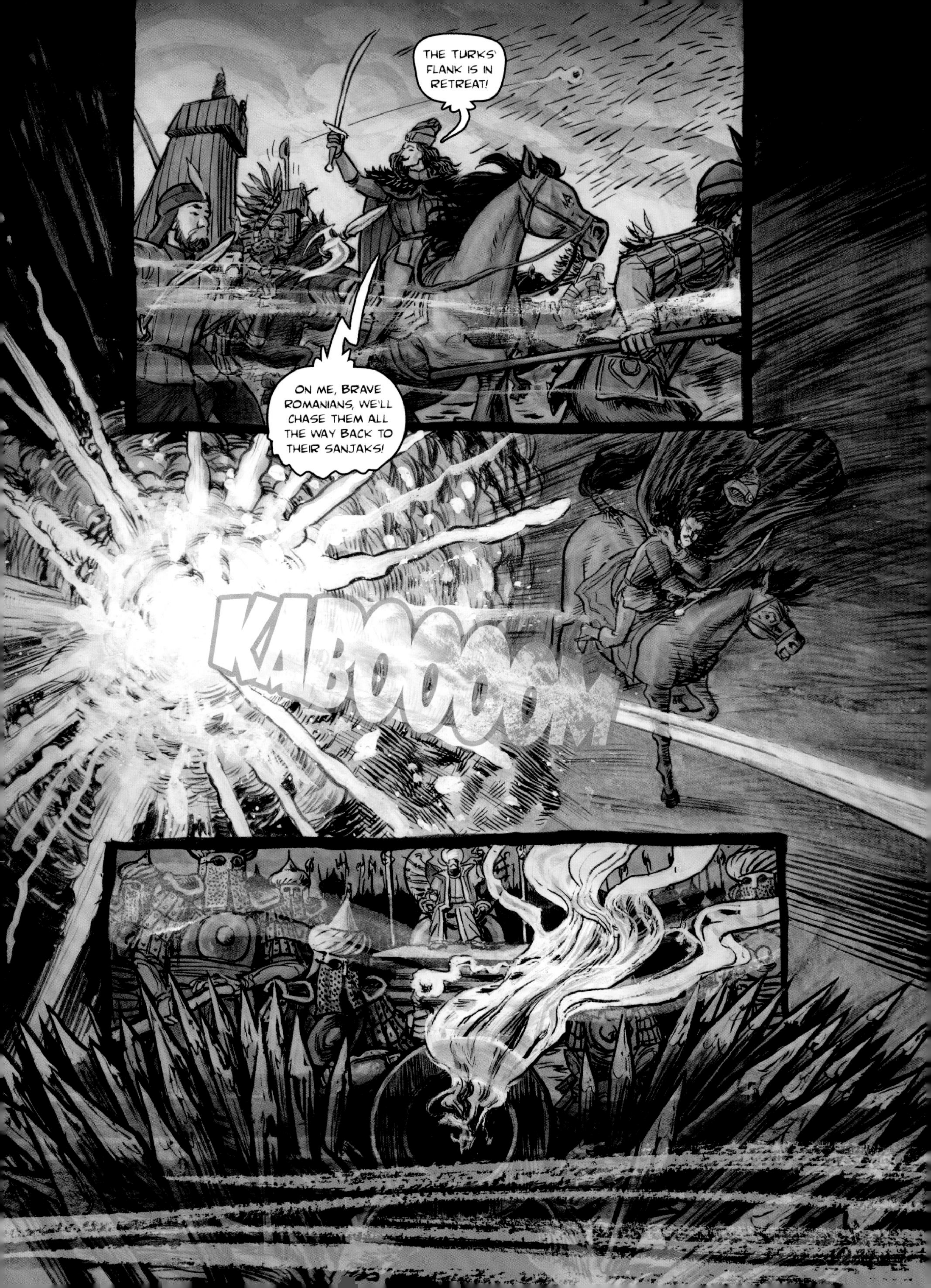
THE TURKS' FLANK IS IN RETREAT!
ON ME, BRAVE ROMANIANS, WE'LL CHASE THEM ALL THE WAY BACK TO THEIR SANJAKS!
KABOOOOOM

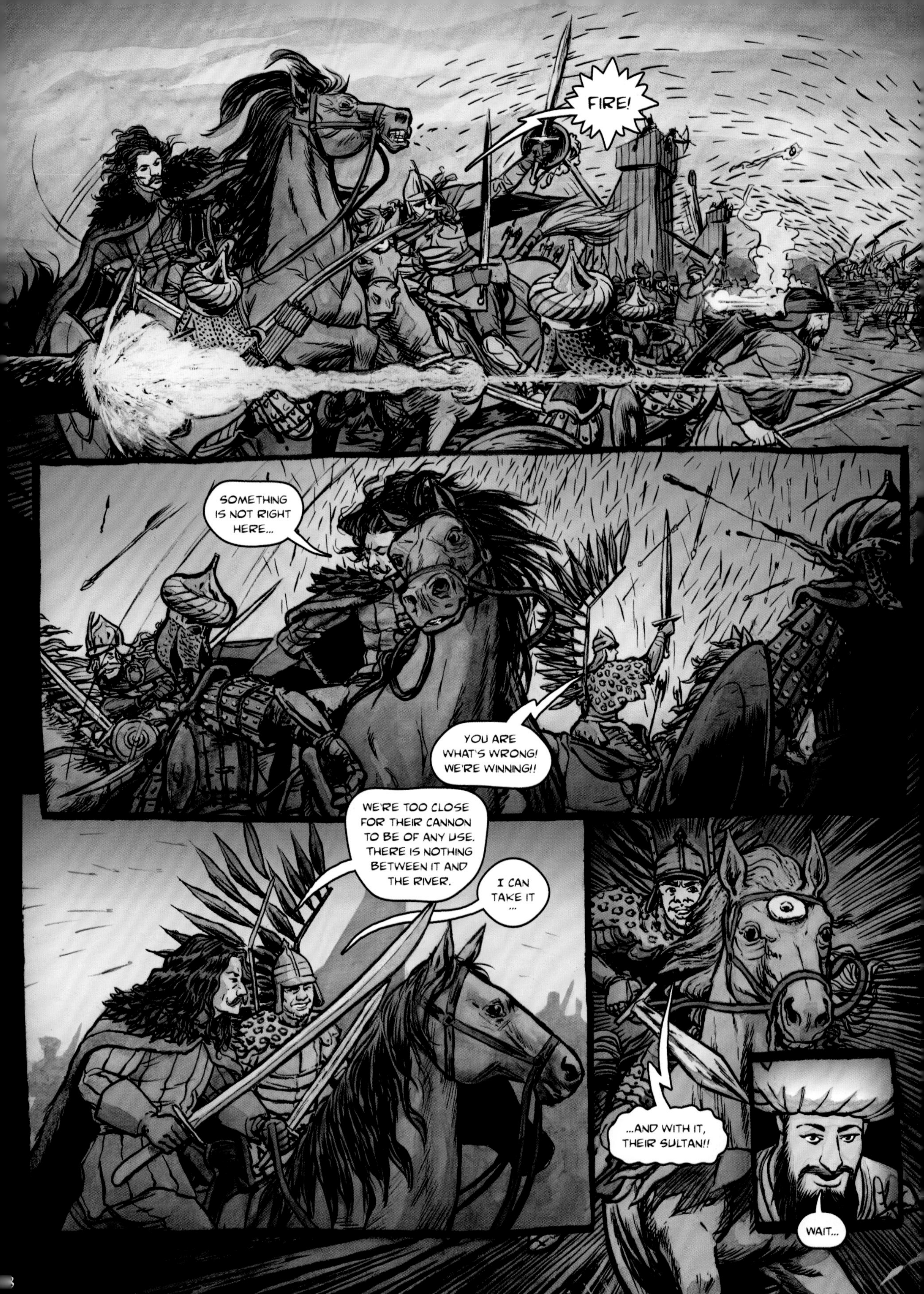
FIRE!
SOMETHING IS NOT RIGHT HERE...
YOU ARE WHAT'S WRONG! WE'RE WINNING!!
WE'RE TOO CLOSE FOR THEIR CANNON TO BE OF ANY USE. THERE IS NOTHING BETWEEN IT AND THE RIVER.
I CAN TAKE IT ...
...AND WITH IT, THEIR SULTAN!!
WAIT...

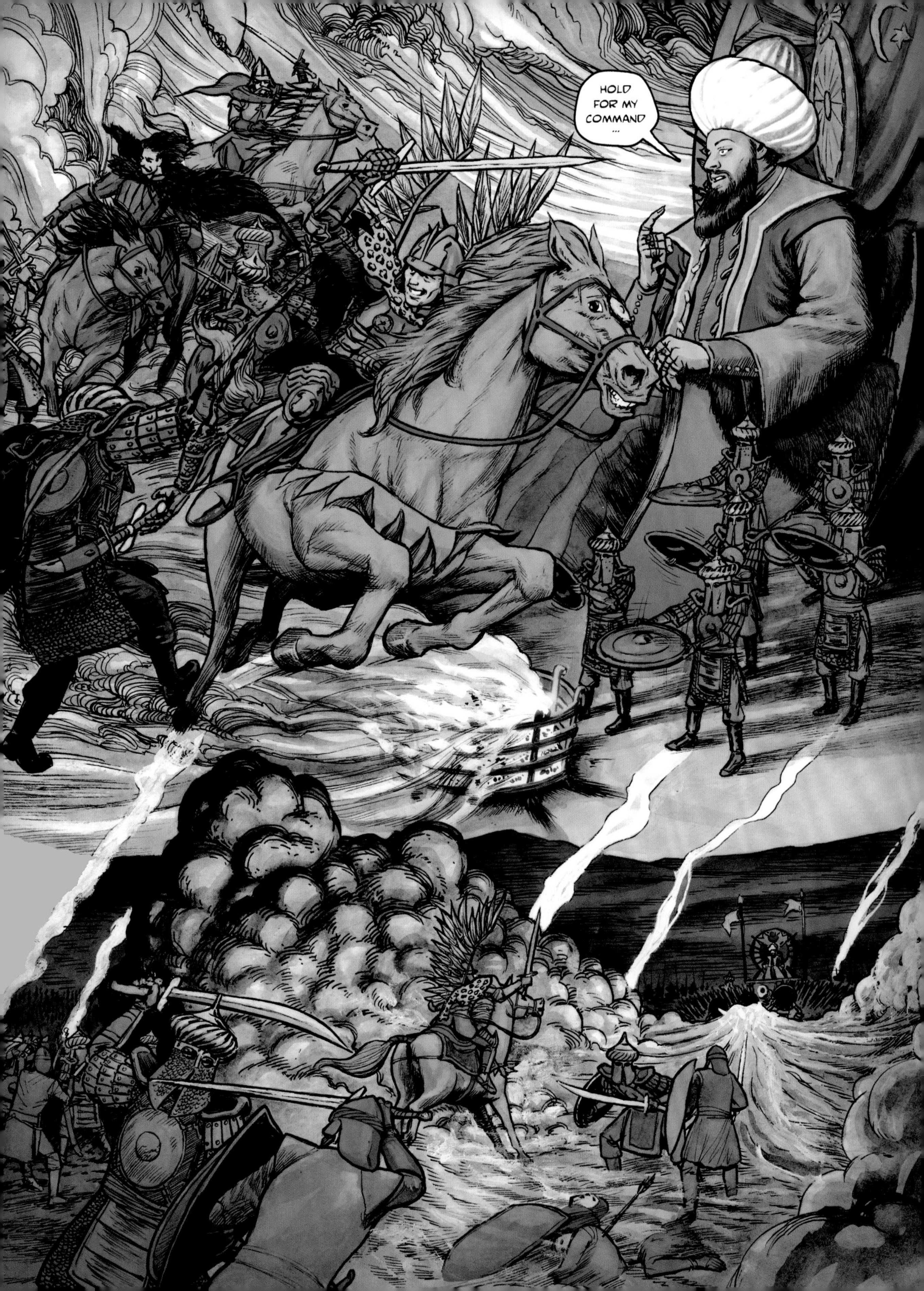
HOLD FOR MY COMMAND ...

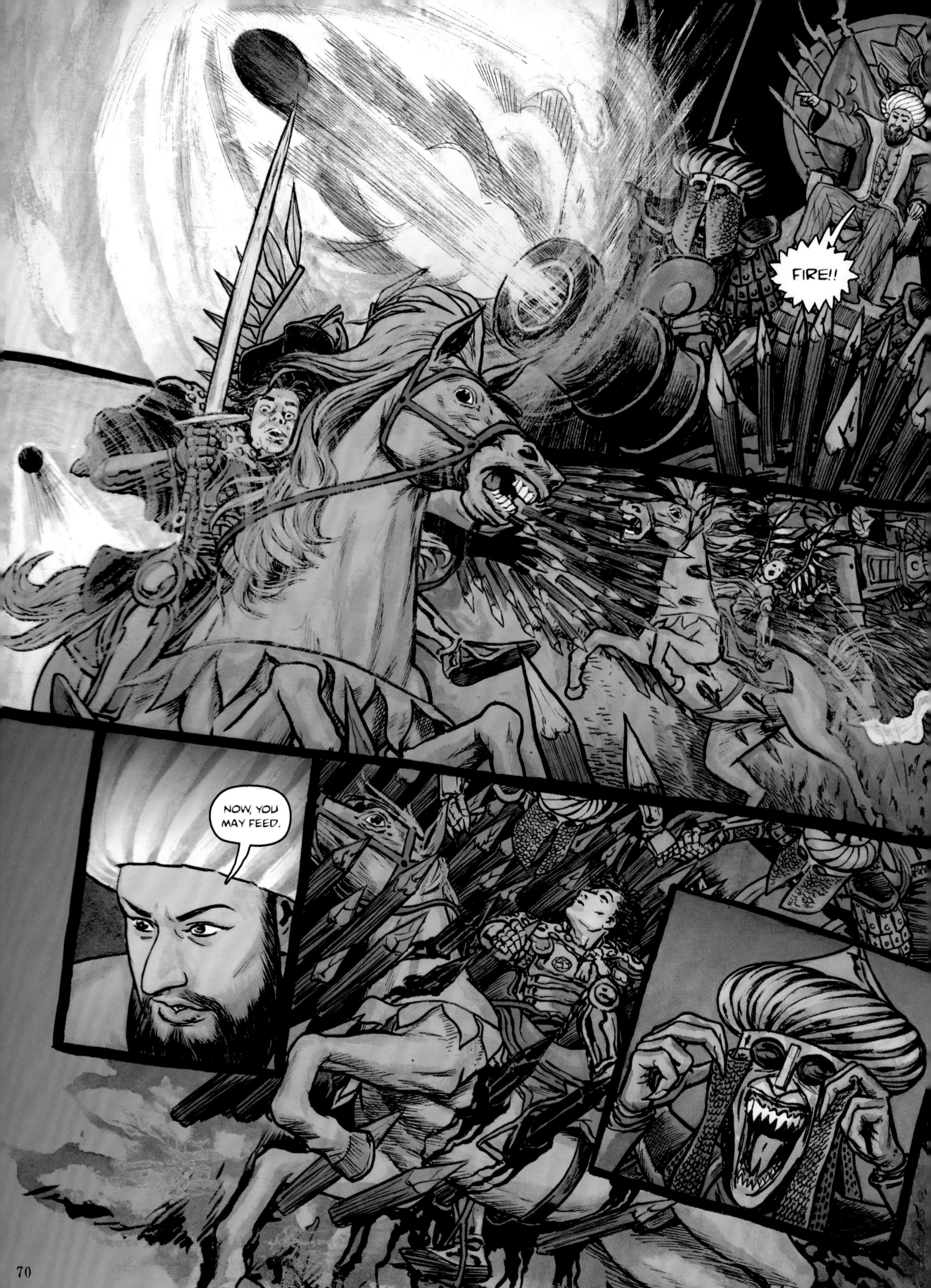
FIRE!!
NOW, YOU MAY FEED.

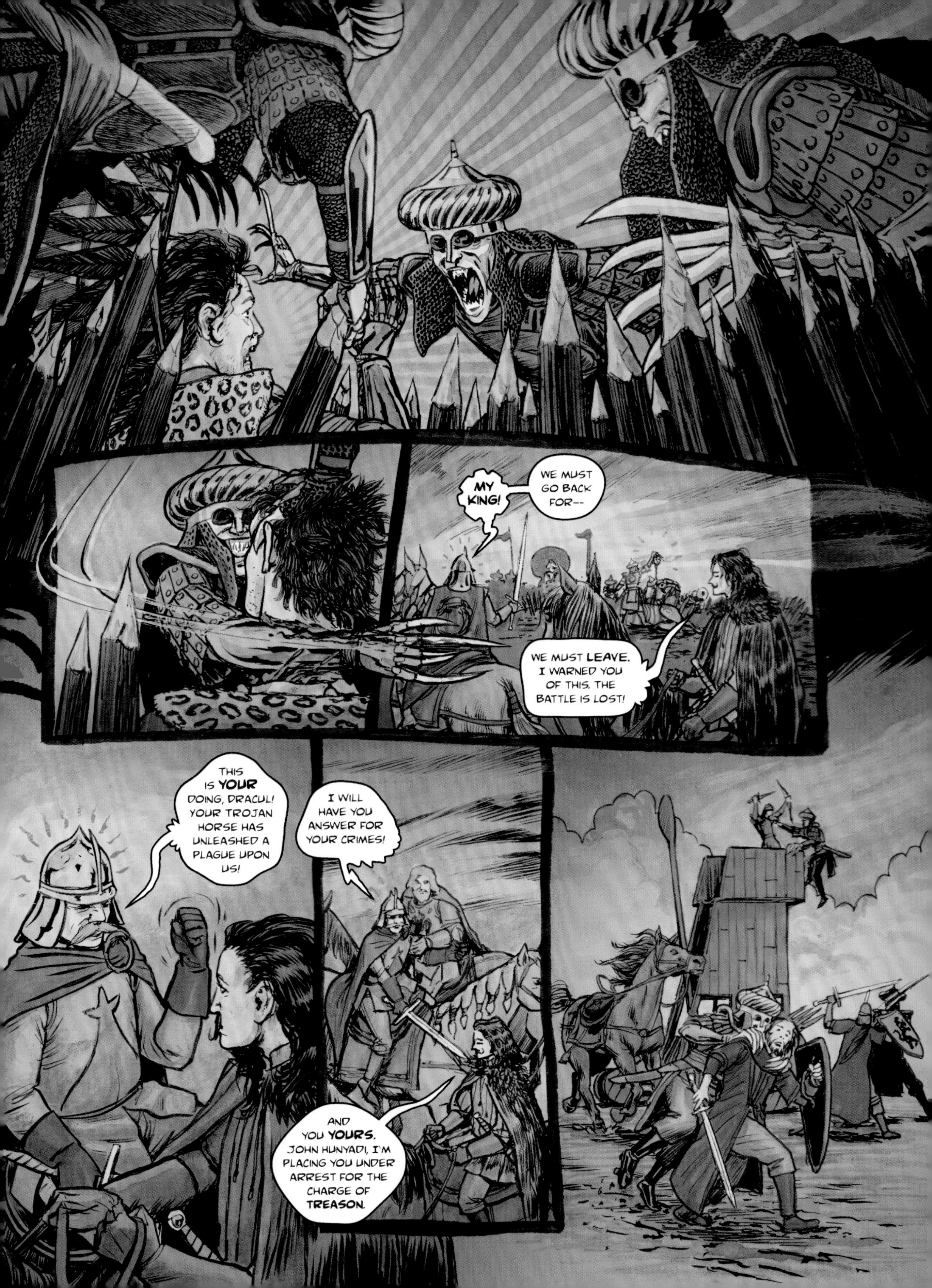

MY KING!
WE MUST GO BACK FOR--
WE MUST LEAVE. I WARNED YOU OF THIS. THE BATTLE IS LOST!
THIS IS YOUR DOING, DRACUL! YOUR TROJAN HORSE HAS UNLEASHED A PLAGUE UPON US!
I WILL HAVE YOU ANSWER FOR YOUR CRIMES!
AND YOU YOURS. JOHN HUNYADI, I'M PLACING YOU UNDER ARREST FOR THE CHARGE OF TREASON.

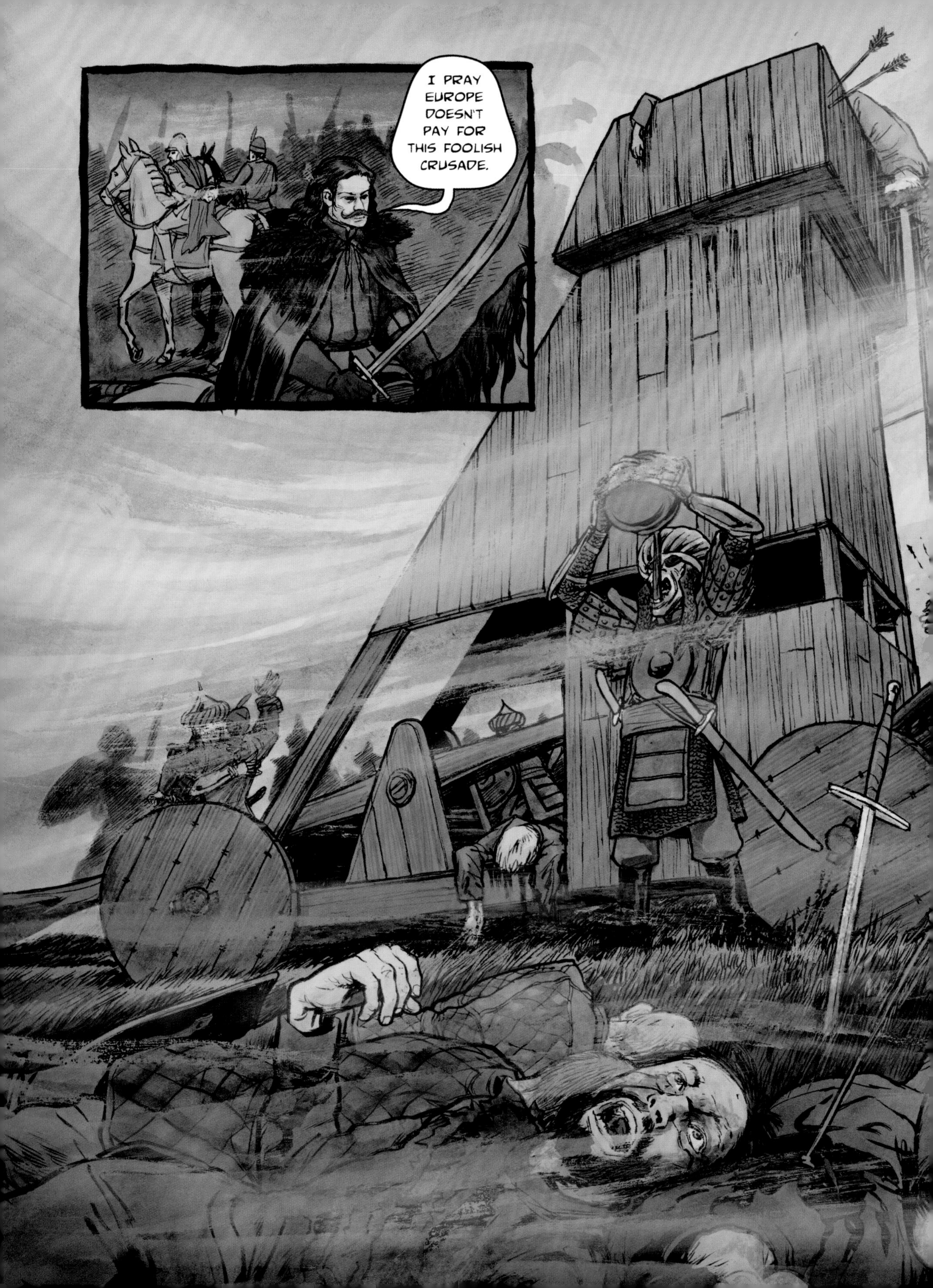
I PRAY EUROPE DOESN'T PAY FOR THIS FOOLISH CRUSADE.

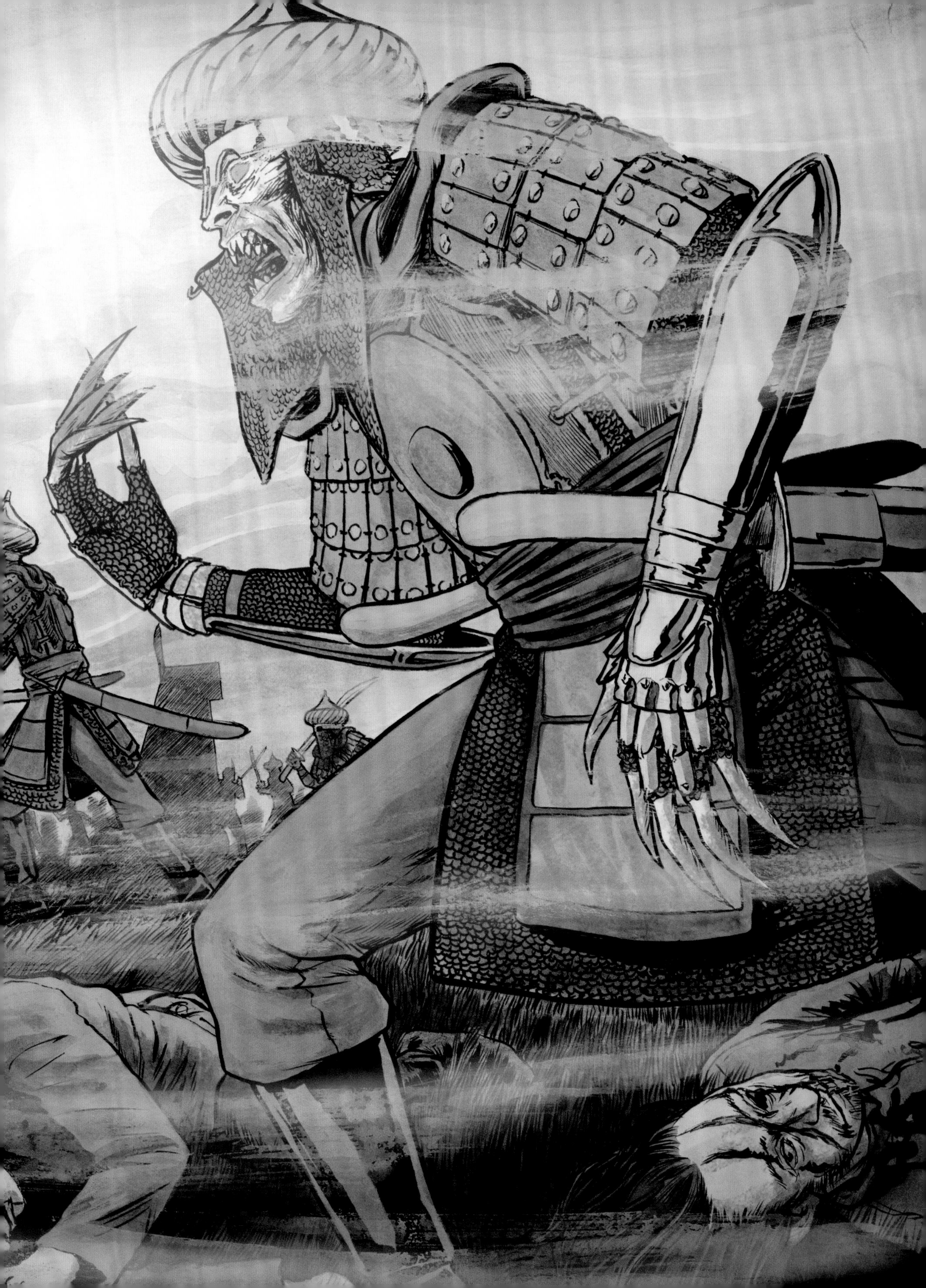

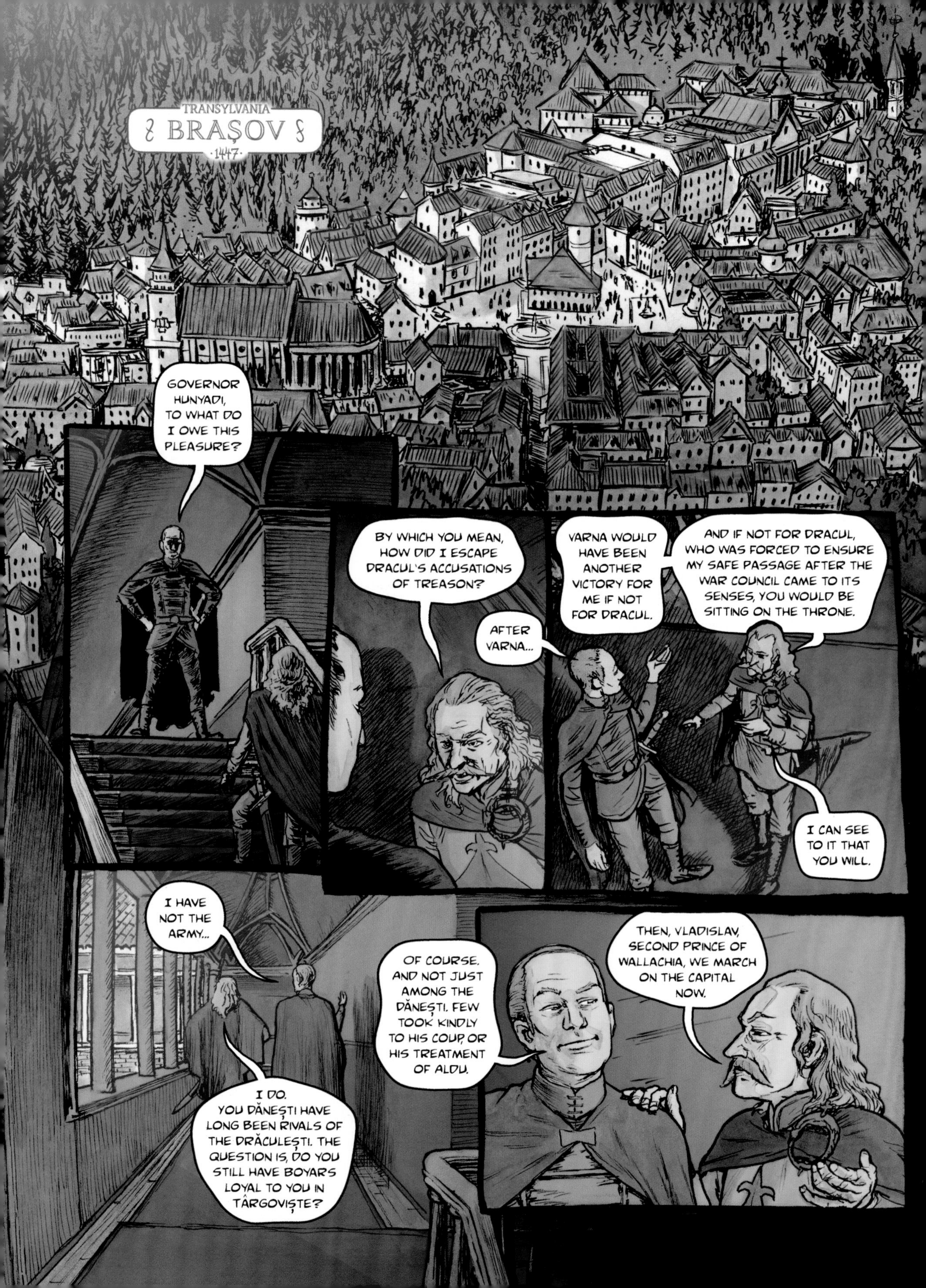
TRANSYLVANIA
BRAȘOV
1447
GOVERNOR HUNYADI, TO WHAT DO I OWE THIS PLEASURE?
BY WHICH YOU MEAN, HOW DID I ESCAPE DRACUL'S ACCUSATIONS OF TREASON?
AFTER VARNA...
VARNA WOULD HAVE BEEN ANOTHER VICTORY FOR ME IF NOT FOR DRACUL.
AND IF NOT FOR DRACUL, WHO WAS FORCED TO ENSURE MY SAFE PASSAGE AFTER THE WAR COUNCIL CAME TO ITS SENSES, YOU WOULD BE SITTING ON THE THRONE.
I CAN SEE TO IT THAT YOU WILL.
I HAVE NOT THE ARMY...
I DO. YOU DĂNEȘTI HAVE LONG BEEN RIVALS OF THE DRĂCULEȘTI. THE QUESTION IS, DO YOU STILL HAVE BOYARS LOYAL TO YOU IN TÂRGOVIȘTE?
OF COURSE. AND NOT JUST AMONG THE DĂNEȘTI. FEW TOOK KINDLY TO HIS COUP, OR HIS TREATMENT OF ALDU.
THEN, VLADISLAV, SECOND PRINCE OF WALLACHIA, WE MARCH ON THE CAPITAL NOW.

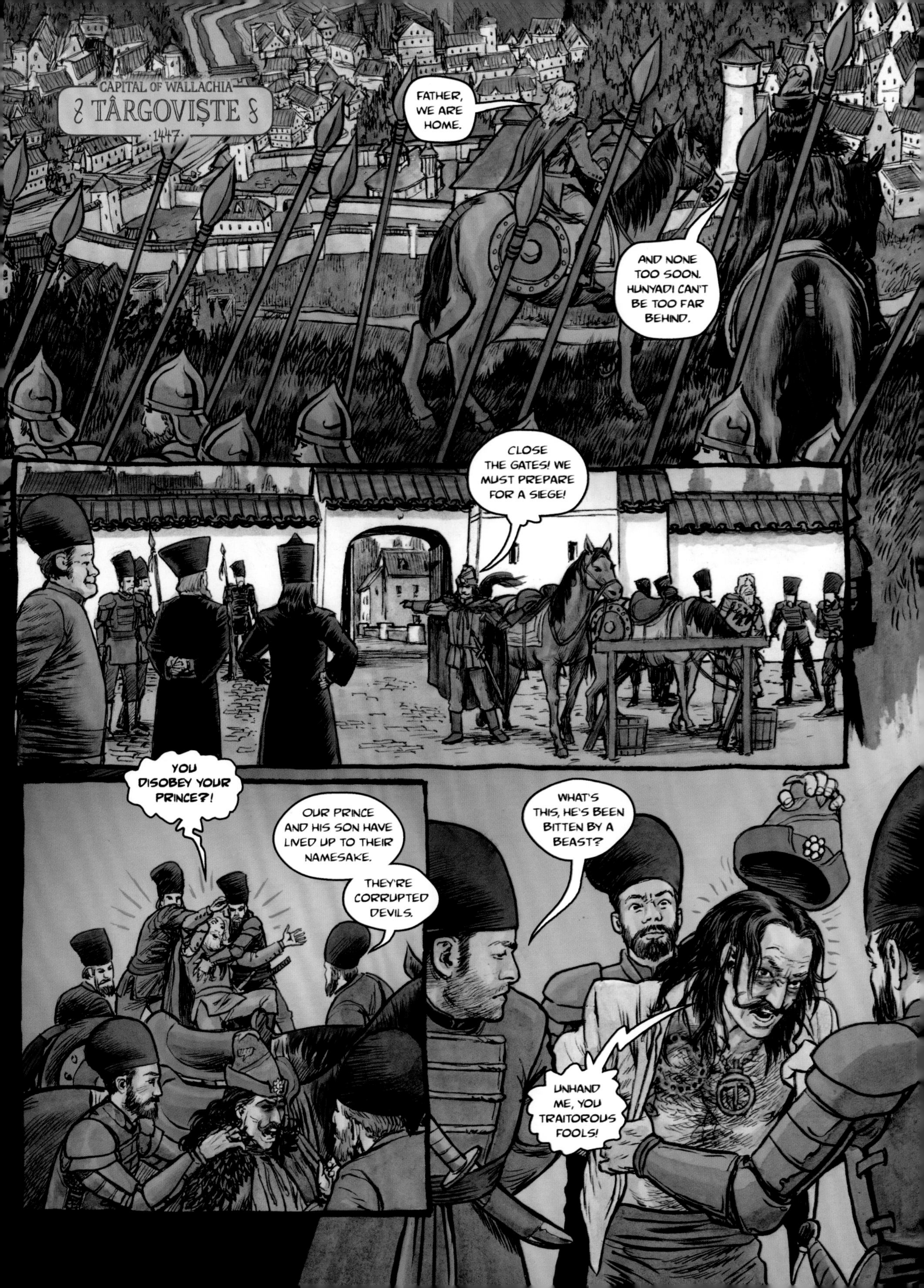
CAPITAL OF WALLACHIA
TÂRGOVIȘTE
1447
FATHER, WE ARE HOME.
AND NONE TOO SOON. HUNYADI CAN'T BE TOO FAR BEHIND.
CLOSE THE GATES! WE MUST PREPARE FOR A SIEGE!
YOU DISOBEY YOUR PRINCE?!
OUR PRINCE AND HIS SON HAVE LIVED UP TO THEIR NAMESAKE.
THEY'RE CORRUPTED DEVILS.
WHAT'S THIS, HE'S BEEN BITTEN BY A BEAST?
UNHAND ME, YOU TRAITOROUS FOOLS!

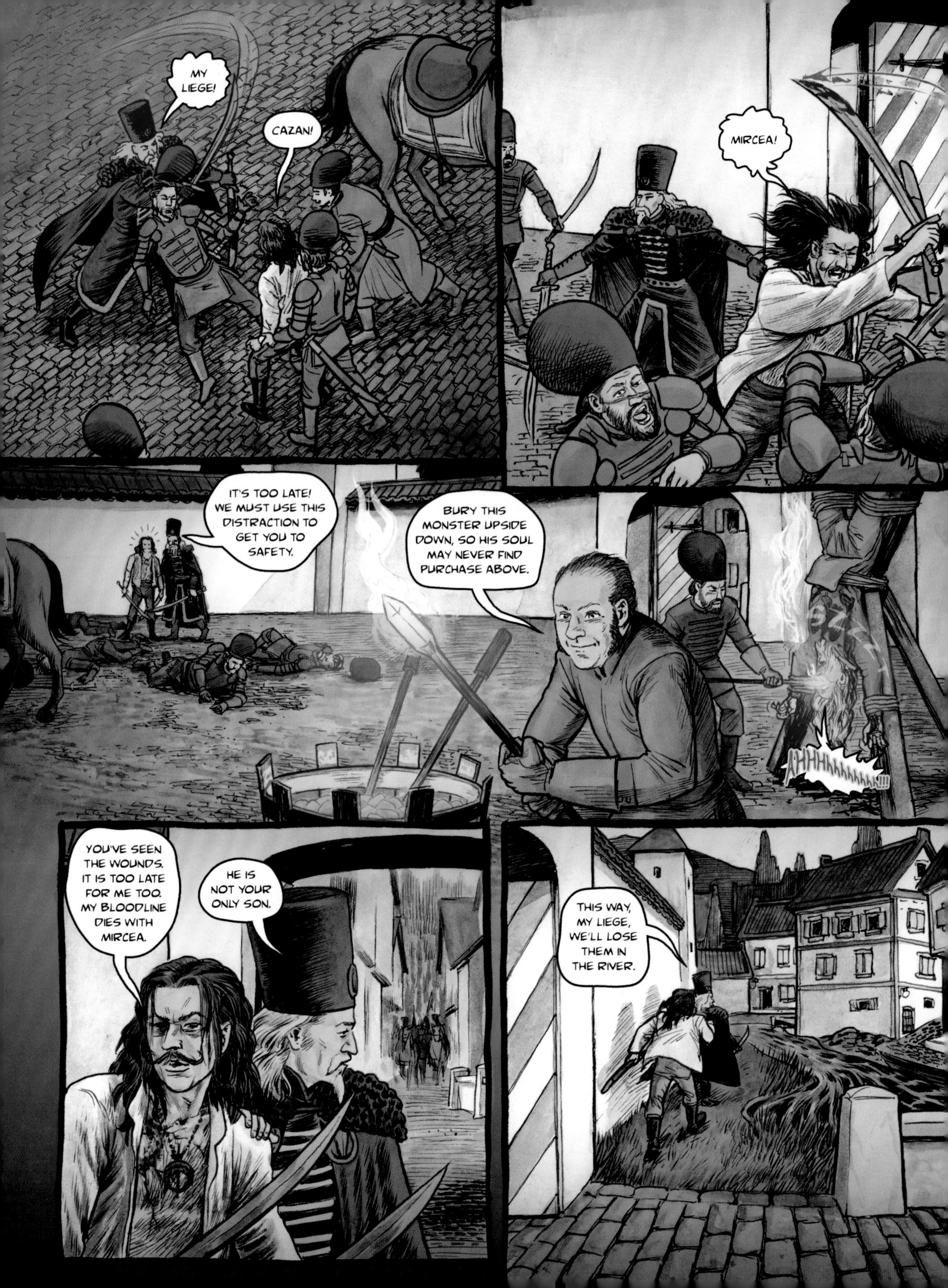
MY LIEGE!
CAZAN!
MIRCEA!
IT'S TOO LATE! WE MUST USE THIS DISTRACTION TO GET YOU TO SAFETY.
BURY THIS MONSTER UPSIDE DOWN, SO HIS SOUL MAY NEVER FIND PURCHASE ABOVE.
AHHHHHHHHHH!!!
YOU'VE SEEN THE WOUNDS. IT IS TOO LATE FOR ME TOO. MY BLOODLINE DIES WITH MIRCEA.
HE IS NOT YOUR ONLY SON.
THIS WAY, MY LIEGE, WE'LL LOSE THEM IN THE RIVER.

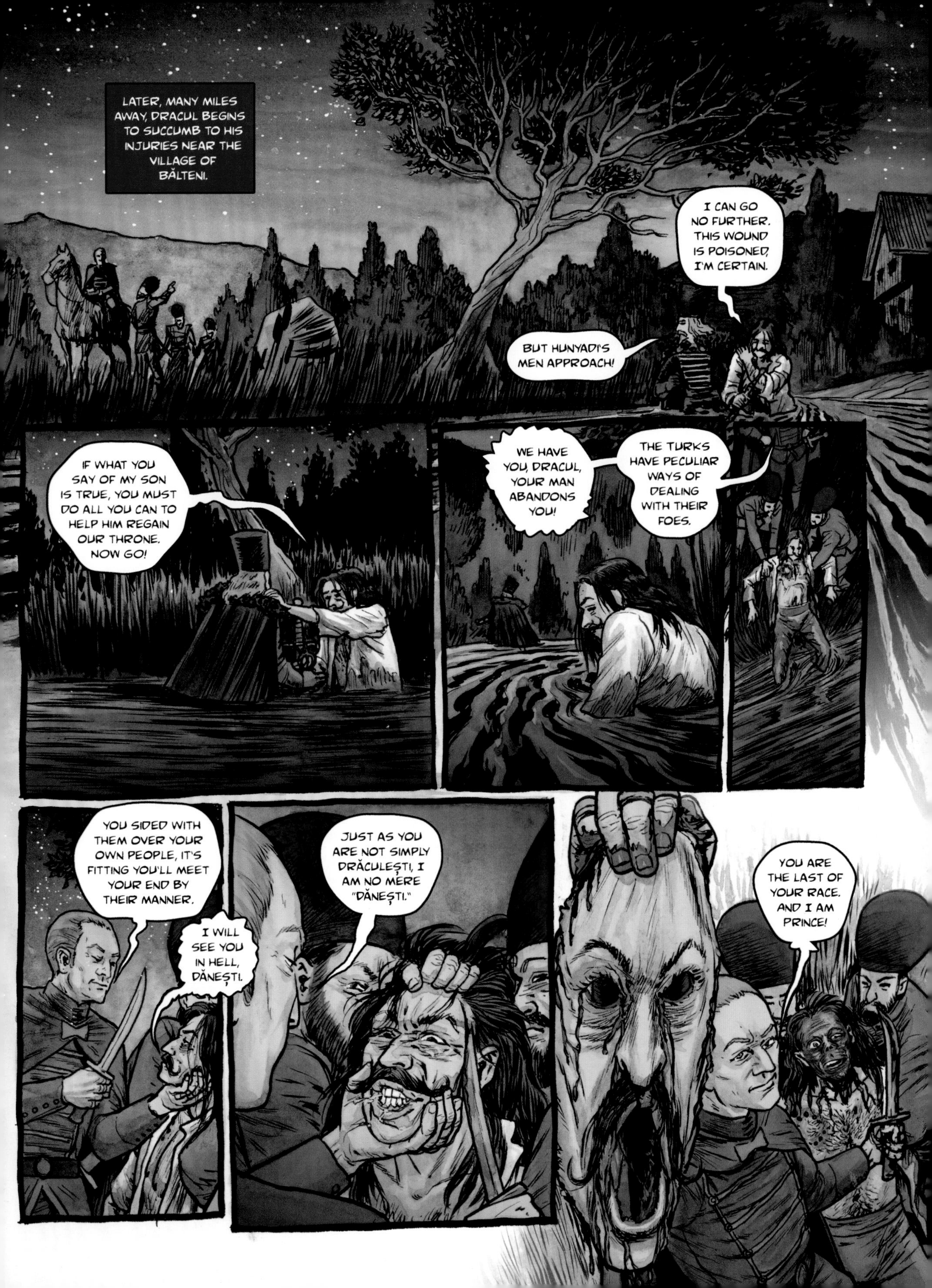
LATER, MANY MILES AWAY, DRACUL BEGINS TO SUCCUMB TO HIS INJURIES NEAR THE VILLAGE OF BĂLTENI.
I CAN GO NO FURTHER. THIS WOUND IS POISONED, I'M CERTAIN.
BUT HUNYADI'S MEN APPROACH!
IF WHAT YOU SAY OF MY SON IS TRUE, YOU MUST DO ALL YOU CAN TO HELP HIM REGAIN OUR THRONE. NOW GO!
WE HAVE YOU, DRACUL, YOUR MAN ABANDONS YOU!
THE TURKS HAVE PECULIAR WAYS OF DEALING WITH THEIR FOES.
YOU SIDED WITH THEM OVER YOUR OWN PEOPLE, IT'S FITTING YOU'LL MEET YOUR END BY THEIR MANNER.
I WILL SEE YOU IN HELL, DĂNEȘTI.
JUST AS YOU ARE NOT SIMPLY DRĂCULEȘTI, I AM NO MERE "DĂNEȘTI."
YOU ARE THE LAST OF YOUR RACE. AND I AM PRINCE!

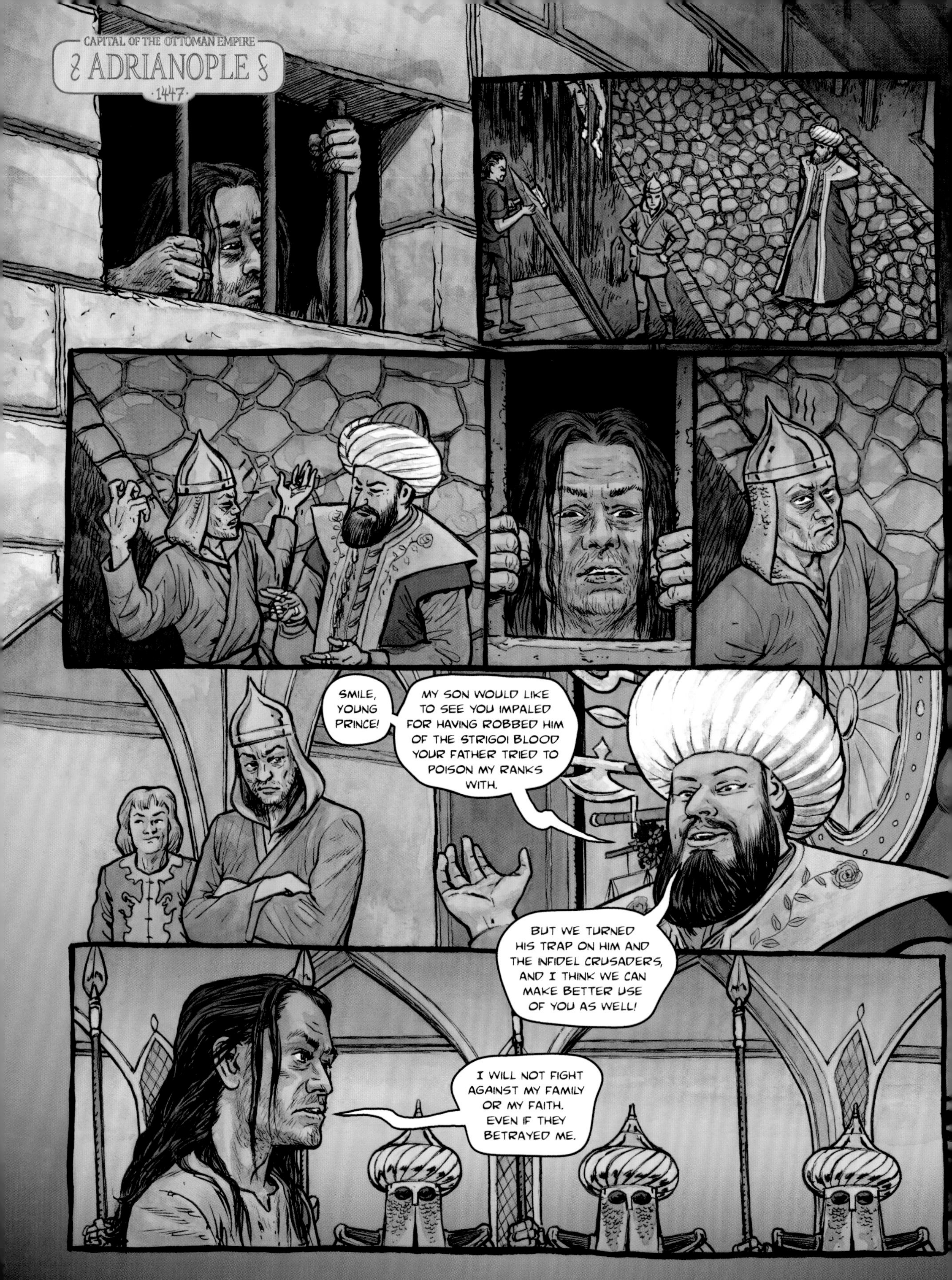
CAPITAL OF THE OTTOMAN EMPIRE
ADRIANOPLE
1447
SMILE, YOUNG PRINCE!
MY SON WOULD LIKE TO SEE YOU IMPALED FOR HAVING ROBBED HIM OF THE STRIGOI BLOOD YOUR FATHER TRIED TO POISON MY RANKS WITH.
BUT WE TURNED HIS TRAP ON HIM AND THE INFIDEL CRUSADERS, AND I THINK WE CAN MAKE BETTER USE OF YOU AS WELL!
I WILL NOT FIGHT AGAINST MY FAMILY OR MY FAITH. EVEN IF THEY BETRAYED ME.

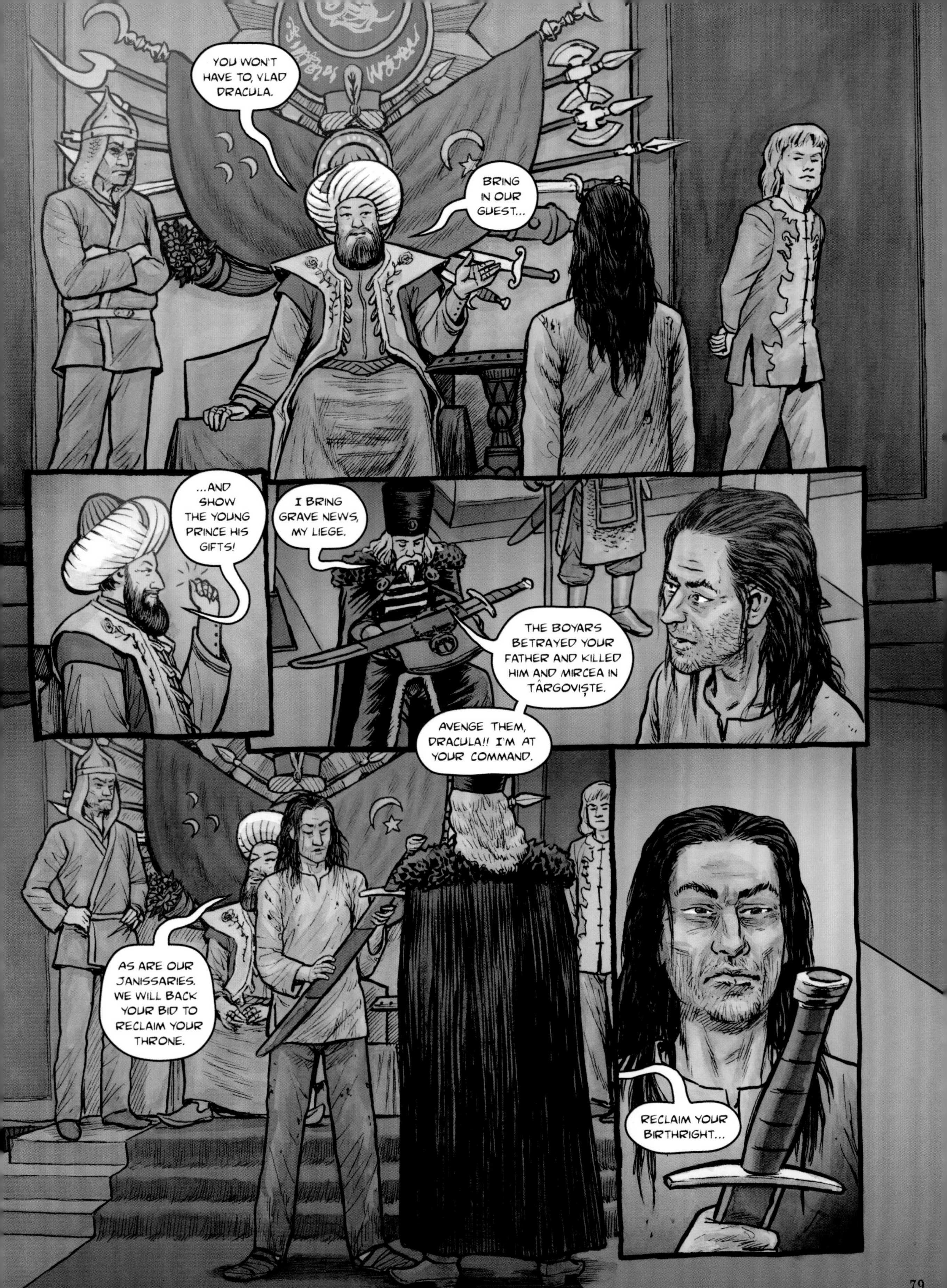

YOU WON'T HAVE TO, VLAD DRACULA.
BRING IN OUR GUEST...
...AND SHOW THE YOUNG PRINCE HIS GIFTS!
I BRING GRAVE NEWS, MY LIEGE.
THE BOYARS BETRAYED YOUR FATHER AND KILLED HIM AND MIRCEA IN TÂRGOVIȘTE.
AVENGE THEM, DRACULA!! I'M AT YOUR COMMAND.
AS ARE OUR JANISSARIES. WE WILL BACK YOUR BID TO RECLAIM YOUR THRONE.
RECLAIM YOUR BIRTHRIGHT...

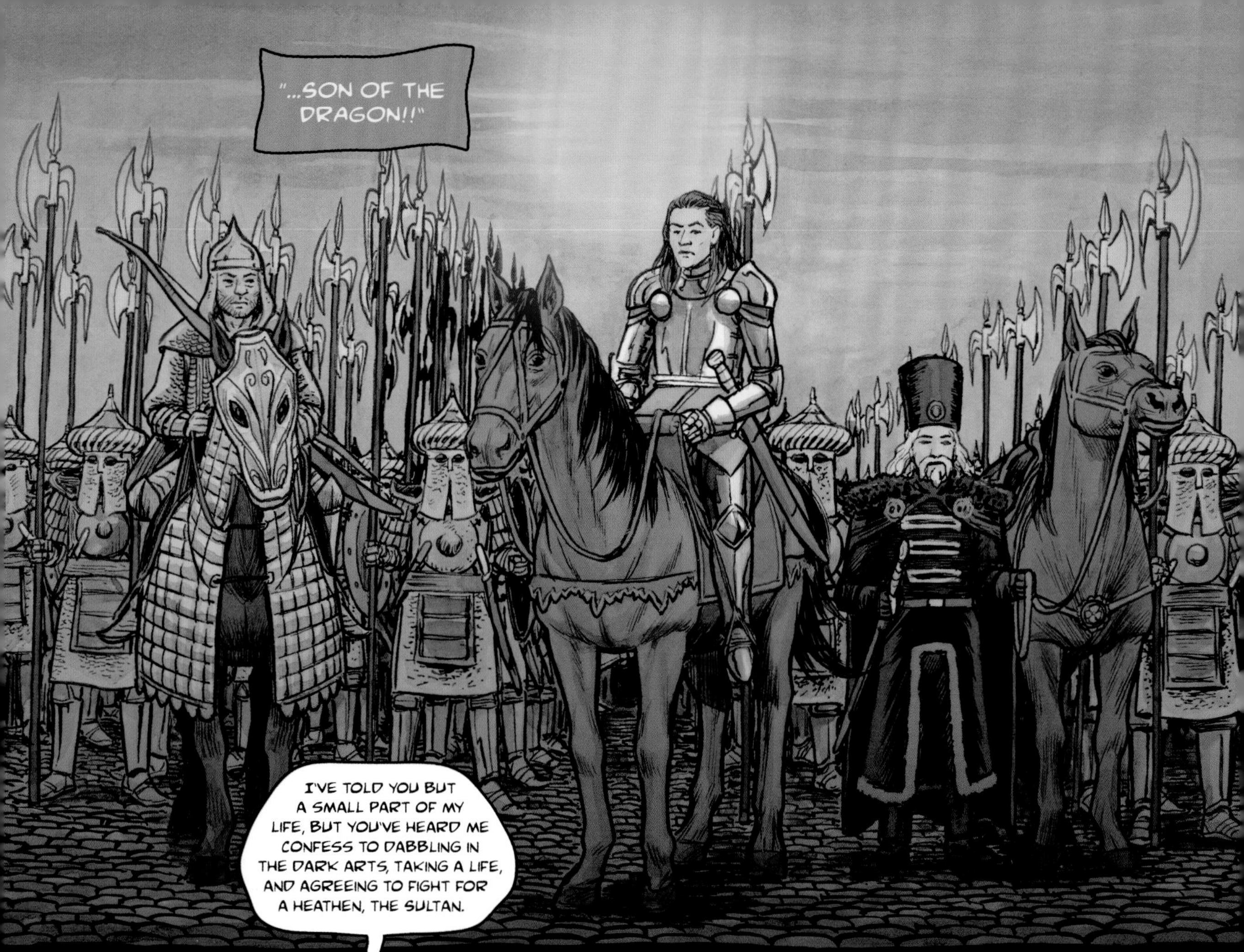
"...SON OF THE DRAGON!!"
I'VE TOLD YOU BUT A SMALL PART OF MY LIFE, BUT YOU'VE HEARD ME CONFESS TO DABBLING IN THE DARK ARTS, TAKING A LIFE, AND AGREEING TO FIGHT FOR A HEATHEN, THE SULTAN.

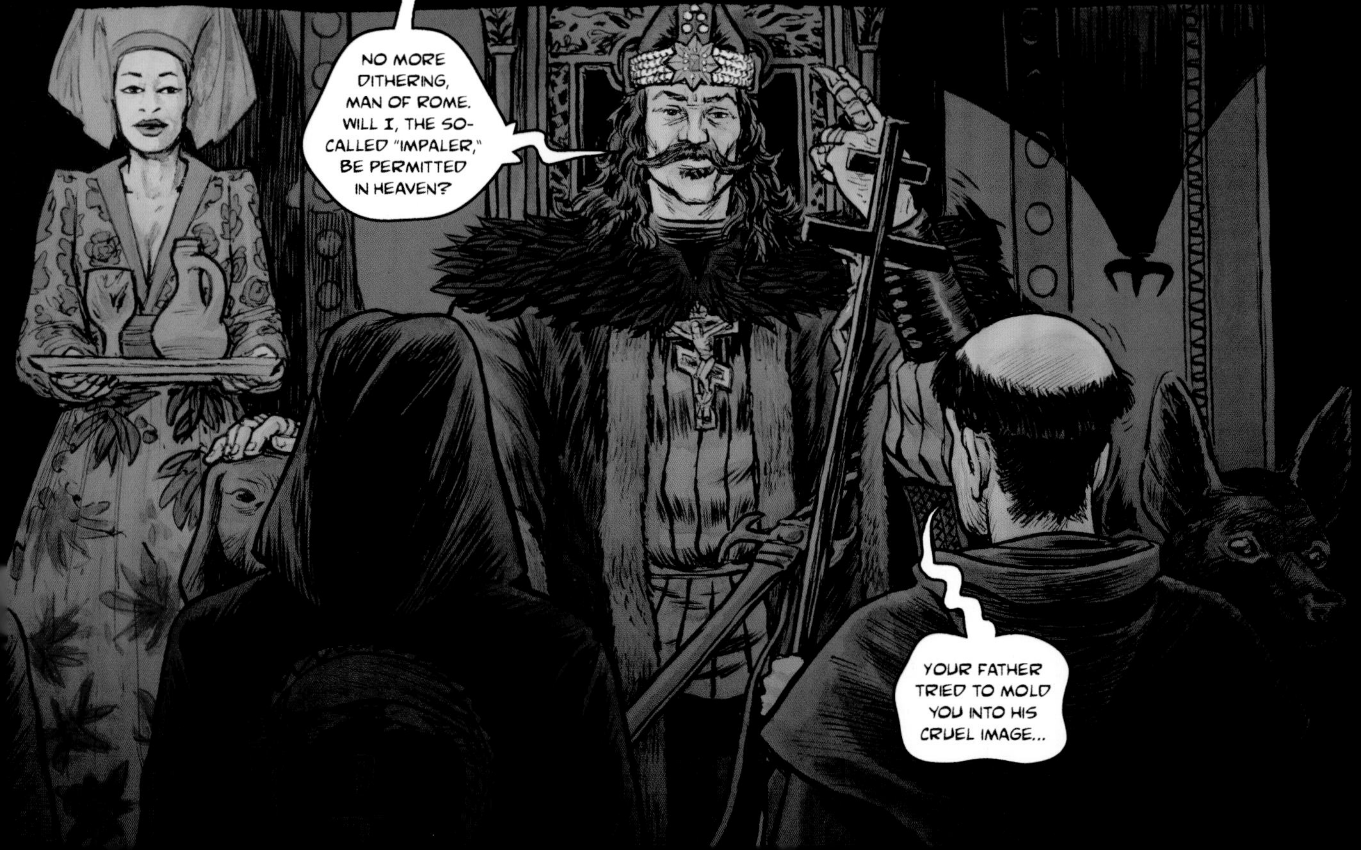
NO MORE DITHERING, MAN OF ROME. WILL I, THE SO-CALLED "IMPALER," BE PERMITTED IN HEAVEN?
YOUR FATHER TRIED TO MOLD YOU INTO HIS CRUEL IMAGE...

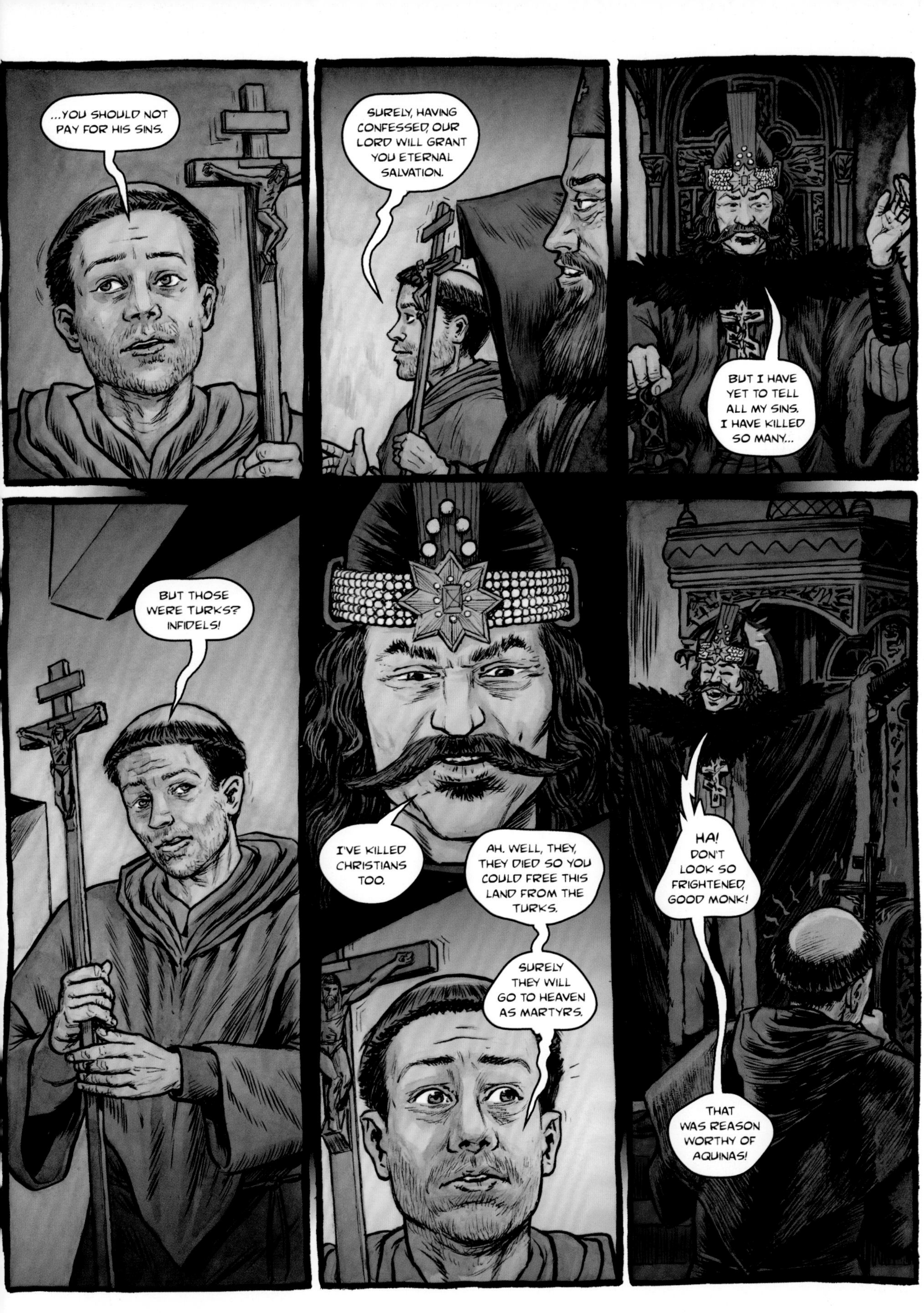
...YOU SHOULD NOT PAY FOR HIS SINS.
SURELY, HAVING CONFESSED, OUR LORD WILL GRANT YOU ETERNAL SALVATION.
BUT I HAVE YET TO TELL ALL MY SINS. I HAVE KILLED SO MANY...
BUT THOSE WERE TURKS? INFIDELS!
I'VE KILLED CHRISTIANS TOO.
AH. WELL, THEY, THEY DIED SO YOU COULD FREE THIS LAND FROM THE TURKS.
SURELY THEY WILL GO TO HEAVEN AS MARTYRS.
HA! DON'T LOOK SO FRIGHTENED, GOOD MONK!
THAT WAS REASON WORTHY OF AQUINAS!

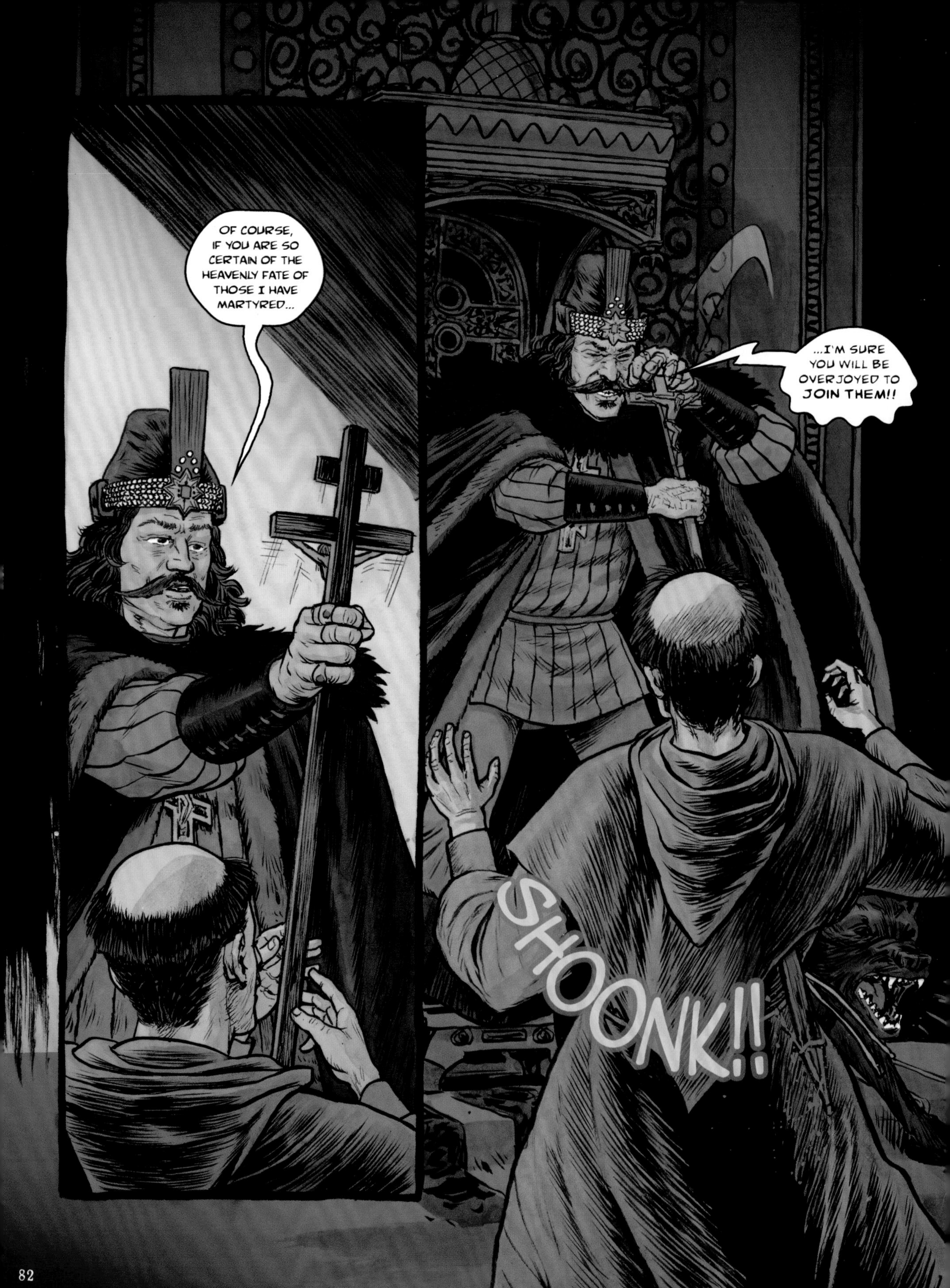
OF COURSE, IF YOU ARE SO CERTAIN OF THE HEAVENLY FATE OF THOSE I HAVE MARTYRED...
...I'M SURE YOU WILL BE OVERJOYED TO JOIN THEM!!
SHOONK!!

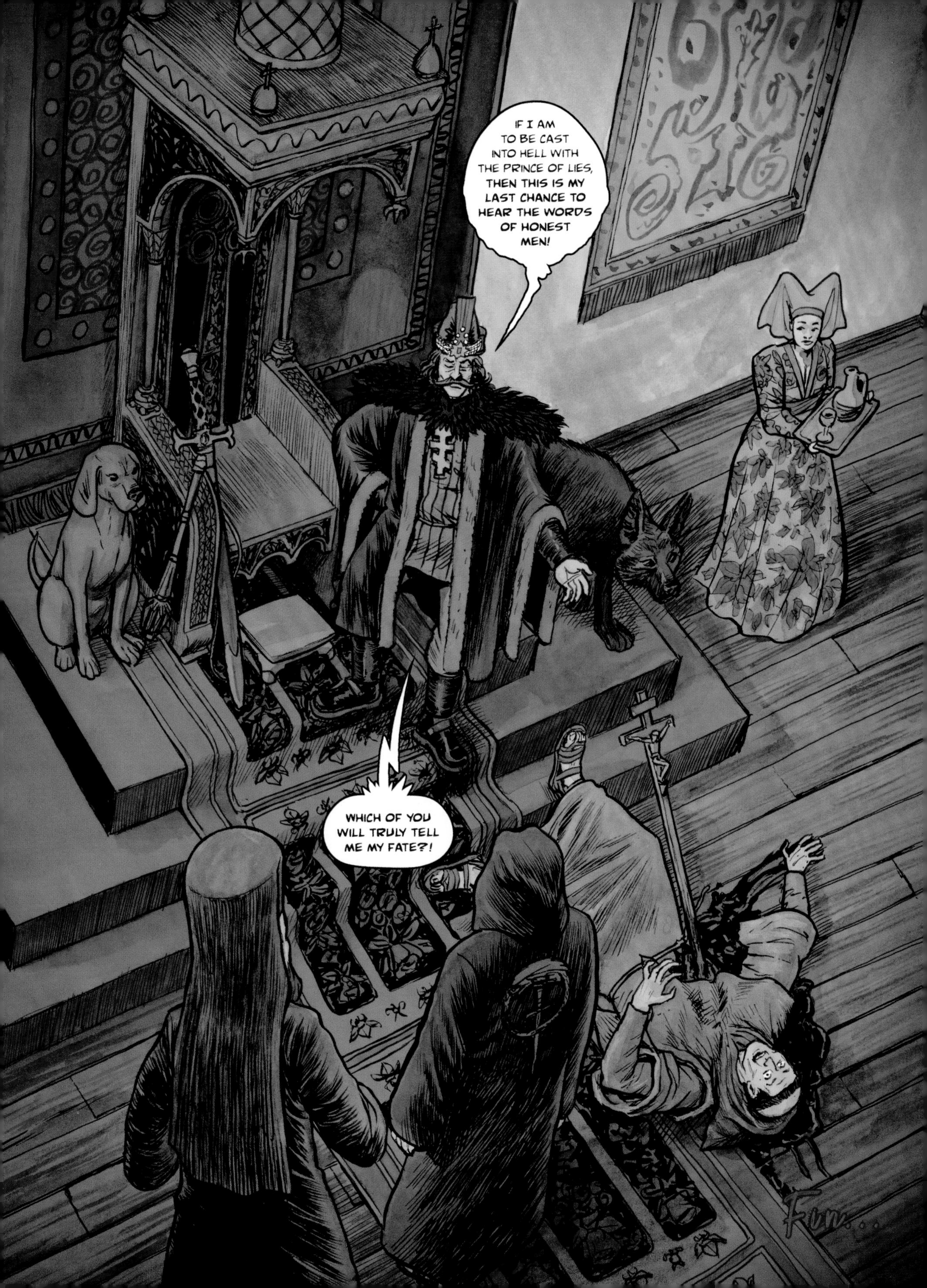
IF I AM TO BE CAST INTO HELL WITH THE PRINCE OF LIES, THEN THIS IS MY LAST CHANCE TO HEAR THE WORDS OF HONEST MEN!
WHICH OF YOU WILL TRULY TELL ME MY FATE?!
Fin...

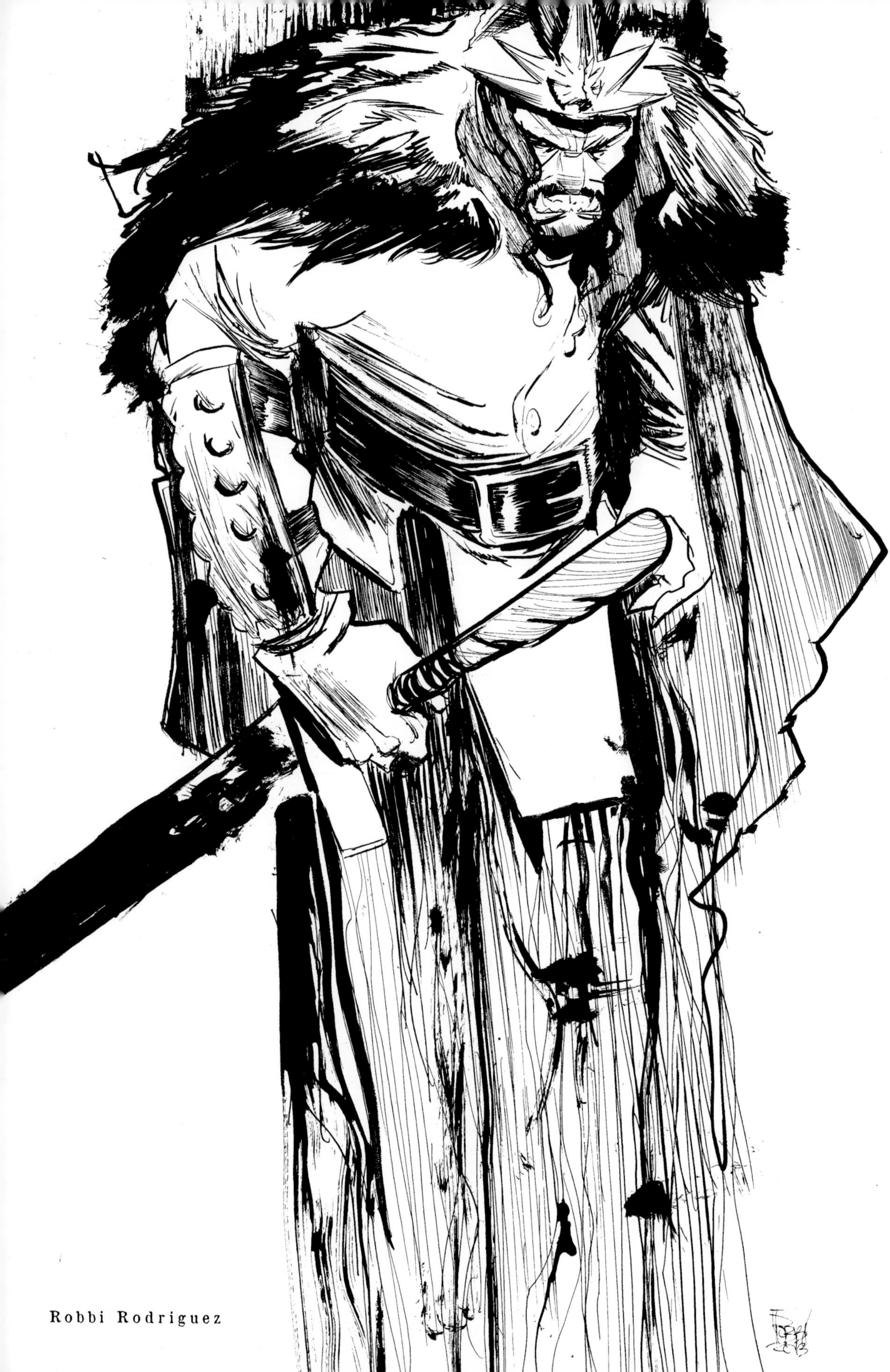

Robbi Rodriguez

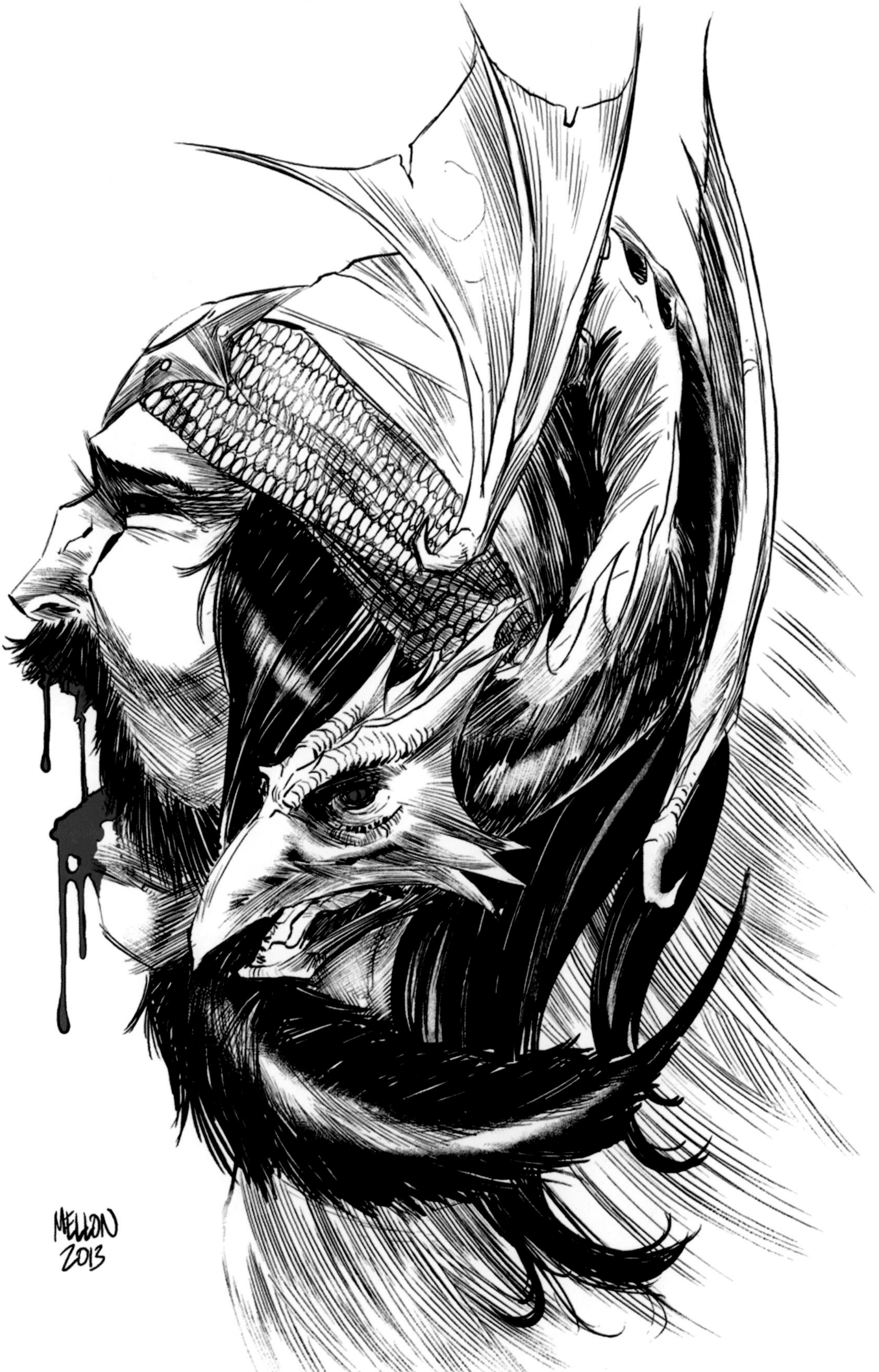
MELLON
2013

Kevin Mellon

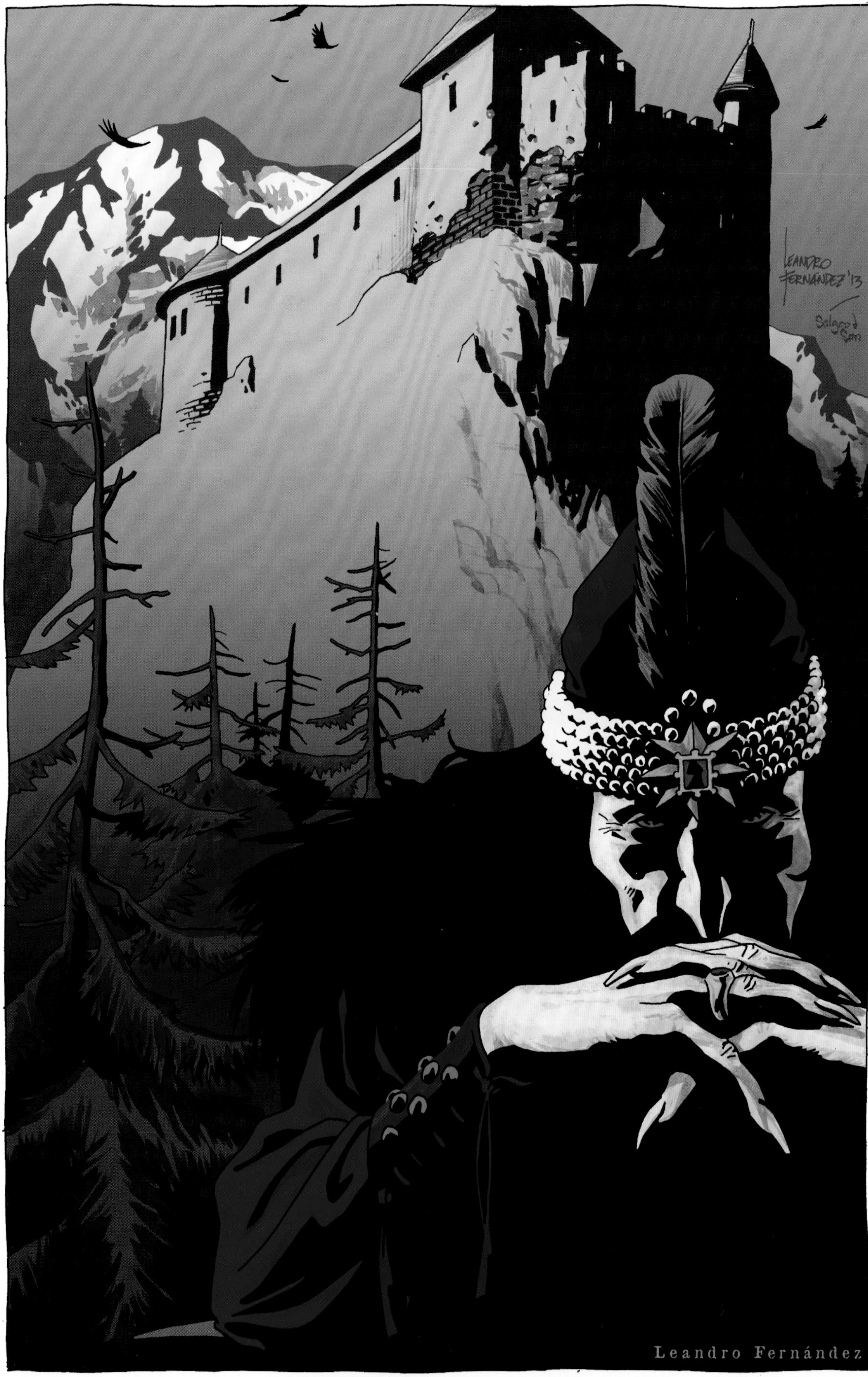
LEANDRO FERNÁNDEZ '13
Salgood Sam

Leandro Fernández

ENDNOTES

Page 1
Castle Dracula

Whether or not Bram Stoker's Dracula was based on the historical Dracula—Vlad Dracula, a.k.a. Vlad Țepeș (Vlad the Impaler)—is a matter of controversy.

The connection between the two was first made by scholars Radu Florescu and Raymond T. McNally in their book *In Search of Dracula* in 1972. One of their greatest pieces of evidence was that Vlad belonged to the House of Drăculești, and he was referred to as Vlad Dracula.

Historians like Elizabeth Miller have tried to discredit their work, saying that Bram Stoker was not knowledgeable about Vlad Țepeș's history.

How well Bram Stoker knew the real Dracula's history is not important to me. In chapter 18 of the novel, Stoker writes of Dracula: "He must, indeed, have been that Voivode Dracula who won his name against the Turk, over the great river on the very frontier of Turkey-land." That proves that he at least had some knowledge of the historical Dracula. For me, that was enough of a connection to create a new story that fused fiction and non-fiction.

Still, artist/cocreator Salgood Sam and I tried to be as faithful to both history and Stoker's novel as possible. Sometimes we were forced to choose between the two.

One such example is Castle Dracula. Bram Stoker is vague about the castle's location, simply placing it near the Borgo Pass in Transylvania. Bran Castle near Brașov—a Romanian town that has its place in history and *Dracula: Son of the Dragon*—has been marketed as Dracula's castle since 1997. Bran is a beautiful piece of architecture and resembles many of the film versions, particularly those in Hammer films. But there's no evidence that Vlad Țepeș ever did anything but pass through the area.

We instead chose Castle Poenari as our Castle Dracula. While there's no proof that Stoker knew of either Bran or Poenari, the real Vlad used Poenari as his fortress. It will play a dramatic role in the events in later volumes of this story.

"Much of what we know of Dracula is from the story of Brother Jacob, a German Catholic monk of the Benedictine order. Much of what we know of Dracula is a lie."

Even the life of the historical Dracula is in dispute.

Vlad Dracula was indeed an impaler, reportedly responsible for at least one hundred thousand deaths (twenty thousand alone in the so-called "forest of the impaled" pictured here).

But with any historical figure you have to consider the source. In this case, some of the accounts of Dracula's legendary atrocities came from German Catholic monks. Dracula confiscated the holdings

Castle Poenari

of the Catholic Church and made enemies of German Saxon traders, who he considered rivals and persecuted as a result. This gave those monks at least two reasons to fear and hate Dracula.

The opening sequence in *Dracula: Son of the Dragon* was inspired by the story of three such monks that visited Dracula in 1461, according to a historical poem by Michael Beheim. Beheim writes that the monks—Brothers Hans, Jacob, and Michael—were returning from collecting alms for their abbey when they were summoned by Dracula, an offer they could not refuse.

Dracula asked the no doubt intimidated monks whether he could be considered a saint, since he'd sent the souls of the many he put to death to heaven. He further asked if there were therefore a "place in paradise" for him.

Brother Michael allegedly answered that Dracula had hope of salvation, as God had spared the lives of those who'd repented, even at the moment of death. This carefully worded answer likely saved the monk's life.

But Dracula pressed another monk, Hans the Porter, asking him, "What will be my fate after death?" Hans answered more honestly, calling Dracula "a demented tyrant" and saying it was "conceivable the devil himself would not want you. But if he should, you will be confined to hell for eternity." Dracula impaled him on the spot.

Whether or not the historical Dracula truly believed in heaven or hell, or cared for the opinions of others on this matter, this story was part of the genesis of *Dracula: Son of the Dragon*. Our version of Dracula very much believes that he is doomed to an eternity in hell, making immortality through vampirism his only escape.

One change we made to the story of these monks was making them men of different faiths. I felt this

was justified because Romania (at the time divided into Wallachia and Transylvania) was very much divided by religion. There was the division between the Catholic Church of the Holy Roman Empire and the Eastern Orthodox Church of the remnants of the Byzantine Empire. In addition there was a conflict between Christianity and the Muslim faith of the ever-expanding Ottoman Empire on Dracula's borders.

The plan for *Dracula: Son of the Dragon* is that this volume will be the first of three books. Each will be bookended with an interaction between Dracula and the three monks in this story. We see a Roman Catholic and an Eastern Orthodox monk. The third monk's faith or identity has yet to be revealed, but hints are there for those who look hard enough.

Page 4
Saxon merchants
trafficking in blood

As mentioned, the Saxon merchants in Transylvania were enemies of Vlad Dracula. In addition to their religious and ethnic differences, they supported a rival to Dracula's throne. It is also likely Dracula craved their wealth, as they had a monopoly on trade in areas under his control and defied his attempts to tax them.

In response, Dracula engaged in genocidal massacres and impalings of the Saxons. This left a deep and lasting stain on the country. Much later, after the fall of Communism in Romania, most of the Saxon population left for what was then West Germany. But Dracula's fight against merchants and noblemen and his perceived support of the peasantry made him a populist hero to some, a belief which persists to this day.

Later in this volume, you'll see that vampire blood is a prized commodity as, among other things, a weapon of mass destruction. In later volumes, we'll see the Saxon merchants seize on that notion and literally start a blood trade. Germans were also arms manufacturers during Dracula's time, so the blood trade will serve as a metaphor for their arms dealing.

Page 5
Hunyadi, Dracul, and a female admirer

This scene is based on a number of historical events, which we combined for dramatic purposes.

They include the following:

•Dracula's father Vlad Dracul and John Hunyadi, Hungarian ruler and Dracul's ally (and later enemy), were both pages at Sigismund's court and members of the real-life Order of the Dragon.

•Dracul jousted at a tournament and unhorsed an opponent.

•A woman was said to have thrown a gift to Dracul, a golden buckle, which Dracul left to his son Dracula upon his death. Historian Radu Florescu claimed his uncle, archaeologist George Florescu, discovered this buckle in what he thought was Dracula's tomb. Proving that fact can be stranger than fiction, the grave's contents—including the clasp and Dracula's bones—disappeared from the history museum in Budapest where they had been stored.

•In 1976, workers restored the house of Vlad Dracul in Sighișoara on the five hundredth anniversary of his son Dracula's death. They unearthed a mural which shows a woman presenting Dracul with a golden cup, which Florescu and McNally believe is a reference to the woman at the tournament.

•Dracul would take on a mistress, Călțuna, who was once a boyar (a Wallachian noblewoman), who then became Mother Eupraxia the Abbess, head of an abbey. Călțuna was thought to be the mother of Vlad the Monk, Dracula's illegitimate brother and rival to the throne. You can see that rivalry in this volume, and in future volumes he will be a major antagonist.

I don't recall why we changed the buckle to a scarf, other than it looked better floating through the air, and did a better job showing the symbol of the Order of the Dragon. The reasoning behind the other changes was clearer. Making Hunyadi the opponent Dracul unseated helped set up the rivalry between them. And it did not seem a great leap to think that the noblewoman who gave Dracul a gift might be the same one who took her vows as an abbess and later birthed his illegitimate son and Dracula's rival.

Page 9
The Order of the Dragon

The Order of the Dragon was a real medieval society. Discovering its existence was a key moment in the development of *Dracula: Son of the Dragon.*

I originally planned on titling this story "Dracula:

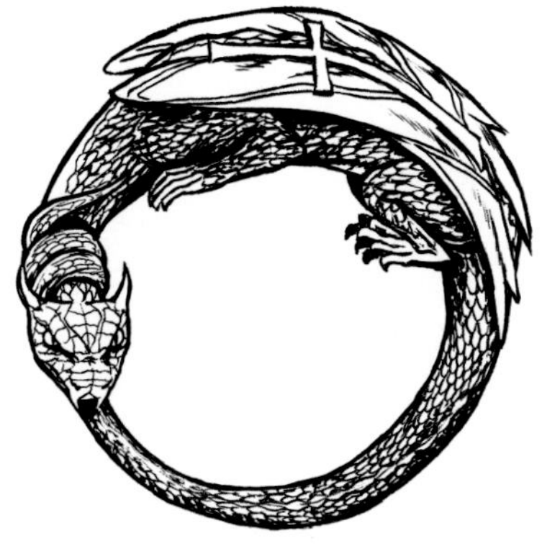

Order of the Dragon". . . which is still a possibility when all the volumes are completed. Here was a real, mysterious organization like the Knights Templar that had a monster both in its name and in its ranks. Best of all, when I started writing about this, no one else had really incorporated it into a work of fiction.

The actual Order of the Dragon was founded by the Holy Roman Emperor Sigismund von Luxembourg in 1408. A religious and military order, its stated purposes were to protect the emperor and defend Catholicism against both heretics within and "infidel Turks" without. According to Florescu and McNally, its "secret" nature was to help advance the emperor's royal family, the House of Luxembourg, politically within Europe. That's why its initial membership was made up of royalty.

Its secret nature made it fertile ground for an occult conspiracy in our comic. *Dracul* means both "dragon" and "devil" in Romanian, with *Dracula* meaning "son of the dragon." That a religious order would use a monster and Satan himself gave me the opportunity to create an organization that made a literal deal with the devil.

As for its membership, some of those mentioned here were truly "Draconists," which sounds sinister but is just another name for someone belonging to the order. Serbian despot Durad Branković was a real Draconist. His sons, who, like Dracula, are hostages of the Ottomans, become important later in the story.

The Bathory family had the order's symbol, an ouroboros—a dragon eating its own tail—in its coat of arms. The Bathorys would rule Transylvania after Dracula. The Bathory family is perhaps most well known for Countess Elizabeth Bathory, the so-called "Blood Countess," sometimes called "Countess Dracula."

A Hungarian noble, Countess Bathory was convicted of torturing and killing maids, servants, and members of the lower gentry. Her sentence was solitary confinement behind a bricked-up wall. After her death, legends spread that she bathed in the blood of her victims to maintain her youth. There is dispute over whether she was additional inspiration for Count Dracula in Stoker's novel. Regardless, there's an undeniable parallel between the folklore surrounding her horrific acts and Count Dracula drinking blood for immortality. Of the many Draconists I could have chosen to represent the order, I specifically chose Bathory because of that association.

The other members listed are fictional. Franckenstein is a reference to Frankenstein. There really was a Castle Frankenstein in Darmstadt, Germany. One of Castle Frankenstein's inhabitants was Johann Konrad Dippel, an alchemist who believed he could restore life through the use of blood. Mary Shelley, author of *Frankenstein*, visited the area near Castle Frankenstein prior to writing the novel. Whether or not Dippel's story inspired *Frankenstein* is subject to the same debate as Count Dracula's origins. But like Bathory, the name evokes horror and the supernatural yet still touches history.

Gévaudan is an allusion to the so-called "Beast of Gévaudan." Between 1764 and 1767, there were allegedly an estimated two hundred attacks by a man-eating wolf in Gévaudan, France (modern-day Lozère). Accounts of this were highly influential on werewolf legends, particularly the idea they could be killed by silver, as Jean Chastel claimed he slew the beast with silver bullets he forged. It is worth remembering that Stoker's Count Dracula could transform into a wolf, and that Dr. Abraham Van Helsing said he could be killed by a "sacred bullet."

There was no Van Helsing in the order, but like Bathory, Gévaudan, and Frankenstein, his name sets up potential meetings between the vampire Dracula and later figures in future stories I hope to tell. This is an ancestor who in the script is named Arminius Van Helsing. The scholars Florescu and McNally claim that a man named Arminius Vambery was both a source for Stoker's historical research and a model for the character Van Helsing. Others, like Elizabeth Miller, dispute this. I thought it was a nice little Easter egg for Dracula scholars, though.

The heretic Jan Hus

Jan Hus was a Czech Catholic Church reformer, or in the church's eyes, a heretic . . . something Draconists were sworn to fight. His followers would engage in the Hussite Wars against Emperor Sigismund. They would use "Wagenburg" tactics, chaining wagons together as mobile forts from which they fired artillery such as gunpowder. John Hunyadi would later adopt this and teach it to Dracula. Later in this volume, we can see the devastating effects of gunpowder on all sides in the battle between Hunyadi, the Draculas, and the Turks at Varna.

Page 10
"Conversion from your heretic 'church'"

In an earlier note, I mention that Eastern Europe in Dracula's time was riven by the schism between the Roman Catholic and Eastern Orthodox faiths.

It is not clear what religion Dracula, or his father Vlad Dracul, practiced. This is important because whichever religion either ruler chose, it presented a conflict. Eastern Orthodoxy was the official religion of Wallachia, and therefore its ruler was required to belong to that church. On the other hand, the Dracula family required the aid of the much more powerful Catholic Church against the Ottomans.

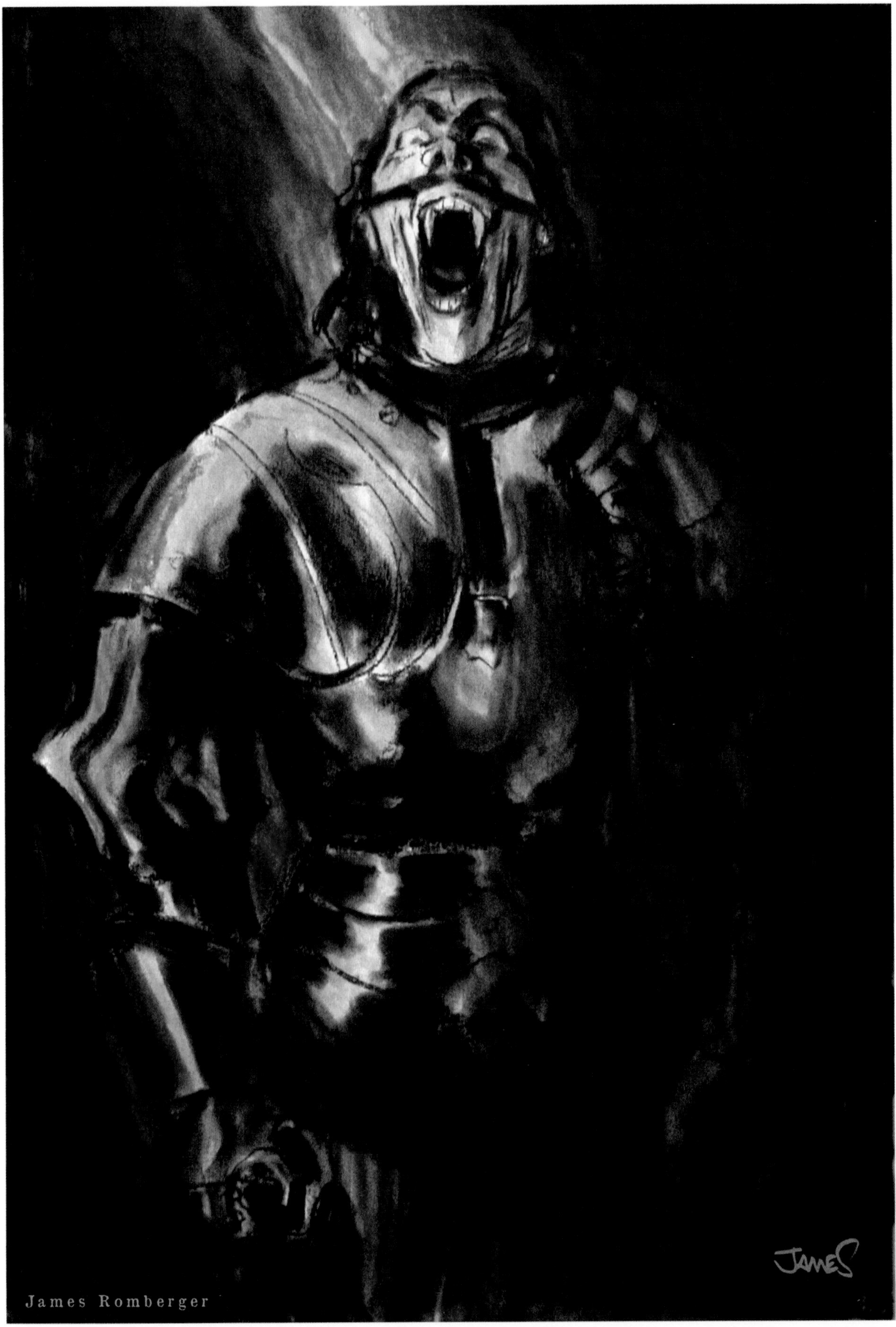
JAMES
James Romberger

Dracul was likely born into the Eastern Orthodox faith. Florescu and McNally claim that when Emperor Sigismund described Dracul as having been "educated at our court," it implied his "conversion to Roman Catholicism."

As for Dracula, both his parents were likely Catholics. Florescu and McNally speculate he may have been secretly baptized in an Eastern Orthodox Church. It's unclear when he made the shift to the Orthodox Church, but it must have at least been when he was crowned prince after his father's death (again, something we'll see in a future volume). Still later, Dracula would be forced to convert back to Catholicism in order to escape imprisonment by his father's one-time ally, John Hunyadi.

Interestingly, there doesn't seem to be any evidence that the Ottoman sultan tried to impose Islam upon Dracula when he was a prisoner at the Turkish court.

Pages 10–11
Lake Hermannstadt, St. George, and the dragon

I'll explore the significance of Lake Hermannstadt further when we look at the Scholomance (page 27), the school in which Dracula was educated in the dark arts, perhaps by the devil himself. Here, I've set it as the location for the myth of St. George and the dragon.

According to Jacobus de Varagine's *Legenda aurea* (*The Golden Legend*) from the 1260s, the legend of St. George concerned a town named Silene plagued by a venom-spewing dragon. Silene was supposedly located in Libya, but I relocated the story to a lake in Transylvania.

To prevent the dragon from destroying the town, a lottery was conducted where a youth from the town would be sacrificed to appease the dragon. One day, the lot fell to the king's daughter, and she was sent out to the lake dressed as a bride. (If this sounds familiar, it may be because this story was the basis for the 1981 movie *Dragonslayer*, which left a deep impression on me as a kid and was one of the many inspirations for this book).

St. George arrived, and the princess tried to send him away. He refused, made the sign of the cross, and impaled the dragon with his lance. In our version, St. George killed the beast. In the legend, he only seriously wounded the creature. St. George then asked the princess to throw a girdle onto the beast. The girdled dragon followed St. George and the princess like a "meek beast" to town, where it terrified the people.

St. George offered to kill the dragon if the townsfolk consented to become Christians and were baptized. Again, according to legend, fifteen thousand people, including the king of Silene, converted. St. George then beheaded the dragon, a church was built on the spot, and flowers sprung forth from the altar that could cure any disease.

There are a number of connections between this myth, the history we present, Bram Stoker's

Dracula and the original mythology of *Dracula: Son of the Dragon.*

The historical Order of the Dragon was modeled after the Hungarian Order of St. George (Societas militiae Sancti Georgii), and the Order of the Dragon itself had St. George as its patron saint.

The story of the woman throwing the girdle in some ways parallels the noblewoman throwing a gift to Dracul at the tournament. (As the "girdle" of the

legend likely referred to a belt, had we kept the gift a buckle it might have made that parallel clearer). Dracul is a metaphorical dragon who is girdled into service of the church.

In chapter 18 of Bram Stoker's *Dracula*, Van Helsing writes, in relation to Transylvania and Dracula's supernatural origins, "Perhaps the most important day of the year is the feast day of St. George, 23rd of April, the eve of which is still frequently kept by occult meetings taking place at night in lonely caverns or within ruined walls, and where all the ceremonies usual to the celebration of a witches' Sabbath are put to practice."

In chapter 1, an old woman gives Jonathan Harker a warning as he travels to meet Count Dracula. "It is the eve of St. George's Day. Do you not know that to-night, when the clock strikes midnight, all the evil things in the world will have full sway?"

These quotes firmly tie St. George to the novel and to dark magic.

More importantly, it is here that we begin to create the mythos for Dracula's vampiric origins in *Dracula: Son of the Dragon.*

Page 16
Aldea

Alexander I Aldea was Vlad Dracul's half brother, the illegitimate son of their father. As we can see by the fact he ruled before Dracul, legitimacy wasn't a requirement for rulership in Romania. This becomes an issue for Dracula when we meet his half brother Vlad the Monk, who would prove to be a rival for the Wallachian throne.

Aldea was on his fifth rule when Dracul succeeded him as voivode (Slavic for "warlord") of Wallachia.

Wallachia changed hands through violence eighteen times in the 1400s, making his death from natural causes unusual.

"A plague can be a weapon in the right hands"

Here "plague" alludes to the vampire Vlad Dracul later hides among the boys he's forced to send to the Turkish sultan as tribute. Dracul then uses the vampire "Trojan horse" to infect the Turks with the plague of vampirism.

Page 17
Cazan

Cazan was one of both Dracul and Dracula's advisers. In addition, he served the aforementioned Aldea and Vladislav II, who succeeded Dracul to the Wallachian throne after he assassinated Dracula's father. Vladislav II will serve as a major antagonist in volume 2.

As Matei Cazacu notes in his book *Dracula*, Cazan's longevity shows that he was astute politically. The fact that Dracula kept Cazan as an adviser even after he served the man responsible for his father's death shows shrewdness on both their parts.

Cazan will play a minor but important role later in this story, witnessing Dracul's death and bringing word of it—along with Dracul's Toledo sword— to Dracula.

Dănești vs. Drăculești

There were two main lineages that ruled—and fought over—Wallachia. Both were from the House of Basarab, descendants of Basarab I. The Drăculești line was founded by Vlad Dracul, from whom the line gets its name. The aforementioned Vladislav II, who killed and succeeded Dracul, was the House of Dănești.

Wallachia and Transylvania

Wallachia and Transylvania are regions that, along with Moldavia, compose what is now Romania. Although Bram Stoker's novel briefly mentions Wallachia, it cites Dracula's homeland as Transylvania, which is what most people associate with the fictional count.

Transylvania is nicknamed "the Land beyond the Forest."

Transylvania was also the historical Dracula's birthplace, but in life he only ruled Wallachia. Unlike Wallachia, which was an independent state before it became part of Romania, Transylvania was ruled for much of its existence by Hungary. John Hunyadi was its military governor at the start of the story. When Emperor Sigismund favors Aldea over Vlad Dracul for voivode of Wallachia, he makes Dracul military governor. This is in part because Aldea allowed the Turks to use Wallachia to stage attacks into Transylvania.

Dracul chose to govern from the Transylvanian city of Sighișoara—Dracula's birthplace—because it was a fortress town with a strategic location. From there, Dracul plotted to retake the Wallachian throne he considered his birthright.

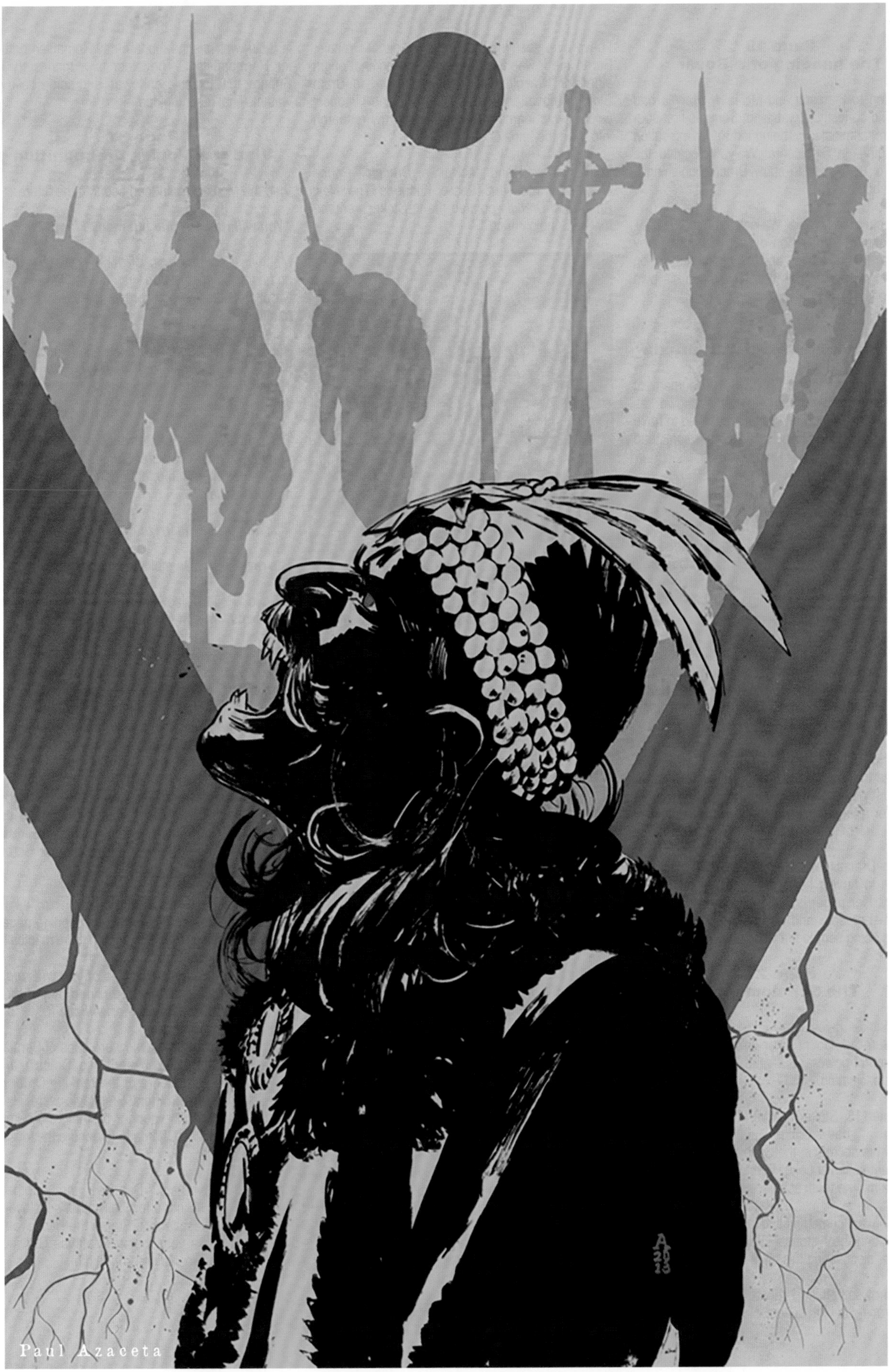

Paul Azaceta

Page 19
The hanging of a Boyar

According to Florescu and McNally, Dracula had a "morbid curiosity in watching, from his first-floor bedroom, criminals . . . being led to . . . execution by hanging" in Sighișoara. We've relocated the scene to Târgoviște to show Dracul punishing a disloyal boyar.

Whether in Transylvania, Wallachia, or later Turkey, executions were common during this time. They must have made a deep and lasting impression on the young Dracula. This doesn't excuse his own executions, but may help explain them.

Page 21
The Monk and Mother Eupraxia

Mother Eupraxia is, as noted in the tournament scene, the noblewoman formerly known as Călțuna. More importantly, she is believed to have given birth to Vlad Dracul's illegitimate son, Vlad the Monk, Dracula's half brother.

Dracula's discovery of and reaction to his half brother is completely our invention. He had to know Vlad, whether he was a "monk" or not, would be a potential rival to the Wallachian throne. Indeed, the Monk would one day rule Wallachia after Dracula's death. The Monk will be an antagonist in later volumes of our story, although you can see the seeds of this in volume 1.

Likewise, we don't know how Dracula's mother would have reacted. In fact, there is still debate over who his mother was. We've opted to identify her as Princess Cneajna, daughter of Alexander the Good, prince of Moldavia.

Sadly, the lives of women are not always valued by those that record history, and their stories are erased. It was a goal of ours to try to give women a greater role, although both the historical record and the lack of space to tell this epic limited this.

As with Dracula, we tried to give her a human reaction to having her son reveal her husband's infidelity. Her anger is not only with her husband but with her son, and she seems indifferent to Dracula being sent to the Scholomance.

Page 27
The Scholomance

Bram Stoker gives very little information about the nature of Count Dracula's vampirism and supernatural powers. But what little he did share I found fascinating.

In chapter 18, Stoker has Van Helsing say, "The Draculas . . . had dealings with the Evil One. They learned his secrets in the Scholomance, amongst the mountains over Lake Hermannstadt, where the devil claims the tenth scholar as his due."

When I was contemplating creating an original story linking the historical Dracula to the fictional vampire, discovering this bit of text was key.

It was not something I recalled from when I first read *Dracula* in high school. Nor was it something

I have ever seen in any other work either *Dracula*. But to me it was the genesis of an original origin story for Dracula that wasboth rooted in Bram Stoker's novel and compatible with the historical world I was learning about through my research into Vlad the Impaler.

Both Florescu and McNally's *Dracula, Prince of Many Faces* and Leslie Klinger's *The New Annotated Dracula* pointed me to Stoker's source for the Scholomance.

Emily Gerard's 1885 work "Transylvanian Superstitions" describes the Scholomance as a "school supposed to exist somewhere in the heart of the mountains, and where all the secrets of nature, the language of animals, and all imaginable magic spells and charms are taught by the devil in person."

"Only ten scholars are admitted at a time, and when the course of learning has expired and nine of them are released to return to their homes, the tenth scholar is detained by the devil as payment, and mounted upon an Ismeju (dragon) and he becomes henceforth the devil's aide-de-camp, and assists him in 'making the weather,' that is to say, preparing the thunderbolts."

This gave me the basis to build new lore for Dracula's supernatural background that was still rooted in the same research that Stoker conducted.

You can see a great deal of that lore here. We have the underground school, where the students learn magic, including the ability to command animals. We see the students flee in terror since they know that the last of them will suffer a terrible fate, which they believe is to serve the devil. We see a dragon, who it appears Dracula's half brother Vlad the Monk will serve. While we don't see Satan in his traditional form, as we've already established, "Dracul" means dragon, so we can speculate about the nature of the beast.

Page 27
The monastery

The monastery depicted above the Scholomance is a combination of two locations. One is a monastery

in Sibiu, which is the modern-day Romanian name for Hermannstadt. The other is a monastery in Snagov that Dracula endowed and some believe was his final resting place.

Page 31
Vlad the Monk's precognition

Vlad the Monk does indeed see into the future.

"You will rule not one but many kingdoms . . ."

Matthias Corvinus, son of John Hunyadi, would go on to rule at least two kingdoms—Hungary and Croatia. There is no record of Matthias Corvinus meeting Dracula in their youth.

But later in life Corvinus would imprison Dracula before releasing him and unleashing him on the Turks. This would result in Dracula's last reign as Wallachia's prince.

The conceit of the Scholomance presented a way to bring these characters together earlier and make their friendship and conflict deeper and more personal.

". . . if you can learn to command the raven"

The raven here has multiple meanings.

Kosovo Polje, also known as "the Field of Blackbirds," was the location of two battles fought between East and West. The first was fought in 1389 between the Ottomans and the Serbs. Tactically inconclusive, it resulted in devastating losses for the Serbs and a strategic victory for the Turks. The second was fought in 1448, where Sultan Murad II and his son Mehmed defeated John Hunyadi, resulting in Hunyadi's capture by the Serbs.

Both battles have mythic importance to Serbs, who invoked them in their war in Kosovo in the 1990s. They view them as fatal events in Serbian history resulting in the loss of Kosovo for Serbia and Christianity.

The House of Hunyadi has a black bird as its symbol, and as you see in the succeeding pages Matthias Corvinus tries to summon them magically.

"As for the Brankovićs, one of you will rule the Serbs. One will be dethroned by young Corvinus. And neither will see it."

Grgur and Stefan Branković were sons of Serbian despot Durad Branković and, like Dracula and Corvinus, were members of the real-life Order of the Dragon. The brothers Branković were also, like Dracula and his younger brother Radu, kept as hostages by the Ottomans to ensure the loyalty of their fathers.

Unlike the brothers Dracula, the brothers Branković were blinded for their father's disloyalty to the sultan. Despite this, Stefan the Blind would rule Serbia for a year, before Matthias Corvinus and the king of Bosnia dethroned him.

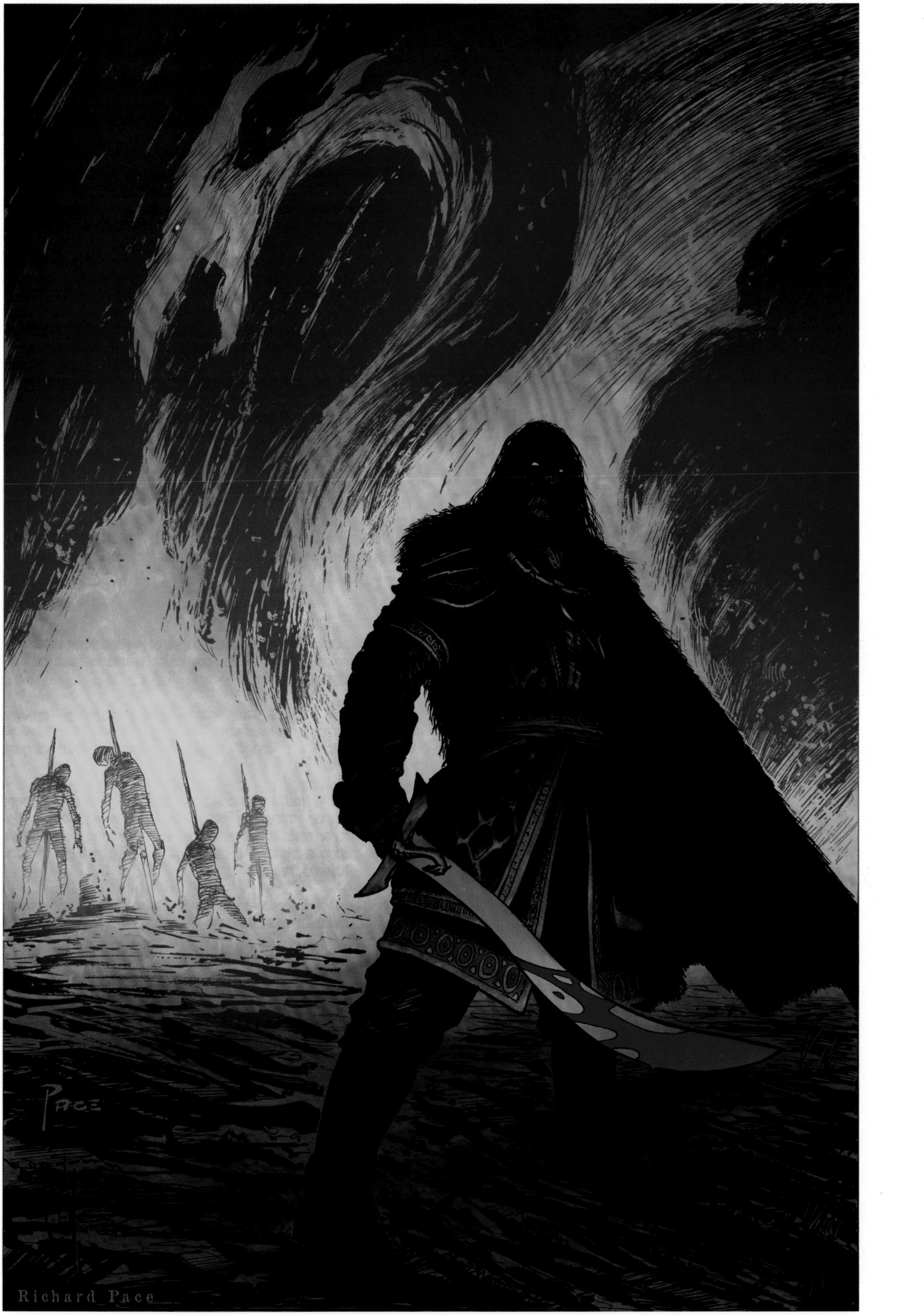
PACE

Richard Pace

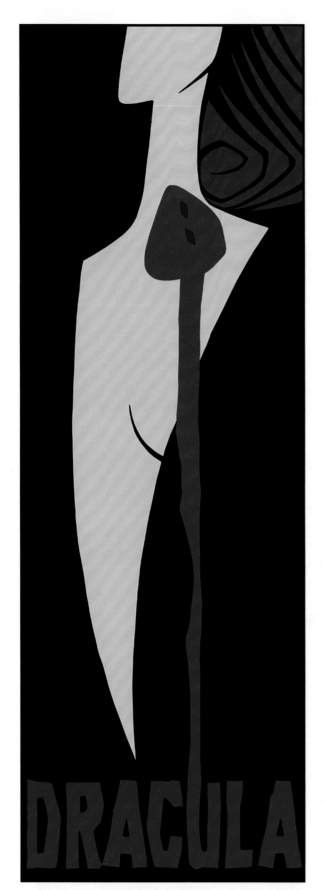

Jeremy Haun

Page 32
Zmeu (dragons)

Zmeu is the correct Romanian spelling of "Ismeju," the dragon described by Bram Stoker's source Emily Gerard as the animal that the tenth Scholomance scholar would ride as "the devil's aide-de-camp."

Page 33
Wallachia, Târgoviște, and King Władysław III

We cut from the fictional education of Dracula and Matthias Corvinus at the Scholomance back to the historical events concerning their fathers.

Vlad Dracul, caught between warring Christian states to the West and the Ottomans to the East, was constantly trying to appease the two, a dangerous game.

In 1441, Hunyadi was sent to the Wallachian capital of Târgoviște by the king of Hungary, Władysław III of Poland.

Here, we see him asking Vlad Dracul to renew his Crusade against the Turks. Under the rule of Vlad Dracul's half brother Alexander Aldea, Wallachia had abandoned the Crusade, allowing the Turks to use Wallachia to stage attacks on Transylvania. This is referenced on pages 17–18, when Dracul takes the Wallachian throne after his brother's death.

Hunyadi appealed to Dracul to fulfill his oath of Crusade as a fellow member of the Order of the Dragon. But, according to Florescu and McNally, there was another reason Dracul might agree to help Hunyadi. While Hunyadi had officially supported Dracul as prince of Wallachia, he was giving secret assurances to Dracul's rival, Dan II Basarab in Transylvania.

Page 36
Strigoi

There are a number of different terms for vampires and other supernatural beings in Romanian folklore. The one which seems to have influenced Bram Stoker the most is *strigoi*.

In chapter 1 of Stoker's novel, when Jonathan Harker is traveling to meet Count Dracula, he overhears Transylvanian peasants use the word *stregoica* for both "witch" and "vampire." In chapter 18 Van Helsing uses that word again.

Strigoi can be the troubled dead who rise from the grave or living people with supernatural attributes. These include invisibility, the ability to transform into animals, and draining the life from living victims through the consumption of blood. The latter two are abilities we see the Count possess in Stoker's *Dracula*.

The methods of killing them—according to gypsies—also appear in *Dracula*: exhumation, removing their hearts, placing garlic under their tongues, etc.

Living strigoi, *strigoi viu*, are kinds of "sorcerers," according to Adrien Cremene, in his book *Mythologie du vampire en roumanie* (Mythology of the vampire in Romania). The living strigoi "steals the wealth of farmers, that is to say, wheat and milk. But it can also stop the rain, drop hail and give death to men and cattle."

Dead strigoi, *strigoi mort*, have a dual demonic and human nature, and are considered more dangerous. Their nature is ambiguous, both human and demonic. They emerge from their grave, preying on their family until dying in their turn.

The distinction between living and dead strigoi would prove important to *Dracula: Son of the Dragon*. Later in this volume we see that the Ottomans use strigoi viu, living vampires, as elite soldiers. Using vampirism as a weapon of mass destruction is a theme we'll see through the entire series.

We haven't met our first strigoi mort, or what I view as a "true" vampire, yet. This is the kind of vampire that Dracula will become. We know in the novel that such vampires prey on those they love. Given the historical Dracula's later feuds with his brothers, this will allow us to add supernatural horror to his family's struggles over the Wallachian throne.

In this volume though, the first strigoi will be Alexandra of Nussdorf. She is a fictional creation, but is inspired by those women we believe Dracula to have loved later in his life. His childhood crush and her tragic fate leave an imprint on him.

When we first meet Alexandra, she fears becoming a *strigoaică*, Romanian for "witch." While it is confusing that the terms for vampire and witch overlap in meaning, it helps further flesh out the connection between dark magic and vampirism that the Scholomance represents.

Page 37
"Then why regain humanity? If mortality means condemnation to hell, why would a vampire give up the gift of immortality for it?"

Without giving away too much of what will appear in future volumes, this phrase is highly important to my idea of why the historical Dracula might choose to become a vampire. You can see from the bookends that he's an impaler. By the beliefs of the church he might very well be condemned for those acts, even if they were done in God's name. Immortality, even the cursed immortality of vampirism, could seem a much more attractive option than an eternity in hell. Especially, as we'll see, when Dracula comes to learn the supernatural is real.

Solomonari

In Romanian folklore, Solomonari are dragon-riding wizards or alchemists that control the weather. If that sounds familiar, it's because that's the same description given to graduates of the Scholomance. Florescu and McNally believe that the German term *Scholomance* derived from the same root word as *Solomonari*. They describe a spot close to Hermannstadt known as Pietrele lui Solomon, or "Solomon's Rocks," where wandering students traditionally took scholarly oaths.

In real life, such students may have been ascetic mystics, which fits the appearance of Vlad the Monk. In Romanian folklore, they are often described as strigoi who studied underground in caves, further bolstering the Scholomance myth.

There are a number of suggested origins for the term *Solomonari*, one of them being that it comes from the biblical King Solomon, renowned for his wisdom. We have Vlad mention that here to muddy the waters of whether the use of the Scholomance's magic is necessarily evil.

Page 39
"Vukodlak!"

Here, Matthias Corvinus tries to summon the raven that Vlad the Monk prophesied would help him rule "many kingdoms." But instead he summons a vukodlak.

In *Dracula: Son of the Dragon* we show a vukodlak

as an undead bird. The inspiration for this was from a role-playing game supplement for Dungeons and Dragons called *Vlad the Impaler: Blood Prince of Wallachia*. However, there was some confusion because that term can mean other things, particularly "werewolf."

Further research led me to some sources to back my interpretation up. One is the Slavic legend of kudlaks, beings born human but with a connection to the supernatural. They could transform into animals such as birds and choose to be good or evil, and if they chose the latter, they would be black in appearance. Kudlaks in bird form could create clouds of pestilence not that different from what Matthias summons.

There is also the Slavic belief that the soul could leave the body as a bird such as a raven, who would hover around the living for forty days. Windows were left open to let these spirits depart, and generally there were friendly relations between the spirits and the living, with food left out for them. But the spirits of sorcerers, sinners, murderers, suicides, and those that did not get a Christian burial could enter households as unclean animals and were feared as the cause of droughts, bad crops, and disease.

Bodies of these unclean spirits were disposed of in similar ways to those of vampires. In addition, the idea that sorcerers could suffer this fate further ties into the peril the students of the Scholomance might find their souls in.

Page 44
The dragon

The appearance of a literal dragon here raises intriguing questions, only some of which will be answered in this volume. Is it a zmeu that Vlad the Monk and other Solomonari may command? Or, given that *Dracul* means "dragon" and "devil," is it the headmaster of the Scholomance, some form of Satan himself?

There is a definitive answer for this that will be revealed in later volumes.

"I think I'll stay for a drink"

This is a reference to Count Dracula's famous line "I never drink . . . wine." This comes not from Stoker's book but instead is uttered by the great Bela Lugosi in Tod Browning's classic 1931 film.

Page 49
Letting the Turks
pass through Wallachia

Dracula's father, Vlad Dracul, switched sides many times during his rule. While he was certainly Machiavellian, Wallachia was in a precarious situation, situated between the Holy Roman Empire and the Ottoman Empire.

In 1437 Dracul signed an alliance with the Turks, after Holy Roman Emperor Sigismund died and Sultan Murad II had quashed the independence of the Christian nations of Serbia and Bulgaria on Wallachia's borders. In 1438 he even accompanied Murad himself on a raid into Transylvania, where the Turks took seventy thousand prisoners. The Transylvanian town of Sebeș surrendered to Dracul personally, hoping for better treatment from a Christian ruler than the Muslim Turks. According to Dracul's oath to the Order of the Dragon, he was obligated to protect Christians from "pagans."

As we saw earlier, John Hunyadi—now king of Hungary—came to visit Dracul in Târgoviște to implore him to fulfill his oath and renew his Crusade against the Turks. But the Turkish position in Eastern Europe had gotten stronger, and Hunyadi had made secret assurances to Dan II Basarab, Dracul's rival to the Wallachian throne.

Dracul decided to remain neutral, allowing Turks to pass through Wallachia and attack Transylvania. There, the Turks suffered heavy losses and defeat.

Page 50
"Ten thousand gold ducats and five hundred boys for the sultan's Janissary corps"

Since Dracul was still technically a vassal of Murad, the sultan did not view Dracul's neutrality as fulfilling his treaty obligations. He summoned Dracul to his court in Gallipoli. Dracul took Dracula and Radu, his youngest sons, with him, leaving his oldest son, Mircea, in charge.

Dracul was also required to make a tribute of ten thousand ducats. In addition, the sultan demanded five hundred young boys for his Janissary corps.

Janissaries, which in Turkish means "new soldiers," were an elite corps of young Christian slaves who were kidnapped by the Ottomans and converted to Islam at a young age. Despite their status as slaves, they were educated and paid regular salaries. Still, they were forbidden to marry or trade and were expected to show undying loyalty to the sultan.

Perhaps because of indoctrination at such an early age, they were renowned for their discipline and unit cohesion. As we'll see later, their high level of training included such things as engineering and artillery as well as archery.

Turning over Christians for forced conversion would clearly be a violation of Dracul's oath to the Order. However, we can get our first hint here in our fictional telling that Dracul is not just going to lie down for the sultan and has something up his sleeve.
Dracul mentions that the Ottoman Empire was built on the ruins of Troy. This is a reference to the Trojan horse. In the last panel of page 51, we see our first hint of what's inside this horse with the tattoo of the Order of the Dragon on a hooded prisoner. A prisoner Dracula recognizes as Alexandra, his classmate at the Scholomance who we last saw fall victim to the dragon.

The tattoo is first shown on page 36. I wanted Vlad Dracula—and the reader—to be able to tell that Alexandra was among the hostages sent to the sultan. And, as we saw her dying . . . that she was likely a vampire. The script specifies that she has green eyes, but the tattoo allows her to be recognized in black-and-white versions.

Pg. 52
Dracul in chains and the imprisonment of his sons

Despite Dracul's tribute, he was seized near the sultan's gates at Gallipoli and bound in chains. He was made to swear an oath on both the Bible and the Koran, but given that Dracul had not kept his word to rulers of any faith, more was required. While Dracul was released, his sons Dracula and Radu were taken as prisoners and sent to the desolate mountain fortress of Eğrigöz.

As we'll see later, Serbian despot Durad Branković would be forced to hand over his children Grgur and Stefan Branković (who we've shown as friends of Dracula at the Scholomance) as hostages also.

Page 53
Adrianople

Thankfully, Dracula and Radu's stay at Eğrigöz was not long. They were transferred to the sultan's court at Adrianople. There, they were by all accounts treated well for a time. They were not forced to convert to Islam, and were educated along with the sultan's heir, Mehmed II.

But that treatment was not to last for Dracula. He was said to be a more difficult hostage than Radu. According to Florescu and McNally, Radu's good looks made him a favorite of the women of the sultan's harem, as well as the men of the court, earning him the name of "Radu the Handsome."

Here, we show Dracula's obstinance in his resistance to Mehmed's entreaties to share the secrets of the Scholomance with him. Dracula still shows loyalty to his father by not revealing the magic he learned.

Dracula's father did not repay that loyalty, however. In 1443, Pope Eugenius IV declared a new Crusade against the Turks to liberate the Balkans from Turkish rule. Led by papal legate Cardinal Giuliano Cesarini, Durad Branković of Serbia, and John Hunyadi, the forces were successful in taking Sofia, Bulgaria. In 1444, Cardinal Cesarini, adding the king of Poland to his crusading army, set his sights on the port city of Varna, in order to prevent the Turks from sending more troops from Asia to Europe.

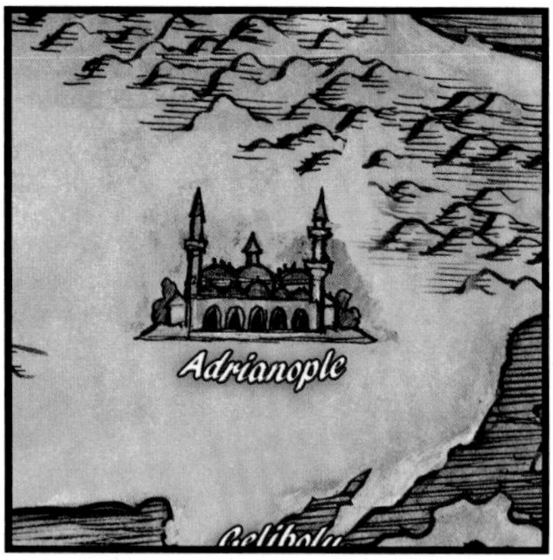
Adrianople

Hunyadi again asked for Dracul's participation. And Dracul once again tried to keep both sides happy, by sending just a token force under his son Mircea.

Dracul had to know that this would endanger Dracula and Radu's lives. While they were not executed, they became true prisoners instead of honored guests.

Page 55
"It is not wine"

Again, a reference to Lugosi's line in Tod Browning's film adaptation of *Dracula*.

Page 56
"They impaled the men who refused to fight"

Impaling was not something Vlad Dracula invented. It has roots that go back to antiquity, with examples from Hammurabi's Babylon and the Egyptian pharaohs. While this scene is our invention, the Turks were known to use impalement before Vlad Dracula, at least as early as the siege of Constantinople.

It is not impossible that Dracula learned the effectiveness of impaling from the Turks, whether as a prisoner fearing it or when he'd later serve in battle with them. I thought it important to show this, as one of the recurring themes of this book is the use of one enemy's brutal tactics against another.

Page 57
The Janissaries march to battle

Aside from being one of my favorite pages, this splash showcases Salgood's unique design for the Janissaries in this book. Their headgear is based on real Janissary helmets, but with the added twist of lenses and chain mail curtains that completely cover the face. While it's not hard to guess at this point, we'll see why we (and the sultan) made those modifications soon.

Page 58
Stefan Branković's fate

As bad as Dracula and Radu's imprisonment was after Dracul broke his oath to the sultan, Grgur and Stefan Branković suffered an even worse fate when Durad Branković joined Hunyadi's Crusade. They were blinded with hot irons, despite the fact that their sister Mara was the sultan's wife.

Where we take historical license is by making that punishment a result of the Branković brothers' refusal to share the secrets of the Scholomance as well.

Page 60
Radu's betrayal

Florescu and McNally cite the Byzantine chronicler Laonicus Chalcocondyles as well as Turkish documents for their depiction of Prince Mehmed as a drunken hedonist who made sexual advances to Radu the Handsome, to which Dracula's brother "eventually succumbed." In return, Mehmed would make Radu his "protégé" and eventually his preferred candidate for the Wallachian throne.

We've added a further betrayal, as well as a deeper motivation for Mehmed, in Radu spilling the secrets of the Scholomance. Here, we see Mehmed use the raven-summoning magic we saw Matthias Corvinus use in the Scholomance.

Page 61
Dracula scaling a wall upside down

With Mehmed in possession of the dark knowledge of the Scholomance, Dracula fears there's no reason for him to be kept alive.

Dracula's escape here by scaling the wall upside down is something taken from Bram Stoker's *Dracula*. In chapter 3, Stoker has Dracula's prisoner Jonathan Harker observe:

"I saw the whole man slowly emerge from the window and begin to crawl down the castle wall over the dreadful abyss, face down with his cloak spreading out around him like great wings. At first, I could not believe my eyes. I thought it was some trick of the moonlight, some weird effect of shadow, but I kept looking, and it could be no delusion. I saw the fingers and toes grasp the corners of the stones, worn clear of the mortar by the stress of years, and by thus using every projection and inequality move downwards with considerable speed, just as a lizard moves along a wall."

This was an image that was seared into my mind from both books and film. It was such a powerful visual that it was on the cover of the 1902 edition of Stoker's novel.

Since the novel tells us that he studied magic at the Scholomance before becoming a vampire, I thought that meant he would have acquired some powers in life. Careful readers may notice that Dracula was studying a climbing spell when he first arrived at the Scholomance, on the second panel of page 29.

Page 63
Dracula killing Alexandra in strigoi form

As Dracula tries to escape, he sees another prisoner and thinks he's found the brothers Branković. Instead, he sees Alexandra, the student he failed to save from the dragon at the Scholomance. Her worst fear has come true . . . the dragon has transformed her into a strigoi.

Alexandra is the "gift" inside of Dracul's Trojan horse. His plan in hiding her among the hostages was to infect the Janissaries with the plague of vampirism she carries. We'll soon see how that backfires.

This scene is important for a number of reasons. It establishes that vampires can be killed by beheading, which is consistent with the novel. It shows Dracula having to kill someone he cared for, which foreshadows even harder choices for him ahead in future volumes.

Many of Dracula's cruelties later in life were inflicted on women. While this scene is in no way meant to excuse them, it is intended to foreshadow, and perhaps explain, those as well.

Alexandra as a vampire was inspired by the Tomas Alfredson film *Let the Right One In*. Eli, the vampire in that movie, appears to be a young girl capable of astounding vampiric violence . . . and also love. (She is biologically a young boy who was castrated. My recollection of the movie is that she identifies as female.) I wanted that same dichotomy here.

Page 64
"The source"

Killing Alexandra destroys what Mehmed refers to as the "source." Mehmed and the Janissaries have been drinking Alexandra's blood.

As we'll learn in the Battle of Varna following this page, what Vlad Dracul saw as a biological weapon, the Ottomans see as a source of power.

For Mehmed, the heir to the throne, it's also a source of exquisite pleasure. This fits with the historical notion of him as a hedonist in his youth. It also fits with Bram Stoker's sexualization of vampirism. In chapter 21, Count Dracula says he wants to use Mina as his "bountiful wine press."

One thing I wanted to do with *Dracula: Son of the Dragon* was to play with the many interpretations of vampirism. Power, pleasure, plague . . . the fact that vampirism can serve as a metaphor for all of these is why vampire fiction in general and Dracula in particular have endured.

Page 65
The Battle of Varna

Future volumes will show Dracula in epic battles first to gain the Wallachian throne and then to defend it against hordes of Ottoman troops. But I wanted to give the reader a taste of Renaissance/ early modern warfare. As Dracula is a prisoner, we cut here to the last great battle of his father, Dracul.

As noted earlier, the papal legate Cardinal Cesarini, John Hunyadi, and Dracula's elder brother Mircea were joined by Władysław III and Vlad Dracul himself outside the Black Sea port of Varna. There, they hoped to stop an invading force led by Sultan Murad. .

The Ottomans had fifty thousand men. Hunyadi led between twenty thousand and thirty thousand crusaders made up of Hungarians, Poles, and Bohemians with smaller units of Czechs, papal knights, Teutonic Knights, Bosnians, Croatians, Bulgarians, Lithuanians, and Ruthenians.

Dracul and Mircea led about seven thousand Wallachians.

The outnumbered crusaders suffered a fatal blow when King Władysław's horse was speared. (The winged hussars we depict here are likely an

anachronism, but I loved the visual and thought they'd help differentiate the Polish king's forces from the Transylvanians, Wallachians, Hungarians, etc.).

He fell and was beheaded by what McNally and Florescu describe as "elite Turkish troops." I interpreted this to mean Janissaries. And as you can see, I further decided that the Janissaries, having drunk Alexandra's vampiric blood, were now strigoi viu, living vampires. This is the moment we learn what the Janissaries' masks hide (and protect from sunlight).

As with the Janissary vampires' modified armor, Salgood did a great job with the vampires themselves. I called for them to have jaws that were unnaturally wide to show a reptilian nature. This reflects their shared heritage with the dragon we saw at the Scholomance.

Seeing Władysław fall, Hunyadi rushed forward with the Wallachian cavalry to save his body. He was unable to, and the body was never found. Cardinal Cesarini suffered a similar fate, left naked and dead.

What happened next is a matter of debate. Some, like eyewitness Andrea de Palatio of Parma, accused the Wallachians of betraying Hunyadi. In our fictional version, Hunyadi blames Vlad Dracul for giving the Turks vampiric power instead of spreading a plague among them.

Florescu and McNally argue that if it weren't for Dracul and the Wallachians, Hunyadi would not have escaped. What is not up for debate is that, despite suffering terrible losses, the Ottomans routed the crusaders, ensuring more Turkish conquests in the Balkans.

In both real life and fiction, Dracul and Mircea held Hunyadi responsible for the defeat, since Hunyadi did not heed Dracul's warnings about attacking a numerically superior foe. Mircea argued for Hunyadi's arrest, trial, and execution. Dracul spared his life and gave him safe passage. This would turn out to be a mistake.

Page 74
Brașov

Spurred on by the humiliation of his defeat at Varna, Mircea's accusations, and ambition, Hunyadi invaded Wallachia. Before doing so, in November of 1447 he met with Vladislav II, a member of the rival Dănești line, in Brașov, Transylvania. Hunyadi was planning to install him on Vlad Dracul's throne.

Page 75
Târgoviște and Bălteni

As Hunyadi and Vladislav approached the Wallachian capital of Târgoviște, Vlad Dracul ordered the gates closed. But boyars loyal to the Dănești line revolted. Mircea was captured, tortured, and buried alive.

Dracul was able to escape, but his freedom was short lived. He was killed in the marshes at Bălteni.

The bite, which Dracul sustained in battle with the vampire Janissaries, was a fictional invention. As far as his scalping, I can't find any research to back it up, so that may also have come from my gruesome imagination.

Page 78
"Reclaim your birthright . . ."

With Vlad Dracul's death, Vladislav assumed his throne.

Dracula was informed of his father's death in the manner depicted in these pages. Sultan Murad made him an officer in the Turkish army, and he replaced Radu as the sultan's favorite for the Wallachian throne . . . for now.

This provides a conclusion to the first chapter of Dracula's life. It also sets us up for the next one, which will center on Dracula reclaiming his birthright. Of course, in a world where we've seen vampires and other supernatural horrors, he'll have to contend with more than just his mortal enemies.

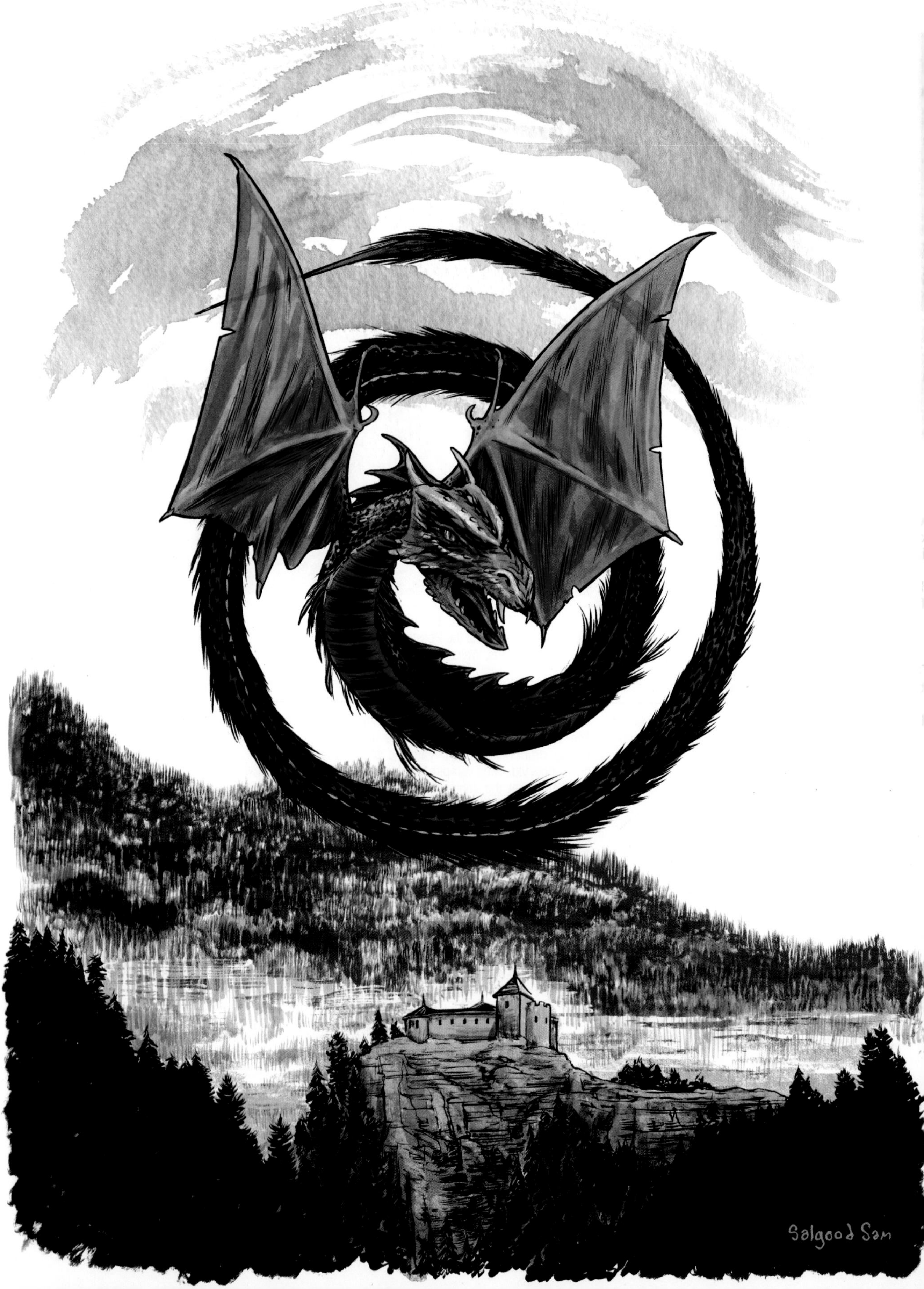
Salgood Sam

Page 81
"But I have yet to tell all my sins."

We end this story where we began, with the bookend of Dracula and the monks of three faiths. He again asks the Roman Catholic Benedictine monk whether his acts of cruelty will bar him from heaven. The monk says that Dracula was born in his father's "cruel image" and "should not pay for his sins." Aside from the "forest of the impaled," we've really only seen Dracul's sins, not Dracula's. But anyone familiar with the history of Vlad the Impaler knows what's coming.

In Romanian folklore, there are many stories of Dracula punishing liars. As he perceives the Benedictine monk to be lying, he impales him on his cross. This foreshadows Dracula's future atrocities. His disregard for the Christian faith leads us to believe he will not seek immortality through religious redemption.

There are still many mysteries left, the biggest of all being how Vlad the Impaler became the vampire we know ifrom the pages of Bram Stoker's *Dracula*. There have been many hints, but sharp readers should note the symbol on the mysterious third monk's back . . . that of the Order of the Dragon.

I look forward to answering these mysteries in future volumes. In the meantime, I hope you've enjoyed this one, and found these notes to be enlightening.

Mark Sable

PARTIAL BIBLIOGRAPHY

Vlad the Impaler. John Bianchi, with Dan Minculescu and Steve Schifani. Nottingham, UK: Games Workshop, 2006. Print.

Vlad the Impaler: Blood Prince of Wallachia. Dr. Mike Bennighof and John R. Phythyon Jr., Virginia Beach, VA: Avalanche Press, 2002. Print.

Bram Stoker's Dracula. Francis Ford Coppola. Perf. Gary Oldman. Columbia Pictures, 1992. Film.

Bram Stoker's Dracula: The Film and the Legend. Francis Ford Coppola and James V. Hart. New York, NY: Newmarket Press, 1992. Print.

Dracula. Tod Browning. Perf. Bela Lugosi. Universal Studios, 1931. Film.

Dracula. Terence Fisher. Perf. Christopher Lee, Peter Cushing. Hammer Films, 1958. Film.

Dracula, Prince of Many Faces: His Life and Times. Radu R. Florescu and Raymond T. McNally. New York, NY: Back Bay Books/Little, Brown and Company, 2009. Print.

In Search of Dracula: The History of Dracula and Vampires (Revised). Radu R. Florescu and Raymond T. McNally. New York, NY: Houghton Mifflin, 1994. Print.

Dracula: A Biography. Radu R. Florescu and Raymond T. McNally. London: Robert Hale & Company, 1973. Print.

The Origins of Dracula. Clive Leatherdale. Westcliff-on-Sea, Essex: Desert Island Books, 1987. Print.

The Enchanted World: Wizards and Witches. Brendan Lehane and the editors of Time-Life Books. Alexandria, VA: Time-Life Books, 1984. Print.

Let the Right One In. Tomas Alfredson. Perf. Kåre Hedebrant, Lina Leandersson. Sandrew Metronome, 2008. Film.

A Dracula Handbook. Elizabeth Miller. United States: XLibris, 2005. Print.

Bram Stoker's Dracula Role Playing Game. Barry Nakazono. Pasadena, CA: Leading Edge Games, 1993. Print.

Armies of the Ottoman Turks 1300–1774. David Nicolle; illustrated by Angus McBride. New York, NY: Osprey Men-at-Arms, 1983. Print.

Hungary and the Fall of Eastern Europe 1000–1568. David Nicolle; illustrated by Angus McBride. New York, NY: Osprey Men-at-Arms, 1988. Print.

The Janissaries. David Nicolle; illustrated by Christina Hook. New York, NY: Osprey Men-at-Arms, 1995. Print.

Dracula. Bram Stoker. Edited and with notes by Leslie S. Klinger; introduction by Neil Gaiman. New York, NY: W.W. Norton & Company, 2008. Print.

Nathan Fox

thank you, KICKSTARTER BACKERS!

Kevin Carrier, Bryan Hickok, Raymond Mullikin, Steve LeCouilliard, Alex Leung, Russell Nohelty, Leilani Coughlan, J.D. Dresner, Tony Donleyv, Cynthia Pelston, Dean Haspiel, Michael Walsh, Gabriel LLanas, Dave Howard, Alison Maxhuni, David McCluskey, B. Alex Thompson, Jesse Alexander, Luiz Pimenta, Nicole Rodrigues, Tim Twelves, Dennis Coyle, Ian Hodgkinson, Josh Schwartz, Jason Phillips, Keith Grachow, Stephen Napolitano, Allan Silburt, Angela Morato, Zane Grant, Darren Hupke, Anita Giraldo, Mark Taormino, Kyle Strahm, Ivan Brandon, Paul Nelson, Ellen Fleischer, Marie Mint, Omaha Perez, Alejandro Bruzzese, Jamie Tanner, Rus Wooton, Sara Michelle Tan, Joel Enos, Samuel Crider, Roxanna Bennett, Steve Bevan, Ryan Closs, David Russo, Mark Andrew Smith, Liam "GhostPockets" Byrne, Thomas Mauer, Josh Gorfain, Daniel

Scholz, Lindsey Hollands, Kristopher Volter, Eoin Hurrell, Zuhur Abdo, Justin Massion, Myke Bakich, Matt Shepherd, Jed Alexander, Sam Wright, Steven Dwyer, Kieron Gillen, Sean van der Meulen, Ed Dunphy, Brandon Perlow, James Leask, Paul J Mendoza, Gary Arkell, Mario Boon, Javina Chaudhry, Andrew Walsh, Gerry Duggan, Drazen Kozjan, Taryn O'Neill, JR Rothenberg, Abhay Khosla, Stephen Eric Johnson, Nick Ahlhelm, Chris Burnhamv, Roy Cowing, Mark Landry, Valentina Mezzacappa, Michael May, Rachael Carpenter, Michael Ferrara, Anastacia Visneski, David Accampo, Lauren Epstein, Evan Young and Lou Iovino, Alberto Hernandez, Nicole Fisher, Andrew Martin, Katie Walder, Julian Orr, Tim Seeley, Ian A, Kim Krizan, Petros Koutoupis, Fred, Scott Rothman, Heather Donnell and Chris R. Smith, Keith Perkins, Joe Keatinge, Jason A. Quest, Nick Filardi, Rick Remender, Jeremy Haun, Ashley Funkhouser, Devi Bhaduri, Corey Blake, Christina Blanch, Johnny Michael Hunter, Buster Moody, Dan Hooper, Haley Cristea, Caleb Michael Smith, Stacey Aragon, Kevin Walsh, Tony, Cheryl Stanford Smith, John Burton and Scott Boyce, Erin Stark, Caleb Monroe, Sam Humphries, Derek Anderson, Cheese Hasselberger, Rebecca Edwards, Aya, C Eberle, Splatstick, Caroline Harris, Mark Cook, Marcin Czaplicki, Jason Ramsay-Brown, Jack Tempest, DMir Anda, Philip Dunne, Stephan Schmidt, Calliope den Ouden, Andy MacDonald, Nathan Fox, John Parkin, Matthew Morris, Jason White, Cass Sherman, Jonathan L. Davis, Bill Sorensen, Dale Wilson, Karl Okerholm, Kerry Roeder, Eric Palicki, Sam Gem, Fifth World Studios, Brandon, Chris Hansbrough, Robert Pincombe, Jessica Singleton, Steve Orlando, Anthony Walsh, Trace Slobotkin, Andy Jewett, Dann Vondenkamp, Joshua Fialkov, Troy Carlson, Kevin Rubin, Allan Morato, Joanna Spilker, Arna Selznick, Ryan Garland, Connie Chung, Miranda Salomon, Anthony Peruzzo, Batton Lash, Matt Allen, Matt Pizzolo, Jason Copland, Stephen Bissette, Jonathan Flicker, Alison Benowitz, John Lacorazza, Leef Smith, Chance Murphy, Diana Tamblyn, Gail Garcellano, Shael Hawman, James Hagans, Justin Nafziger, Frank Salinas, Charles Drost, Dan Hess, Adam Debany, Nicholas Clayton, Jonathan Zylberberg, James Turner, Jeff Amano, Conor McCreery, Doug Mayo-Wells, Adam Luptak, Stephan Vladimir Bugaj, Monique Kundahl, Leonard Kirk, Mike Aragona, Ron Vink, Stephen Molnar, Ryan French, Nicholas Reichle, Wood, James Hoare, Richard, Daniel Ha, Fred Mahieu, Timothy Martin, Damian Gordon, Edward Kaye, Ken Lashley, Richard Pace, Peter Halasz, Brian Skene, Dalton Sharp, J.T. Lampman, Kim Holm, Tom Kerkhove, Janice Chiang, Scott Andrews, Raina Ebel, Matthew Crehan, Guilherme Chaves Corrêa, Michelle Breslin, jellybelly, Jessica Smallwood, Brandon Eaker, Patrick Michael McNamara, Brett Schenker, Ryan Browne, BAD KARMA, Pierluigi Cothran, Rob McKittrick, Wei Jen Seah, Shlomo Roman, Victor Andrade, Ty Buttars, Edgardo Ceballos, Bora Sela, Jim Lesniak, Eugen Sasu, David Leimbach, Jean Ly, Mark Pawziuk, demifiend, Michael Schwartz, Jillian Venters, Emily McCabe, James Robinson, Sergio Luis Ferre, Uyen Le, Christian Scott, Kris Dresen, John Santo, Jose Vargas, Teresa Raschilla, Tim Baldwin, Tracy Fehr, Chris Ryall, Jeff Simpkins, Stephanie DiRubbio, Stephane, Paul Cook, Andrew Burrell, Timothy Giganti, Sharon I, Kathy Vandenheuvel, Will Miller, Kristin Rozum, Deane Aikins, Adam Pottier, Lord Bob and minion, James Moses, Charisse Vizcarra, Kyle Smith, Jared Stern, Josh A Cagan, Cat Lissfelt, Marco Piva, Matt, Blaze De'Nosferatu, Justin Bernstein, Ashley P Quach, The MFA Visual Narrative dept @ SVA NY, David Clarke, Gregory Benton, Robert Windom, Shawn Demumbrum, Jason Pritchett, Dale and Dave Cox, and Ian Wood!

COMIXOLOGY COMES TO DARK HORSE BOOKS!

JASON LOO
CHIP ZDARSKY
AFTERLIFT

ISBN 978-1-50672-440-9 / $19.99

JUSTIN JORDAN
TYASSETA
BREAK LANDS
SARAH STERN
RACHEL DEERING
VOLUME I: THE CHASE

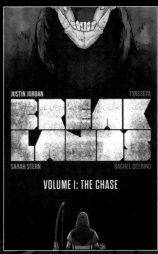

ISBN 978-1-50672-441-6 / $19.99

curt pires
alex diotto
dee cunniffe
micah myers
Youth

ISBN 978-1-50672-461-4 / $19.99

THE BLACK GHOST
HARD REVOLUTION
ALEX SEGURA
MONICA GALLAGHER

ISBN 978-1-50672-446-1 / $19.99

THE PRIDE
OMNIBUS

ISBN 978-1-50672-447-8 / $29.99

JIM ZUB • MAX DUNBAR
STONE STAR
VOLUME I:
FIGHT OR FLIGHT

ISBN 978-1-50672-458-4 / $19.99

AFTERLIFT

Written by Chip Zdarsky, art by Jason Loo

This Eisner Award–winning series from Chip Zdarsky (*Sex Criminals*, Daredevil) and Jason Loo (*The Pitiful Human-Lizard*) features car chases, demon bounty hunters, and figuring out your place in this world and the next.

BREAKLANDS

Written by Justin Jordan, art by Tyasseta and Sarah Stern

Generations after the end of the civilization, everyone has powers; you need them just to survive in the new age. Everyone except Kasa Fain. Unfortunately, her little brother, who has the potential to reshape the world, is kidnapped by people who intend to do just that. *Mad Max* meets *Akira* in a genre-mashing, expectation-smashing new hit series from Justin Jordan, creator of *Luther Strode*, *Spread*, and *Reaver*!

YOUTH

Written by Curt Pires, art by Alex Diotto and Dee Cunniffe

A coming of age story of two queer teenagers who run away from their lives in a bigoted small town, and attempt to make their way to California. Along the way their car breaks down and they join a group of fellow misfits on the road. travelling the country together in a van, they party and attempt to find themselves. And then . . . something happens. The story combines the violence of coming of age with the violence of the superhero narrative—as well as the beauty.

THE BLACK GHOST SEASON ONE: HARD REVOLUTION

Written by Alex Segura and Monica Gallagher, art by George Kambadais

Meet Lara Dominguez—a troubled Creighton cops reporter obsessed with the city's debonair vigilante the Black Ghost. With the help of a mysterious cyberinformant named LONE, Lara's inched closer to uncovering the Ghost's identity. But as she searches for the breakthrough story she desperately needs, Lara will have to navigate the corruption of her city, the uncertainties of virtues, and her own personal demons. Will she have the strength to be part of the solution—or will she become the problem?

THE PRIDE OMNIBUS

Joseph Glass, Gavin Mitchell and Cem Iroz

FabMan is sick of being seen as a joke. Tired of the LGBTQ+ community being seen as inferior to straight heroes, he thinks it's about damn time he did something about it. Bringing together some of the world's greatest LGBTQ+ superheroes, the Pride is born to protect the world and fight prejudice, misrepresentation and injustice—not to mention a pesky supervillain or two.

STONE STAR

Jim Zub and Max Zunbar

The brand-new space-fantasy saga that takes flight on comiXology Originals from fan-favorite creators Jim Zub (*Avengers*, *Samurai Jack*) and Max Dunbar (*Champions*, *Dungeons & Dragons*)! The nomadic space station called Stone Star brings gladiatorial entertainment to ports across the galaxy. Inside this gargantuan vessel of tournaments and temptations, foragers and fighters struggle to survive. A young thief named Dail discovers a dark secret in the depths of Stone Star and must decide his destiny—staying hidden in the shadows or standing tall in the searing spotlight of the arena. Either way, his life, and the cosmos itself, will never be the same!

AVAILABLE AT YOUR LOCAL COMICS SHOP OR BOOKSTORE / To find a comics shop near you, visit comicshoplocator.com
For more information or to order direct, visit darkhorse.com

DARK HORSE BOOKS

COMIXOLOGY ORIGINALS